...ca Walter (née Hampson)*

...dra Leigh
...-1827

Leonora
b. 1732

*Rebecca Hampson had first married William Walter

William Hampson Walter m. Susanna Weaver

James   three other sons   Philadelphia m. George Whitaker.

...ht m. Elizabeth Bridges
1773-1808

George   eight other children

Henry
1771-1850
ob.s.p.

m. (1) Eliza de Feuillide
1761-1813

(2) Eleanor Jackson

Cassandra
1773-1845

JANE
1775-1817

Charles m. (1) Frances Palmer
1779-1852   1790-1814

three daughters

(2) Harriet Palmer

The
Double Life
of
JANE AUSTEN

The
Double Life
of
JANE AUSTEN

JANE AIKEN HODGE

HODDER AND STOUGHTON

LONDON SYDNEY AUCKLAND TORONTO

FOR

MISS MARY M. LASCELLES

I wish to acknowledge the kindness of the Oxford University Press in allowing extensive quotations from *Jane Austen's Letters to her sister Cassandra and others*, collected and edited by R. W. Chapman.

I have also received much help, advice and encouragement from my husband, Alan Hodge, and from Sir Zachary Cope, Milton Crane, John Murray, W. O. P. Rosedale and B. C. Southam.

J.A.H.

Contents

Illustrations

Introduction

IN JANE AUSTEN'S LIFETIME, IT OCCURRED TO NO ONE THAT SHE would one day be famous, that future generations would be eager for details of the intensely private life of " 'tother Miss Austen". Burying her, in 1817, in Winchester Cathedral, her grieving family paid due tribute to "the benevolence of her heart, the sweetness of her temper, and the extraordinary endowments of her mind", but did not think to mention the six novels that would bring people from all over the world to look at the plain, stone slab that marks her grave.

When *Persuasion* and *Northanger Abbey* were published posthumously in 1818, her brother Henry contributed a brief *Biographical Notice* that is more a laudatory character sketch of the lost, beloved sister than an attempt to give the facts of her life. He sums up his view thus: "A life of usefulness, literature and religion, was not by any means a life of event." And he disposes of such events as he cares to notice in under two printed pages.

It was more than fifty years before a fuller attempt was made at a biography, and by then all of Jane Austen's own generation were gone, her last brother having died, at a great age, in 1865. The two oldest nieces, Fanny Knatchbull and Anna Lefroy, who might have remembered the Aunt Jane of the Steventon period, were old ladies. The author of the 1870 *Memoir*, her nephew, James Edward Austen-Leigh, had been only nineteen when she died, so that most of his memories, like those of his sister Caroline Austen, were inevitably of the last years of their aunt's life. And when he applied to his older cousin, Lady Knatchbull, for a sight of their aunt's letters, most of which had been bequeathed to her by Jane's sister Cassandra, he was put off with excuses. The letters were missing. Lady Knatchbull, Jane Austen's beloved niece Fanny, was too old and too ill to be troubled about them. Though unfortunate, this is hardly surprising. Jane Austen, writing, years before, both to Fanny herself and to her sister and close confidante Cassandra, had talked freely about Fanny's frivolous youth. There had been various young men to be discussed, seriously or otherwise, and one of them, comically described by Jane to Cassandra, had been, in fact, an apothecary. In Regency, and still more, no doubt, in Lady Knatchbull's elegant Victorian circles, apothecaries were not at all the thing. It is no wonder if Fanny Knatchbull, remembering these letters, and others, in which her aunt had advised her over a serious affair with a young gentleman of an Evangelical turn, decided to take the standard Victorian lady's refuge in illness. At all events, the letters were not available to James Edward Austen-Leigh, and his *Memoir* is the poorer for their lack, though it does include a few that had passed to other members of the family.

To do her justice, Lady Knatchbull kept the letters, and when she died, her son, Lord Brabourne, published them, with a dedication to Queen Victoria and his own explanatory text; but by then it was 1884. When his *Letters of Jane Austen* came out, she had been dead sixty-seven years. Lord Brabourne himself was two generations away from his subject, and, still more important, he had lost touch with the Hampshire branch of the family, to which his great-aunt had belonged. For the Austens, like their most illustrious member, had a kind of double life. Lord Brabourne's grandfather, Jane Austen's brother Edward, had been adopted by rich relations in Kent and had finally taken their family name of Knight, while James Edward, son of her brother James and author of the *Memoir*, remained in Hampshire, inherited money and an extra name from the distaff side, and so became Austen-Leigh. It was members of his family, W. and R. A. Austen-Leigh, who finally published, in 1913, the *Life and Letters* of Jane Austen, which sums up family records and tradition. Another invaluable source book is the *Austen Papers, 1704–1856*, edited by R. A. Austen-Leigh, which appeared in 1942, and is a perfect goldmine of miscellaneous family letters and documents.

But the dates of these books show how far they are removed from their subject, and there are, in fact, great gaps in the story they tell. This is because it is largely based on Jane Austen's own surviving letters, the best source of all for her life, and they were ruthlessly pruned by Cassandra before her own death. In *My Aunt Jane Austen, A Memoir*, Caroline Craven Austen records that Cassandra "looked them over and burnt the greater part (as she told me), two or three years before her own death . . . of those that *I* have seen, several had portions cut out". And, again, in *Personal Aspects of Jane Austen*, Mary Augusta Austen-Leigh tells us that Cassandra, who shared her sister's strong sense of privacy, saved only such of the letters as she thought to contain "nothing sufficiently interesting to induce any future generation to give them to the world". In fact, the gaps in the letters can be expected to correspond with crises in their author's life, or in her family's. Cassandra's hand was a heavy one. We can only respect, and regret it.

What remains is suggestive of Jane Austen's own description, in *Sanditon*, of a sea mist and "something white and womanish" just visible through it. Ever since the *Memoir* was published, people have been peering through the mist. Relatives and connections have added a fact or conjecture here, an anecdote there; contemporary sources have been combed for comment and criticism. As the Austen cult grew, devotees pursued "dear Aunt Jane" from place to place, happily discovering here a ballroom where she probably danced, there a double hedgerow that may have inspired her. It does not add up to very much.

The family's devoted, if belated, recollections give us a kind of framework of a life, but they tend to paint a character at once too good to be true and far too good to have written either the six brilliant novels or the equally surprising letters. I have no doubt that this is largely Jane Austen's own fault. She played, supremely well, the part that was expected of her. She *was* "dear Aunt Jane", beloved of children, who never said a sharp thing. Or hardly ever. There are sharp things in her letters, and there must have been in her conversation, but Cassandra burned many of the letters, and the family preferred to forget the conversation. In her lifetime, Jane Austen did her best to conform to the conventions of her day, and after her death the family touched up the picture. Somehow, in their devotion, they succeeded in superimposing their legendary dear aunt on the other figure of Miss Jane Austen, the author. One must always distinguish between these two ladies. Dear Aunt Jane seldom said an unkind thing. She nursed the sick, looked after the children, gave way to her brothers' convenience. She was, rightly, a beloved aunt and sister. One is not quite so sure how she stood as a daughter.

But Miss Jane Austen, who commenced as an author at about twelve years old, was something very different. What depths of intellectual and moral despair must she have plumbed before she achieved the extraordinary ironic moral vision that has been compared, with justice, to Chaucer's? No use going to her family's records for evidence or clues about this. They will simply tell us that Aunt Jane played the piano before breakfast — and rather easy tunes at that. While she sat there, every inch the maiden aunt, she was doubtless wrestling, like every other artist who has created something that endures, with her vision of the universe. It was a fortunate thing for her family that the highly polished surface of the six novels, their sheer artistry, concealing tension, makes it easy to miss the depth and bitterness of what they are often saying.

Jane Austen looked at the world around her, and found it wanting. She wrote at a time like ours, when the established moral code was under question, and the whole fabric of society changing. The gay, romantic plots that have delighted generations of teenagers are only the surface tune behind which beats the great rhythm of her moral and ironic argument. She had to choose between laughter and tears, and I think sometimes the choice was a very near thing. There are not many easy answers in her novels. There is curiously little religion either. One of the reasons, I think, why her books continue so readable is that her characters make their moral decisions in the same kind of climate of unknowing, or even of unbelief, that we are used to today. She did try, once in *Mansfield Park*, to write a book cn a religious theme, and produced a flawed masterpiece. It is no wonder if the Victorians found her doubtful reading. How much more respectable to be Lucy Snow and rush to confession (even to a Roman Catholic priest) than to be Elizabeth Bennet or Anne Elliot, and deal with despair alone.

Naturally, dear Aunt Jane would have told you, and with perfect truth, that she was a good churchwoman. A few of the prayers that she wrote survive. Her letters of condolence on family deaths say the proper things, properly. Dying, she had the comfort of two clergyman brothers at her bedside, and insisted on receiving the last rites of the Church when she was still conscious enough to understand them. I hope Miss Jane Austen, the author, was also conscious enough to find it ironic that of the two clergymen brothers, one was James, whom she had always liked the least, and the other Henry, who had turned to the Church as a *pis aller* after failing elsewhere.

Ironic laughter was Jane Austen's own answer to the *tragédie humaine*, and we must look for the real evidence about her character not in the censored reminiscences of Victorian relatives, but in the books and the letters themselves. We have all that remain now, brilliantly edited in R. W. Chapman's definitive Oxford edition, to which I have referred throughout, but without page references which would have entailed a perfect jungle of footnotes. All quotations are from Jane Austen, unless otherwise identified. Peering, in my turn, through the mists of a hundred and fifty years, I have tried for my own picture of the person who could write those seven extraordinary novels (including *Lady Susan*), and those significant and delightful letters. Where I have allowed myself the luxury of conjecture, I have said so. Elsewhere, I hope, I am solidly grounded in the authorities.

And then, there are the critics. How surprised, and how amused, Jane Austen would have been if she could have known what an immense number of critical works would be devoted to her. "Who, me?" one imagines her saying, with one of her occasional grammatical lapses. "All those books — and so many of them by men!" That would have amused her, I am sure, as much as anything. As it is, I must begin with an apology. Over and over again I have achieved what I thought an original point, only to find it tracked, already, in someone else's snow. By now, the tracks are so thick, the pattern so confused, that I can only say I owe something to almost every author quoted in my inevitably selective bibliography, but a most particular debt to R. W. Chapman, Miss Mary Lascelles, Marvin Mudrick, B. C. Southam and Miss C. L. Thomson.

Her critics have always spent a surprising amount of time contentedly retelling Jane Austen's stories for her. In the text, I propose to pay my readers the compliment of assuming that they know the plots of the novels. But, for quick reference, Appendix III contains synopses of the six major novels. I like to think that these may tempt or infuriate readers into going back to the books themselves. I can think of no other author whose books change so much as the reader changes. Read *Emma* at eighteen, and at eighty, and you will have read two different books. But Jane Austen wrote them both.

Finally, this book is written for the general public, not the world of scholarship, though its basis is as scholarly as I can make it. But in the interests of readability I have modernised spelling and usage in all quotations, and have kept my footnotes to a minimum, hoping that any critic who feels I have stolen his thunder may forgive me as a fellow admirer of Jane Austen, and one who claims no more than to be, as she once described herself, "a partial, prejudiced, and ignorant historian".

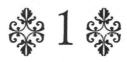

1

WHEN JANE AUSTEN WAS BORN, A STAR DANCED. SHE HAD THE
gift of laughter; and she needed it. And yet, apparently, her prospects were
fair enough. In an age of sharp contrast between the circumstances of rich
and poor, she was born into a reasonably comfortable nook of nearly the
upper middle class. Her father, George Austen, a surgeon's son, had been
left a penniless orphan, it is true, but the Austens of Kent had strong
family feelings. Young George was taken in hand by his uncle, Francis
Austen, a successful attorney of Tonbridge, who sent him to Tonbridge
School. From there he obtained a scholarship to St. John's College,
Oxford, where he seems to have acquired a good deal more education
than many of his contemporaries, in that time of academic dead water. His
son Henry described him as "not only a profound scholar, but possessing
a most exquisite taste in every species of literature". Even allowing for
family prejudice, we can probably accept this as close enough to the truth.
George Austen went back to teach at his old school when he left St.
John's, but returned there later as a Fellow. He was ordained in 1760
and next year another relative, Thomas Knight of Godmersham in Kent,
presented him with the living of Steventon, in Hampshire, to which
his Uncle Francis presently added that of Deane, a mile and a half
away.

It was, comfortably, enough to marry on. History does not relate just
where or when George Austen met his future wife, Cassandra Leigh, but
it seems reasonable to assume that it was through an Oxford connection.
The Leighs were Founder's Kin of St. John's College through their
ancestor, Sir Thomas White, and Cassandra's father, the Reverend
Thomas Leigh, had been a Fellow of All Souls before he received the

college living of Harpsden in Berkshire. Moreover her uncle, Dr. Theophilus Leigh, was Master of Balliol for over half a century, and was praised for his wit by Mrs. Thrale in a letter to Dr. Johnson.

Altogether the Leighs came from a rather higher stratum of the complex society of their day than the Austens. They had baronet blood, and an abbey in the family. Charles I had found shelter at Stoneleigh Abbey when Coventry shut its gates against him, and his portrait still hung there, disguised as a flower-painting. There was money about, too, tantalisingly near, though never, as it turned out, quite near enough.

But for the moment, it all seemed happy ending. Handsome George Austen married witty Cassandra Leigh in Walcot Church, Bath, on April 26th, 1764. The bride went away in a scarlet riding habit and the short honeymoon journey home to Hampshire was unusual in that the happy couple were accompanied by a six-year-old boy. He was another George, the son of Warren Hastings, the famous first Governor-General of British India, and had been in George Austen's care since 1761. This was presumably the result of George's sister Philadelphia's friendship with the great man in India. Orphaned and penniless as her brother, Philadelphia had been shipped off by her friends, like Jane Austen's Miss Wynne in *Catherine*, to make the best marriage she could in India. She had married a surgeon called Tysoe Saul Hancock, considerably older than herself, and it seems reasonable to assume that she had made friends with Warren Hastings' first wife either before or on the voyage out, since the same people stood sponsor for them both. It was to prove an invaluable connection for her.

Little George Hastings, however, died young, that autumn of 1764 of a putrid sore throat (probably diphtheria) and Mrs. Austen, her grandson tells us in his *Memoir*, "always declared that his death had been as great a grief to her as if he had been a child of her own". Those were strong words, for her own family grew fast. By 1772, Mr. Hancock was writing gloomily from India to his wife in England about "the violently rapid increase of the Austens' family". And, again: "I fear George will find it easier to get a family than to provide for them."

He reckoned without the capable Austens and Leighs. George and Cassandra managed, but it was not easy. Like Mr. and Mrs. Heywood, in *Sanditon*, they found that "the maintenance, education and fitting out of their children demanded a very quiet, settled, careful course of life". The honeymoon scarlet riding habit was worn steadily for two years and reappeared, later, cut down into hunting pink for one of the active

Austen boys. Mr. Austen supplemented the income from his two parishes by taking in pupils and farming his glebe.[1] His wife wrote knowledgeably to her sister-in-law[2] about hay and cows, and cheerfully received guests while doing the family mending in the parlour.

The family kept on growing. James was born in 1765, George in 1766, Edward in 1768 and Henry in 1771. Then, in 1773 came the first girl, Cassandra, followed in 1774 by Francis, in 1775 by Jane, and finally, in 1779 by "our own particular brother", Charles. Some biographers of Jane Austen have suggested that Mrs. Austen was a bit of a *malade imaginaire*, needing constant physicking by her daughters. There may be some truth in this as far as her later life was concerned, but as a young woman she must have had a constitution of iron to have borne and reared all those children, running a large household and doubtless helping to run her husband's parish the while, and have come out of it all still capable of writing an entertaining letter, or a reasonably comic poem; still prepared to enjoy the inevitable business of the amateur theatricals the Austens liked to indulge in.

Steventon Rectory, much improved by George Austen, has long since been pulled down, but has been lovingly described for us by a younger generation of Austens. It must have been a pleasant, rambling house, with its seven bedrooms, its garden and elm walk, and the barn where, more economical than the Bertram family, the Austens put on their plays. There were servants, of course, and a carriage, though, like Mr. Bennet, Mr. Austen probably used his horses as much for farming the glebe as for drawing the carriage. There was probably not a great deal of time for social life with a family increasing so fast.

Mrs. Austen writes of Cassandra that she suckled her for the first quarter before weaning her and handing her over to a good woman in the village. This was probably the form with all the children. The phrase "put out to nurse" used in the *Memoir* does not, in fact, mean, as it might seem to, that the children had a wet nurse like little aristocrats. They were just weaned rather early, cared for in the village, visited daily by their parents, and brought home when they were about one, and, presumably, their busy mother had had her next child, or, at least, felt ready to cope with them. As a system, it seems to have worked admirably. With one exception, the young Austens were a quite strikingly bright and successful family. The exception was George, the second son, who was subject to fits. Mrs.

[1] Farmland constituting part of a clergyman's benefice
[2] Susanna Walter, wife of George Austen's half-brother, William Hampson Walter. See family tree.

Austen wrote hopefully about him for a while. Mr. Austen was more realistic, writing in 1770, "We must not be too sanguine . . . we have this comfort, he cannot be a bad or a wicked child." Two years later, Tysoe Saul Hancock wrote another of his gloomy letters home from India. George, his godson, must, he said, "be provided for without the least hopes of his being able to assist himself".

The Austens managed. All we know is that George lived on until 1838, so he must have been well cared for somewhere. A backward brother of Mrs. Austen's, Thomas Leigh, was being quietly looked after in rural seclusion, supported by a small income. In those days of annual child-bearing such cases were almost inevitable. Perhaps George went to live with him, or, perhaps more likely, he may simply have been returned to the "good woman" who had nursed him at Deane. Jane Austen refers in her letters to "talking on her fingers" to a very deaf man, and this may have been the way she communicated with her brother George. Communicate with him, in so far as it was possible, I am sure she did. Miss Brigid Brophy has produced a fascinatingly far-fetched theory by which the Austens suffered from a kind of family guilt complex about their treatment of George, with the most disastrous effects, among other things, on Jane Austen's attitude to sex. But the Austens simply were not that kind of family. We hear no more about George because he was undoubtably one of the subjects Cassandra deleted from her sister's letters, and one the family very likely preferred not to discuss.

The rest of the Austen children grew up gaily enough. At seven, Frank bought a pony called Squirrel with £1 12s. of his own money, hunted it for a couple of years (in his mother's hunting pink), and sold it at a profit. They were a competent family. Mrs. Austen was not quite so capable as usual over the birth of her daughter Jane. She expected her in November, but her husband wrote on December 17th, 1775, to apologise to his half-brother's wife, Mrs. Walter, who must have "wondered a little we were in our old age grown such bad reckoners . . . however last night the time came . . . We have now another girl, a present plaything for her sister Cassy and a future companion. She is to be Jenny, and seems to me as if she would be as like Henry, as Cassy is to Neddy." He was to prove a true prophet on every count.

Jane Austen's godparents were Jane, wife of her father's benefactor, Francis Austen, and the Reverend Samuel Cooke, of Great Bookham, who had married her mother's cousin, another Cassandra, daughter of Theophilus Leigh. No doubt Jane, like her sister, was "suckled . . . through the first quarter", and then "weaned and settled at a good woman's at Deane". And no doubt she, too, was "very healthy and lively", and soon into short petticoats.

But their mother was a busy woman, and, possibly, like other mothers, rather more interested in her boys than her girls. And with seven children, and the pupils, the seven-bedroomed house must have been stretched to bursting. At all events, while the boys stayed at home, to be tutored, along with the paying pupils, by their father, Cassandra and Jane were sent off, at a remarkably early age, to boarding school. Jane was only six, but as Mrs. Austen explained, where Cassandra went, Jane must go too. "If Cassandra was going to have her head cut off, Jane would insist on sharing her fate." Even together, it must have been a sufficiently drastic experience. They went, first, to Oxford, to a school run by a Mrs. Cawley, widow of the Principal of Brasenose. It was a family connection, and not, as it proved, a lucky one. Mrs. Cawley was "a stiff-mannered person", the sister of the Reverend Edward Cooper, who had married Mrs. Austen's own sister, Jane. One of the comforts of the Austen girls must have been that their slightly older cousin, Jane Cooper, went too. It was lucky for them that she did. Mrs. Cawley presently moved her school to Southampton and there the two Austen girls caught putrid fever (no doubt diphtheria again, as in the case of poor little George Hastings). Mrs. Cawley seems to have shrugged her shoulders over the business. What, after all, were a couple of girls? But Jane Cooper was worried about her cousins and wrote to her mother. Mrs. Cooper and Mrs. Austen descended on the school and removed their daughters just in time. Jane Austen nearly died. Tragically, Mrs. Cooper caught the infection, and did die. It was 1783, and Jane was seven.

The three girls then had another, and apparently happier experience of boarding school at the Abbey School, Reading, run by a Mrs. Latournelle, an Englishwoman married to a Frenchman. The place was pleasant, and the discipline light. The three girls could go out and dine at an inn with their respective brothers, Edward Austen and Edward Cooper, and some of their friends, when they happened to be passing through Reading. Family tradition dates their leaving school as 1784 or 1785, when Jane Austen would have been eight or nine—one has, constantly, to remember that her birthday was in December. But Mr. Austen was still making payments to Mrs. Latournelle in 1785, '86 and '87. It seems more likely that the girls were still there than that their father was behind with his payments.

The date of 1787 for the final return home would make sense in other ways. The house would have been much emptier. James had left home long before, having gone up to St. John's as Founder's Kin in 1779 at the early age of fourteen. Henry followed him there, not quite so brilliantly, at seventeen, in the summer of 1788. Meanwhile Edward, the lucky one, had been adopted by those rich cousins, the Knights, who had given Mr. Austen his living of Steventon. Edward had visited them a good deal as a boy, and his father had finally protested that it was interfering too much with his education. But Mrs. Austen had seen things differently. "I think, my dear," she is reported to have said, "you had better oblige your cousins and let the child go." She won the day. Edward kept up his visits to Kent, was formally adopted at last and sent on the Grand Tour, that essential training for a young gentleman of fashion, in 1786–8. He was a sensible choice on the part of the childless Knights. James, the eldest Austen, had expectations of his own on the maternal side. His mother's brother, for whom he was named, had become James Leigh Perrot on inheriting money from a maternal great-uncle. He and his wife, another Jane, had been married since 1764 and were still childless. James seemed their logical heir. Poor George had already disappeared from the scene, and there was Edward, competent and good-looking like all the Austens, but quite evidently not a scholar like his brothers James and Henry. Money and the Grand Tour were just right for him. As for Francis, of the pink coat and the hunting exploits, he was already well-launched on a naval career. He joined the Royal Naval Academy at Portsmouth in 1786 and did so well that he got a chance to go as a volunteer to the East Indies in 1788. Charles followed him to the Naval Academy in 1791, but already there must have begun to be room for the girls.

Aside from the scanty framework of dates, we know nothing about Cassandra's and Jane's education, except its results. The author of the *Memoir* suggests that his own father, their elder brother James, who "was well read in English literature . . . and wrote readily and happily, both in prose and verse . . . had . . . a large share in directing Jane's reading and forming her taste". Very likely he did. Henry, too, probably had his influence on his sisters' education, along with their father and the pupils and family visitors who continued to play a part in the lively and changing family scene. Even their mother may have contributed more to their education than housewifery. And, no doubt, like the Bennet girls, they had visiting masters to teach the really essential female accomplishments. Jane could play the piano; Cassandra could draw; and they both sewed and embroidered beautifully, Jane being particularly good at satin stitch.

A good deal of biographical dust has been stirred up over the question of Jane Austen's education in general, and her knowledge of languages in particular. As so often, it is her own fault. It is so extraordinarily difficult to know when to take her seriously. When she wrote the Prince Regent's librarian that she could "boast herself to be, with all possible vanity, the most unlearned and uninformed female who ever dared to be an authoress", she was probably about as serious as when she described her *History of England* as "by a partial, prejudiced, and ignorant historian". I imagine that she had small Latin and less Greek, but her knowledge of French is established, for me at least, by a casual little phrase in one of her letters about "the *feu* of *bru* the Bishop".

In fact, she and Cassandra had the kind of education she preferred for her own heroines: plenty of books, plenty of time, and plenty of good talk. Those were happy years. The Austens were great ones for charades, and riddles, and impromptu verses of all kinds. At Christmas and midsummer, when the pupils went home and the family came back there, they entertained their friends and relations by putting on their own plays. They did *The Rivals* in 1784, *Which is the Man* and *Bon Ton* in 1787, and *The Sultan* and *High Life Below Stairs* in 1788. Mr. Austen may have been a clergyman, but he was no Edmund Bertram, and Mrs. Austen joined in the fun with a will.

"I like first cousins to be first cousins, and interested in one another," Jane Austen wrote to a niece later in life, and one cousin in particular must have stood out at this time. George Austen's sister, Philadelphia Hancock, had come home from India about 1765 with her daughter Eliza, then four years old. Her husband had come too, but had soon found the cost of living too much for him and had gone sadly back to India in 1769, chasing the forlorn hope of a fortune, and writing regularly to his wife about his beloved daughter's education. He never saw either of them again, but died, still impecunious, in 1775. Fortunately Warren Hastings, who was Eliza's godfather, had come to the rescue in the meanwhile by settling ten thousand pounds on mother and daughter. It makes one wonder, just a little, about the relationship between them, but Hastings was known for his generosity.

Anyway, Eliza was able to grow up as a young lady, with the accomplishments Tysoe Saul Hancock had wanted for her. In 1777, her mother took her to Europe, very likely for reasons of economy as well as of education. By 1870 they were in Paris and moving apparently in the best society. The *Austen Papers* contains letters written by Eliza to her cousin, and Jane Austen's, Philadelphia Walter, daughter of George Austen's half-brother. Eliza went to Versailles and described Marie Antoinette as "a very fine woman . . . most elegantly dressed". And, soon, she married a Frenchman, and a count at that, becoming Madame la Comtesse de Feuillide. Her husband, she told her cousin, adored her, though she was not particularly in love with him. He must at least have been a man of some political acumen. When Eliza became pregnant at the end of 1785, he insisted that she go to England to bear the child. She did so, grumbling a little about the inconvenience of it all (her husband could not accompany her), and the inelegant state in which she must be reunited with her family. Her son Hastings was born in the summer of 1786 and, owing to his father's forethought, would not be liable for military service in France. But poor little Hastings, like his cousin George, was subject to fits. Unlike George, he died young, in 1801.

Eliza's mother, Mrs. Hancock, had always kept in close touch with her brother's family, and, when possible, had seen Mrs. Austen through her many child-bearings. The bond must have been a close one, and Eliza certainly looked on Steventon as a second home when she was in England. James visited her in France in the spring of 1786, and Henry stayed with her in London both in 1787 and 1788, and rather hoped to return to France with her that year, but unfortunately a Fellow of St. John's was so inconsiderate as to die, leaving a place vacant, of which he had to take advantage. The visit to her in London must have been interesting enough. She was on intimate terms with Warren Hastings and his second wife, and probably took Henry, as well as her Cousin Philadelphia, to a session of Hastings' famous trial for "high crimes and misdemeanours" supposedly committed during his term of office as Governor-General in India. This politically-motivated trial loomed large in the public eye between 1788 and 1795 and must have been followed with close attention by the Austens. When Warren Hastings was finally found not guilty, he received, among other congratulations, a rather sycophantic letter from Henry Austen. It must have been small comfort considering the financial straits to which the long trial had reduced him. There would be no more help for Eliza from this quarter.

Eliza, meanwhile, continued "the greatest rake imaginable", as she wrote to her Cousin Philadelphia, but went happily from drawing-rooms and Almack's to join in the Austen family theatricals at Steventon. In November 1787 she wrote on her Aunt Austen's behalf to invite Philadelphia to join them in their Christmas production of *Which is the Man* and *Bon Ton*. "I assure you we shall have a most brilliant party and a great deal of amusement, the house full of company and frequent balls. You cannot possibly resist so many temptations, especially when I tell you your old friend James is returned from France and is to be of the acting party." But Philadelphia must have returned an answer like Fanny Price's. On November 23rd Eliza wrote again about "the strong reluctance you express to what you call *appearing in public*". And then, on a firmer note, she repeated her invitation: "Provided however you could bring yourself to act, for my Aunt Austen declares 'She has not room for any *idle young people*'."

Philadelphia did not go, so we are deprived of one of the faintly disapproving letters she used to write to her own brother James about their cousin and "her dissipated life". We have to imagine the brilliant party and the frequent balls, the crowded, cheerful rectory, and twelve-year-old Jane watching it all, and doubtless drawing her own conclusions as her brilliant cousin the Countess flirted impartially with James and Henry Austen at once. It is interesting in the light of the galaxy of male ones she was to create, that the first flirt Jane Austen is on record as encountering was female.

Did Mrs. Austen breathe a quiet, maternal sigh of relief when Eliza went back to France in 1788? If she did, it was premature. The connection was very far from being ended. About this time we get some rare glimpses of the Austen girls in their youth. Mr. and Mrs. Austen, Cassandra and Jane visited their benefactor, Francis Austen the attorney in Kent that summer, and while there they met their cousin Philadelphia Walter for the first time. Philadelphia wrote to her brother that Cassandra was supposed to be very like herself, and, "I can't help thinking her very pretty ... The youngest (Jane) is very like her brother Henry, not at all pretty and very prim, unlike a girl of twelve." And then, on a warmer note, she went on to describe parents and daughters as all "in high spirits and disposed to be pleased with each other". But, "Jane is whimsical and affected." Those observant eyes may have looked through the new-met cousin a little too obviously. Jane would learn to be more guarded as she grew up.

By 1791, the outbreak of the French Revolution had brought Eliza back to England with her little boy. The fact that her husband soon returned to France does not seem to have dampened her lively spirits, and she was soon writing Philadelphia that Cassandra and Jane "are perfect beauties and of course gain 'hearts by dozens'." Next year, a real disaster struck her in the death of her mother, to whom she was devoted. She went to Steventon to be comforted, and wrote Philadelphia that Cassandra and Jane "are both very much grown ... and greatly improved as well in manners as in person, both of which are now much more formed than when you saw them. They are I think equally sensible, and both so to a degree seldom met with, but still my heart gives the preference to Jane, whose kind partiality to me indeed requires a return of the same nature." And then, with a logical connection that might have alarmed Mrs. Austen, "Henry is now rather more than six foot high ... As to the coolness which you knew had taken place between H and myself, it has now ceased, in consequence of due acknowledgements on his part."

James had proved fickle. He married Anne Mathew, a general's daughter, in the spring of 1792, and the young couple set up house-keeping on an income of three hundred pounds a year. Edward, in Kent, had made the more prosperous match suitable to the adoptive heir of a fortune. He had married Elizabeth, daughter of Sir Brook Bridges in December, 1791, and by the autumn of 1792 Eliza could report to Philadelphia that, "Both Mrs. James and Mrs. Edward Austen are in the increasing way." That winter, the Austen girls' cousin and schoolmate, Jane Cooper, lost her father suddenly just before her intended marriage. She went straight to Steventon and was married from there, in December, to Captain Thomas Williams, R.N., who was to play a grateful part in the naval advancement of his young cousins-in-law, Charles and Francis. It is significant of the atmosphere at Steventon that bereavement and disaster always brought the cousins there. Altogether, what with deaths and births, courtings and marriages, balls and theatricals, there must have been plenty of material at hand for a girl who was beginning to discover the pleasures of writing.

One more description of Jane Austen dates from about this time, though it was recollected, much later, by an acquaintance of the Austens', Sir Egerton Brydges. He remembered Jane as "fair and handsome, slight and elegant, but with cheeks a little too full". Her nephew enlarged on this in the *Memoir*. "In complexion she was a clear brunette with a rich colour; she had full round cheeks, with mouth and nose small and well formed, bright hazel eyes, and brown hair forming natural curls close round her face. If not so regularly handsome as her sister, yet her countenance had a peculiar charm of its own to the eyes of most beholders." Her brother Henry, in the *Biographical Notice* he wrote for the posthumous edition of *Northanger Abbey* and *Persuasion*, misquoted Donne significantly. "Her complexion was of the finest texture. It might with truth be said, that her eloquent blood spoke through her modest cheek." What it spoke, is another question. No description can give the slightest hint of what lay behind her polite, enigmatic smile.

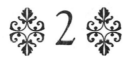

THE WORLD OF STEVENTON RECTORY WAS A PEACEFUL ONE, ITS variety no doubt provided by the coaches that stopped at Deane Gate or Popham Lane and set down an unexpected midshipman brother, or an equally welcome student. But what of the world outside the civilised enclave where Jane Austen was growing up? It was in a state of quite extraordinary social and political upheaval. Change of every kind was in the air. During her lifetime, Dr. Johnson died, and Darwin was born. Her brief forty-one years span the chasm between the eighteenth-century England of Dr. Johnson and Henry Fielding, and the comparatively modern one of the Regency.

Born in the year that "the shot heard round the world" heralded the War of American Independence, Jane Austen lived through the other, brief war with America of 1812–14 as well as the long, grim struggle with France that ended with Waterloo. War was a basic condition of her adult life, and it is not surprising that so many of the men who played a part in her story belong to the clergy. Her two sailor brothers fought for King and Country all over the high seas, and became admirals in the process, though not until after her death. She may not have talked about it much, but the long war must have been almost as steadily at the back of her thinking as the atomic bomb is at the back of ours.

At home, the war meant a steady rise in the cost of living, with prices when it ended eighty-seven per cent up on the pre-war level. Poverty, and the eighteenth-century enclosure of common land, were driving people into the towns; the Industrial Revolution was in full swing, and the machine breakers were out. But this was mainly in the Midlands and the North, where the greatest industrial development was taking place. There were not many Jacobins in Hampshire.

As always, the rising cost of living, which harmed many, helped some. The poor grew poorer, and the rich richer. Between them, a fascinating new phenomenon was growing in size and complexity: the middle class that was to be Jane Austen's special preserve. In the age of Dr. Johnson, there had been the aristocracy, the minor aristocracy, and the poor, with a few borderline cases (the clergy, for instance) in a kind of limbo between them. Younger sons of the aristocracy were provided for by "jobs" in the customs, the tax office, and above all in the exchequer. They could, without losing caste, be bought commissions in the army, or they could act as absentee parsons for a clutch of family livings. At a pinch, like Mr. Hancock, they could seek their fortunes abroad, often with the East India or the Hudson Bay Company. This kind of trade, if it was profitable enough, might pass. A rich nabob would be received in society much more easily than a man who had made money in trade at home. Similarly, medicine and the law might be profitable, but were not elegant.

The difficulty was that there were so many younger sons. By the end of the eighteenth century the supply both of "jobs" and of family livings was running low. Sprigs of the aristocracy were reduced to living in their parishes, like Henry Tilney and Edmund Bertram, and a whole new, literate society was beginning to develop round them. This was largely composed of "new" men, who had made fortunes of one kind or another, small or great, in the industrial expansion of the war years. George Austen's Uncle Francis, who started out with a bundle of quill-pens and eight hundred pounds and made a fortune as an attorney, is a case in point. The Gardiners in *Pride and Prejudice* exactly reflect his position. Fortunes were being made in trade too. I like to think that Mr. Woodhouse's money, which made Emma queen of Highbury, was based on some small, eighteenth-century, unmentionable object like the one in Henry James's *The Ambassadors*. But of course Mr. Woodhouse would not have made it himself, or Emma could not have held the position she did.

Some men were newer than others. The Eltons did not come up to Jane Austen's rigorous social standards (still less to Emma's), and Cobbett launched a fierce attack on new-rich farmers who lived in smart brick houses (often called "Waterloo Farm"), drove a gig and had a piano in the parlour for their daughters. The Martins, in *Emma*, leap at once to mind. I am sure that Mr. Martin bought a piano for his Harriet. On a higher level, "improving" farmers were making the most of the opportunities provided by the agricultural enclosure of the eighteenth century, and following Coke of Norfolk and his like in the intelligent use of their acres. The high price of wheat was no hardship to them. When he was not visiting the Woodhouses, Mr. Knightley was busy improving his land, with William Larkins as his prime minister, and no doubt making a great deal of money in the process. He could afford to be generous with his baking apples, and Emma, living on a fixed income, was lucky to get him.

The great landowners were improving too, but in a different way. It was the age of landscape gardening in the largest sense, of Capability Brown and of Repton, who charged five guineas a day, and whom Mr. Rushworth rather thought of employing at Sotherton. Mr. Rushworth, of course, was a mere Tory minnow compared to the great whales of the Whig aristocracy, who owned so much land, and so dominated society as practically to rule the country, whether they happened to be in or out of office. Most of them were not, in fact, of very ancient family, tending to date from the Glorious Revolution of 1688, or, at the most, from the Tudor upheaval.

We do not need Caroline Austen's information to be sure that Jane Austen, her family, and their friends were all country Tories of the deepest dye. As such, they would tend to look down on the comparatively *nouveau riche* Whigs, and might, often with some grounds, think them worse educated, and no better bred than themselves. Lady Catherine de Bourgh is probably Jane Austen's caricature of a Whig aristocrat. It makes one wonder a little about the politics of the Darcy family. Similarly, when Lady Middleton says there is little chance of their meeting Willoughby in the country, since he "is in the opposition, you know", she presumably means that she and her family are Whigs while his status as anti-hero makes him a country Tory like the Dashwoods.

Other changes were revolutionising social life. Canals and macadamised roads brought the first leap forward in transportation since the time of the Romans. Roads and regular mail services went together. The kind of steady correspondence kept up by Cassandra and Jane Austen had become a possibility for the first time in English history. Where Richardson's Pamela had to hide her letters under a stone, Jane Austen's Lady Susan could put them in the post bag.

Another drastic change was in dress. When Jane Austen was in short petticoats, men wore powder on their hair, knee-breeches, embroidered waistcoats and full-skirted coats, while their ladies were gorgeous in high "heads" and full-skirted gowns. The French Revolution and the Napoleonic War changed all this. Between the time that Jane Austen wrote her first three novels, and their revision for publication around 1809, fashions had changed dramatically, and were still changing. Trousers were coming in, even if the Duke of Wellington was turned away from Almack's for wearing them, and Lady Caroline Lamb was damping her exiguous muslins to make them cling to her figure. Commenting dryly, in her letters, on the new extremes of fashion, Jane Austen also learned a very useful lesson from the changes she had seen. Whether she went through her early work, as she revised it, and struck out any old-fashioned bits of costume, we shall never know, since the original versions do not survive, but certainly, in her books as they stand, there is the barest minimum of reference to dress. It is one of the many reasons why her novels remain so readable. One is not perpetually boggling over a fichu or neck-handkerchief. Only in *Northanger Abbey*, probably the least revised of all the books, do we get Henry Tilney's imaginary diary entry with its "sprigged muslin robe with blue trimmings – plain black shoes – appeared to much advantage". And here, significantly, Mrs. Allen reveals her stupidity by her preoccupation with dress.

Critics have accused Jane Austen of being impervious to the turbulence of the society she lived in, because she does not talk about it much. The answer, if one were needed, lies in the number of references to her novels in modern social histories of her times. She did not speak of these things, as Cobbett did, to praise or blame. They were simply incorporated in the fabric of her thinking, and therefore of her books. An acute reader can find hints of the contemporary scene everywhere. Where Lady Middleton gives the disagreeable Miss Steeles needlebooks made by an emigrant, a social historian would give us a whole chapter on the plight of the French refugees in England. Unluckily for her critics, Jane Austen was not vain enough to imagine being read by generations unaware of the conditions of her own age. Having, for once, set *Persuasion* definitely in 1814, she expected (not unreasonably) that her readers would know all about the brief peace with France that freed Captain Wentworth for his love-making. When she finished the book in 1816, she must have felt no need to underline the pathos of its ending. Describing Anne's happiness, she tells us that, "The dread of a future war was all that could dim her sunshine." Contemporary readers would have known how close that war was.

Religious thought and feeling were changing with everything else. The eighteenth century had fancied itself the great age of reason. Pope, writing his *Essay on Man* in the first half of the century, had described the human situation as, "A mighty maze and quite without a plan"; had been persuaded by his friends that this might, just possibly, give offence; and had changed the line to read, "A mighty maze! But not without a plan." His first version was probably the more characteristic of his time. When he was writing, the seventeenth-century religious crisis of Protestant versus Catholic was over; the Church was Established, taken for granted, and, much of the time, forgotten. It was the great age of pluralism and the hunting parson.

With the turn of the century came a turn of feeling. The age of reason had led to the horrors of the French Revolution. The inertia of the Established Church was challenged by the Dissenters, and, in particular, by the Evangelicals, whose Bible was Wilberforce's *Practical Christianity*, published in 1797. Below the frivolous surface of Regency England, a great groundswell of serious thought was building up, showing itself, notably, in the Bill for the abolition of the slave trade, which was pushed through Parliament by Wilberforce and his friends in 1807. Writing, towards the end of her life, to her niece Fanny, Jane Austen spoke up for the Evangelicals, and there is certainly a contrast between the light-hearted use of the Church as a career in *Sense and Sensibility* and *Northanger Abbey* and Jane Austen's own declared intention of discussing the problem of ordination in *Mansfield Park*. But where she herself stood in the matter remains open to question. The one thing that is certain is that, as always, she was deeply aware of the change of feeling around her.

Dissent and education went together, and the reading public was already growing rapidly when Jane Austen was born. Circulating libraries existed as early as 1742, and by the end of the eighteenth century demand and supply of light reading were growing side by side. Public lending libraries were supplemented by private borrowing groups such as those Jane Austen speaks of in her letters. The mass market that made small fortunes for Miss Burney and Miss Edgeworth, but not for Miss Austen, was already in existence. The libraries, in fact, were such a powerful element in the book market that they were able to insist on the main-tenance of the expensive three-volume format that suited them because each of the volumes could be lent out separately.

It is hard, today, to imagine the amount of free time that the average member of the middle to upper classes had in the late eighteenth and early nineteenth centuries. Even middle-class poverty probably meant being reduced to two maid-servants and a man. Jane and Cassandra Austen may have acted as house-keepers for their ailing mother: it would have been unthinkable for them to act as cook. There was all the time in the world for satin stitch, and morning calls, and novel reading.

Jane Austen could always find time to write to Cassandra when they were separated, not with a fountain pen, or an easy ballpoint, but with a quill pen that constantly needed mending, and with the high cost of postage always in mind. Writing had to be kept small and legible, the lines close together, and sometimes even crossed. The importance of a good, clear hand was one of Tysoe Saul Hancock's reiterated themes as he wrote home to his wife about the education of their daughter Eliza. Jane Austen wrote as beautifully as she sewed, and was glad, late in her life, to note an improvement in the handwriting of a nephew.

It is worth stopping for a moment to consider how different her world really was from ours. Her understanding of human nature was so profound, her cool, realistic outlook on life apparently so like our own, her characters so convincing, that one is in danger of assuming that her (and their) circumstances, too, were like ours. It is an advantage of her books that this mistake is possible, but it is a hazard to our understanding of their author.

When she described a country walk, like the one Anne Elliot took with the Musgroves and Captain Wentworth, what did Jane Austen expect her reader to imagine from the small amount of detail she allowed herself? There are "tawny leaves and withered hedges", and, when the walkers near their destination, Winthrop Farm, where an improving farmer is at work, there are "large enclosures, where the ploughs at work, and the fresh-made path spoke the farmer, counteracting the sweets of poetical despondence, and meaning to have spring again."

It was a quiet countryside, with birdsong and the farmer shouting at his horse where we would expect motor horns and the roar of the tractor. A horse-drawn mail coach might clatter by, but no jet plane would scream overhead. The hedgerows Jane Austen loved would be full of primroses and violets in spring, as they were of hazelnuts in autumn; and when silly Harriet Smith scrambled up the bank to get away from the gipsies, she may have been scratched by a bramble, or stung by a nettle, but she was certainly not impaled on barbed wire. One needs to remember, all the time, the untouched, quiet landscape that Jane Austen knew and loved.

The same chasm yawns between her city experience and ours. Hans Place, where she liked to stay with her favourite brother Henry, was across the fields from London proper, and though Horace Walpole probably anticipated Jane Austen's own views in calling Bath a detestable little city "all crammed together and surrounded with perpendicular hills", it was still one where the Austens' first house was on the edge of open country, and where the worst that could happen to Catherine Morland was to be nearly run down by a badly driven curricle. If Jane Austen disliked Bath in the 1800s, I wonder what she would think of it today.

And then there was the position of woman, into which Jane Austen was growing in the rambling freedom of Steventon. Mary Wollstonecraft's *Vindication of the Rights of Women* was published in 1792, when Jane was seventeen. Some women and, even, men were beginning to talk and think about women's rights, but the leaven of social change was only just starting to work. If there were few ways that a young man could respectably earn a living, there was only one for a young woman. She must marry. The only possible alternative was teaching, either in a school or as a governess. Miserably paid, either position meant that its holder was lost in an even lower limbo than that of the younger sons who became apothecaries or attorneys, and without their chance of redeeming themselves by making a fortune.

This was not all. Before she married, a young woman was imprisoned behind an iron curtain of proprieties. She could not live alone, or travel alone, or, in the higher reaches of society, even walk alone. Lady Harriet Cavendish, walking on her family's country estate, was invariably accompanied by a footman. It is no wonder that the Miss Bingleys were horrified at Elizabeth Bennet's arrival, muddy and cheerful from having walked a few miles across the fields. And, naturally if she must not walk alone, still less must a young woman walk tête-à-tête with a man. If Jane Fairfax had agreed to walk back to Donwell Abbey with Frank Churchill, it would have been as good as announcing their engagement.

Since a woman's only future was matrimony, education in the academic sense was comparatively unimportant. Accomplishments were what mattered. Young ladies must be able to display themselves to advantage. They learned to sing, to draw, to dance, to play the piano, or the harp, if they had good arms and rich fathers; to write a good hand and to listen to the gentlemen talk. Anything else was really supererogatory. When Jane Austen's elder brother James suffered a small diminution in his income, he very naturally cut down on his daughter's education. It is eternally to the credit of her brother, the author of the *Memoir*, that he instantly offered to give up his hunters rather than let her suffer.

But then, the Austens were an unusual family. Even so, young Jane must soon have been aware of the differences between Cassandra and herself and their brothers. While the boys were out in hunting pink risking their necks on cut-price ponies, the girls must graduate from garden and childhood pleasures to the more adult delights of housewifery, morning calls and, for exercise, shared walks and drives. Again, if they were rich, they could ride, with a groom in attendance, but this was well above the Austens' touch. Jane Austen must have learned to ride at some point in her career, no doubt when staying with her brother Edward in Kent, or she would not have been able to manage those sad donkeys when she was ill, but she never speaks of riding in her letters, and her heroines do not indulge in it much. Mrs. Bennet made Jane ride to

Netherfield in the (successful) hope that she would catch cold; Fanny Price rode for health, and Mary Crawford for pleasure, but we seldom see the Bertram girls riding, or the Musgroves. This may simply mean that Jane Austen was artist enough to realise that the kind of conversation at which she excelled is not very conveniently conducted on horseback, but I think it also reflects a condition of her level of society. Horses were for the gentlemen; ladies walked, or, best of all, danced for their exercise. Here, at least, was a socially accepted form of activity, and Jane Austen loved it. Luckily for her, she belonged to a family that almost certainly cared nothing for the elaborate rules of elegant society, by which a young lady could not appear in public until her older sisters were married and she was "out". Mrs. Austen, like Mrs. Bennet, undoubtedly let her daughters join in those gay little balls of which Eliza de Feuillide wrote to her cousin Philadelphia, and when Jane Austen wrote of enough private balls to satisfy any but the insatiable appetite of fifteen, she wrote from experience.

We do not know when she attended her first public ball (they happened once a month all winter at Basingstoke), any more than we know when she wrote her first story, but, for both events, an early date is more probable than a late one. The Austens were a family who enjoyed playing with words. They wrote riddles in the elaborate style of the period, and celebrated family occasions in comic verse. When Jane was growing up, her eldest brother, James, was a Fellow at Oxford, and running his own periodical, *The Loiterer*, (no connection, of course, with *The Rambler* or *The Spectator*), and Henry, also at Oxford, was contributing to it. It has, in fact, been suggested that the thirteen-year-old Jane may have contributed a letter signed "Sophia Sentiment" to the March, 1789, number of *The Loiterer*. At all events, there was writing in the air, and a sympathetic audience ready. So when exactly did young Jane start writing? Long afterwards, when she lay dying at Winchester, she sent a message to her twelve-year-old niece Caroline, who had already started to write. "If I would take her advice," Caroline reported her aunt as saying, "I should cease writing till I was sixteen . . . she had herself often wished she had *read* more, and written *less*, in the corresponding years of her own life."

If we accept the year 1787 for the date of the Austen girls' return home from Mrs. Latournelle's school, it seems reasonable to take this, when Jane was nearly twelve, as the date of the earliest of the minor works that survive in three closely-written notebooks. Jane Austen may have regretted, as she told Caroline, that she had not read more and written less, but she still felt kindly enough towards what she had written to copy and save it, and we must be grateful to her.

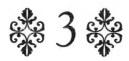

3

EXPERTS AGREE IN ASSIGNING THE MISCELLANEOUS PIECES THAT
Jane Austen copied into her three notebooks to the years 1787 to 1793,
when she was twelve to eighteen. The juvenile hand-writing of the
earliest pieces in *Volume the First* is probably almost contemporary with
their composition, but Jane Austen continued the painstaking copying
of these early works for many years. It is another reminder of how much
time she had. The originals are lost, and the three volumes are not
necessarily copied in chronological order of composition, but B. C.
Southam has worked out a convincing arrangement for them, and
argues that at least all the earliest pieces are, quite evidently, in *Volume the
First.*

The varied and often delightful contents of these three volumes were
written for Jane Austen's whole family. They were a public, not a
private joke. And the dedications with which she furnished them, in
parody of the fashion of the time, showed that the varying family group,
diminished by the absence of some members, was also enlarged from time
to time during this period by visits from friends, relations, and married
brothers. There are dedications to all the immediate members of the
family (except, of course, the unfortunate George), and to the two first
nieces, James's daughter Anna and Edward's daughter Fanny. The family
circle was growing. Fanny and Anna were both born in 1793, so that the
solemn dedications to them must have been by way of christening
presents from their "affectionate aunt".

Two pieces are dedicated to the Austens' cousin, Jane Cooper, and the
best known of all the *Juvenilia, Love and Friendship* to their cousin Eliza,
Madame la Comtesse de Feuillide, no doubt on the occasion of one of her

Christmas visits to Steventon. *Frederic and Elfrida*, the first piece in *Volume the First*, is dedicated to Martha Lloyd, "As a small testimony of the gratitude I feel for your late generosity to me in finishing my muslin cloak ..." while *Evelyn*, in *Volume the Third*, which is dated May 6th, 1792, is dedicated to Martha's sister Mary.

The Lloyd girls were probably Cassandra and Jane's closest friends. Their widowed mother had lived for a few years as tenant of Deane Rectory, moving to a house called Ibthorp, eighteen miles away, in 1792, no doubt because James Austen was marrying and taking over at Deane. The connection between Lloyds and Austens, reinforced in various ways, was to continue through all their lives. Mrs. Lloyd had been one of three Miss Cravens, daughters of a notorious Lady Craven, whose brutal neglect of her children had been an eighteenth-century scandal and whose story probably lies behind both *Lesley Castle* and *Lady Susan*. Mrs. Lloyd's other daughter, Eliza, had already married her cousin Fulwar Craven Fowle, whose brother Thomas had been a pupil at Steventon Rectory and was to be still more closely linked with the Austens.

There were other close friends in those lively, sociable growing years. When the Austen girls went to the monthly Assembly Balls at Basingstoke, they often stayed with their friends the Misses Bigg, daughters of Mr. Bigg Wither of Manydown, and no doubt treated their younger brother Harris, six years younger than Jane, very much as they did their "own particular brother", Charles. Nearer home, there were the Digweed boys, sons of Mr. Digweed who rented Steventon Manor from Mr. Knight, and, most important to Jane, Mrs. Lefroy, wife of the neighbouring Rector of Ashe, a cultivated woman who seems to have acted, to some extent, as mother-substitute for Mrs. Austen, who, though only fifty-three in 1793 seems already to have acquired some of the habits and privileges of old age. She had worked hard, and borne and reared eight children in fourteen years. Now, when Jane and Cassandra went out dancing, chaperoned by friends, she stayed at home with her sixty-two-year-old husband.

Since we have none of Jane Austen's own letters written before 1796, the *Juvenilia* themselves give us our best picture of her teenage years. First and foremost, they show her as an omnivorous reader, despite that caution of hers to her niece Caroline. When she said that she wished she had read more and written less, she very probably meant that she wished she had read more selectively. According to her brother Henry, "Her reading was very extensive in history and belles lettres; and her memory extremely tenacious. Her favourite moral writers were Johnson in prose and Cowper in verse." She preferred Richardson to Fielding, was "enamoured of

Gilpin on the Picturesque", and, later in life, was teased a good deal about her passion for Crabbe's poetry, and recognised Scott at once as the author of *Waverley*.

She and her family were happy addicts of the novel: "great novel-readers and not ashamed of being so," she said herself in a letter of 1798. The greater part of her *Juvenilia* are skits on one kind of contemporary fictional excess or another, and our enjoyment of them is partly, though only partly, dependent on our knowledge of the butt.

Here is Richardson, and the novel in letters:

DEAR SALLY,

I have found a very convenient old hollow oak to put our letters in; for you know we have long maintained a private correspondence. It is about a mile from my house and seven from yours. You may perhaps imagine that I might have made choice of a tree which would have divided the distance more equally—I was sensible of this at the time, but as I considered that the walk would be of benefit to you in your weak and uncertain state of health, I preferred it to one nearer your house, and am your faithful

BENJAMIN BARR.

The contemporary novel of extreme sensibility is another favourite target, but one that seems to have irritated the young author almost beyond humour. *Evelyn*, where everyone acts from motives of the most ludicrous sensibility, is one of the least entertaining of these very miscellaneous pieces. The same is true of Jane Austen's attempts to parody contemporary drama. It is odd that someone who was to write such admirable dialogue should have had so little gift for the theatre, but the dramatic fragments are as disappointing as the occasional attempts at verse:

> When Corydon went to the fair
> He bought a red ribbon for Bess,
> With which she encircled her hair
> And made herself look very fess.

Whose daughter has not produced something like this? It is, of course, one of the very earliest of the *Juvenilia*, dated by Chapman as written between 1787 and 1790, that is between Jane Austen's twelfth and fifteenth years.

The other pieces belonging to this period are particularly interesting for the light they cast on the family circle in and for which they were written. Jane Austen's brother Henry claimed, rather primly, that she liked

37

Fielding less than Richardson because "she recoiled from everything gross. Neither nature, wit, nor humour, could make her amends for so very low a scale of morals." Following his line, Jane Austen's modern detractors like to write of her as a born old maid, who peered myopically at a limited world through blinkers. They must have forgotten about the Johnsons (in *Jack and Alice*) who "were a family of love, and though a little addicted to the bottle and the dice, had many good qualities", and who ended a lively evening at the gaming table by being carried home "dead drunk". And there is Lucy, in the same piece, who began by being caught in a man-trap on her beloved's estate and ended the victim of a rival, "who jealous of her superior charms took her by poison from an admiring world at the age of seventeen".

In her early teens, Jane Austen struck a curiously modern note in her mockery of the kind of contemporary hero and heroine who thought nothing of robbing their benefactors, and believed it their duty to disobey their parents. It seems that the angry young man is not an entirely twentieth-century invention after all. "My father," says a baronet's son in *Love and Friendship*, "is a mean and mercenary wretch!" "Seduced by the false glare of fortune and the deluding pomp of title," this deplorable parent has urged his son to marry the Lady Dorothea, with whom, in fact, he is in love. His answer is inevitable. "Lady Dorothea is lovely and engaging; I prefer no woman to her; but know, Sir, that I scorn to marry her in compliance with your wishes. No! Never shall it be said that I obliged my father." Jane Austen goes on, incorrigibly, to have it both ways in the father's answer. "Where Edward in the name of wonder (said he) did you pick up this unmeaning gibberish? You have been studying novels I suspect." Naturally, the hero refuses to reply to this unfair insinuation, mounts his horse and sets out on a succession of mock-picaresque adventures.

Already, from time to time, in these early works, one hears, clear as a bell, the delicious, unmistakable note of Jane Austen's laughter. "Preserve yourself from a first love," says Lady Williams in *Jack and Alice*, "and you need not fear a second." The heroines of *Love and Friendship* faint "alternately on a sofa", and one of them, dying of a chill, apostrophises the other as follows: "Beware of swoons, dear Laura . . . A frenzy fit is not one quarter so pernicious; it is an exercise to the body and if not too violent, is I dare say conducive to health in its consequences – Run mad as often as you choose; but do not faint."

Love and Friendship is perhaps the most entertaining of the early works, but *Lesley Castle* and *Catherine* are the more significant for Jane Austen's development. They show the young author moving gradually away from her basis in parody towards the novel itself. *Northanger Abbey* is simply a further stage in the same development. Its heroine, incidentally, was originally called Susan, not Catherine.

Throughout the *Juvenilia*, young Jane Austen was quite evidently enjoying herself in her new element, experimenting with sentence structure, with Johnsonian antithesis, and with alliteration, and entertaining her family with topical jokes. "Beware of the unmeaning luxuries of Bath and the stinking fish of Southampton," says Isabel in *Love and Friendship*, and the author, reading aloud, could no doubt depend on her family's sympathetic laughter. There must have been a visit to that stiff Aunt and Uncle Leigh Perrot who divided their time between their house, Scarlets, in Berkshire, and Bath. Jane Austen was later to write: " 'Tis really very kind of my aunt to ask us to Bath again; a kindness that deserves a better return than to profit by it." The Southampton reference may hark further back to that unlucky school episode, but it is more likely to celebrate a happier occasion described in a characteristically arch letter of Eliza de Feuillide's in 1791. "As to Cassandra it is very possible as you observe that some son of Neptune may have obtained her approbation as she probably experienced much homage from these very gallant gentlemen during her aquatic excursions. I hear her sister and herself are two of the prettiest girls in England." Perhaps Cassandra and her parents had accompanied Charles to the Portsmouth Naval Academy, where he was enrolled that year, and where Francis had already distinguished himself. No doubt it was with Francis' older friends that Cassandra made her "aquatic excursions". It is sad to think that Bath and Southampton, so light-heartedly mentioned here, were later to be the setting for the unhappiest and least productive years of Jane Austen's life.

But, for the moment, all was matter for her mirth. An unusual departure was her comic *History of England*, based on Goldsmith's *History* with a few light-hearted side-glances to Shakespeare, and foreshadowing, to a quite surprising extent, Sellar and Yeatman's *1066 and All That*. The *History* runs from the reign of Henry IV, who "ascended the throne of England much to his own satisfaction in the year 1399", to that of Charles I, where the young author leaves off, admitting that, "The recital of any events (except what I make myself) is uninteresting to me." As so often with Jane Austen, it is hard, in this extravaganza, to tell just where the laughter stops. Was she entirely serious, as her family thought, in her defence of Mary Stuart? She certainly anticipated a modern shift of historical opinion by coming out strongly in defence of the House of York, and even of Richard III. After all, as she sagely observes, "If Perkin Warbeck was really the Duke of York, why might not Lambert Simnel be the widow of Richard." She also quotes a surprisingly realistic charade on James I's favourite, Carr. Speech and thought must have been remarkably free at Steventon Rectory.

But the *Juvenilia* also reflect other, sharper experiences of adolescence. Where should we look for the original of Catherine's jealous aunt who so misconstrued the girl's lively friendliness with young men? And who was the source for the great lady in the *Collection of Letters*, who anticipates Lady Catherine de Bourgh's discourteous treatment of Charlotte Collins? We shall never know, but what does become obvious through the ebullience, the exaggeration and the sheer nonsense of the *Juvenilia* is that their young author was very far from being an inexperienced country mouse. Those observant eyes had seen a great deal, that happy spirit had found much to criticise as well as much to laugh at in the world by the time Jane Austen was eighteen.

Then, maddeningly, silence falls for three years. We know from the *Life*[1] that Jane Austen visited Southampton at about this time and apparently went to a ball there, and that she and Cassandra went to stay with Edward and his wife in Kent, and with friends (probably the Fowles) in Gloucestershire. But there are no letters for this period. Cassandra and Jane paid their visits together and undoubtedly wrote home to their parents, but Mrs. Austen was not the kind of mother who saved her children's letters. With seven of them active in the world, it is hardly surprising.

It seems to have been at this time that Jane Austen took a vital step forward in her career as an author. She stopped writing for the whole family and started writing for herself. But what did she write first? Many years later, Cassandra wrote a brief note on the dating of her sister's novels,[2] which suggests that an early version of *Sense and Sensibility* called *Elinor and Marianne* was written about this time, and there is a family tradition that this was a novel in letters. This instantly suggests a connection with Jane Austen's one surviving novel in letters, *Lady Susan*. Experts disagree about the date of *Lady Susan*, but I think it is safe to assume that these two books occupied Jane Austen between 1793 and 1796, when, according to Cassandra, she began work on *First Impressions*, which was to become our *Pride and Prejudice*.

Unfortunately, no copy of *Elinor and Marianne* survives. Jane Austen

[1] Used throughout for *Jane Austen: Her Life and Letters* by W. and R. A. Austen-Leigh.
[2] See Appendix II.

seems to have destroyed her original texts when she was satisfied with her revision. But even in its final form, as *Sense and Sensibility*, the book seems to me to share another significant characteristic with *Lady Susan*. These two are Jane Austen's harshest books. *Lady Susan* would come as a surprise from her pen at whatever age she wrote it. This curiously cold-blooded study of a wicked woman is almost entirely without humour. Until the very end, the laughter is silent. Then, at last, having perhaps written herself into a better temper, Jane Austen allows herself a characteristic note. She abandons the letter form and writes a conclusion in her own unmistakable style. "This correspondence, by a meeting between some of the parties and a separation between the others, could not, to the great detriment of the Post Office Revenue, be continued longer." And she goes on to wind up the affairs of her characters with the kind of brisk, humorous affection that ends *Northanger Abbey*.

Many people find it impossible really to like *Sense and Sensibility*. Elinor is often too sensible to be borne, and Marianne too silly, while the minor characters tend dangerously towards caricature. Even in the final version, a kind of bad temper that we do not readily associate with Jane Austen will keep breaking through. Mr. Palmer's habitual rudeness is not funny, though we try to think it so, and Lucy Steele goes in for a type of psychological cruelty that Lady Susan would have admired. The scenes where she insists on confiding in Elinor about her love for Elinor's beloved Edward are curiously painful, and so is the way Elinor lays herself open to them and, inevitably, to a charge of hypocrisy: "I should be undeserving of the confidence you have honoured me with, if I felt no desire for its continuance, or no farther curiosity on its subject. I will not apologise therefore for bringing it forward again." She may not need to apologise to Lucy, but she should, or her author should, to us. Of course, something stiff in Elinor's tone, here and at other critical points of the book, may be the result of the translation from letter form. But I think there is more to it than this. I think these two books were written during a grave crisis of Jane Austen's life, and very probably helped her through it.

1795 was Jane Austen's twentieth year. Catherine Morland or Marianne Dashwood would have thought her almost on the shelf. And indeed her life must have changed to a quite extraordinary extent since the carefree days of the *Juvenilia*, when there was almost always a brother at home to share the family jokes. By now, James and Edward were married men, James with one, Edward with two children. Charles and Francis were both at sea, and Henry, Jane's favourite brother, must have been rather evidently at sea in another sense. At once the most brilliant and the least successful of the family, he had thought of taking orders, had changed his mind and become a lieutenant of the Oxford Militia in 1793.

It is tempting to connect this change of plan with the final return to England of that brilliant older cousin of his, Eliza de Feuillide. Revealed in her letters as a witty, frivolous, gossiping creature, Eliza thought nothing of the Church, and Henry, quite evidently, thought a good deal of her. Her husband the Count had sent her to England for her safety, while he returned to France, hoping to save at least something of the family estate from the rising tide of the French Revolution. Instead, he was caught trying to help a friend who was already engulfed by it, was convicted of suborning and seducing witnesses, and guillotined in February 1794. His mistress gave evidence at his trial, but then it was twelve eventful years since his wife had written that "he literally adores me."

Jane Austen had encountered death before, when her aunt Jane Cooper caught diphtheria from them, but that had been when she was only a child. The death, under such horrible circumstances, of her cousin's husband, though we do not know if she had ever met him, must have been a considerable shock to the eighteen-year-old girl, who would hate France all her life. It may, perhaps, have been a kind of double shock. None of Eliza de Feuillide's letters to the Austen family survive, but she certainly wrote to them, probably to Jane, who was her favourite of the two sisters, and undoubtedly in the same frivolous tone she used to their cousin Philadelphia Walter. Did she take her husband's death too lightly? After all, she had never pretended to love him, and very likely knew about the mistress he kept in France. Or, perhaps worse still, did she parade a grief everyone knew she did not feel? It must all have been hideously complicated, for the Austens, by the question of Henry. For Jane, it may have been a double disillusionment. Eliza had written Philadelphia about Jane's "kind partiality to me", and Henry was Jane's favourite brother.

Another, closer family death followed in 1795. James Austen's wife Anne had lived only a mile and a half away from the Austens at Deane and must have been, by then, very much a member of the family. Her death was equally sudden and unexpected, and her two-year-old daughter Anna was brought at once to Steventon to be cared for and consoled by her young aunts. That they did this successfully is clear from Anna's long, intimate relationship with them both, but it must have made it a sad year for the Austens.

Something probably much more drastic even than these encounters with death and disillusionment happened to Jane Austen about this time.

Cassandra fell in love. We do not know anything about the development of her relationship with Tom Fowle. He had been her father's pupil long before, and must have kept in touch with the Austens through his brother's marriage to Eliza Lloyd. Now he was a clergyman. Cassandra and Jane had visited his family, and by 1795 he and Cassandra were engaged and she was doubtless busy working on her trousseau. Next year, Mrs. Austen, writing to welcome a new daughter-in-law, mentioned Cassandra's prospective departure for Shropshire. This must have been a reference to a living there promised to Tom Fowle by his relative, Lord Craven, but until it fell vacant, there was no money to marry on. Tom Fowle went to the West Indies in 1796 as regimental chaplain with Lord Craven, and Cassandra stayed at home at Steventon.

And what of Jane? So far, she and Cassandra had always shared everything, whether good or bad. "If Cassandra was going to have her head cut off, Jane would insist on sharing her fate." And here was something Jane could not share. What did she feel? How did she bear it? We have no idea. But it seems to me that whatever precise and painful form it took, this experience must lie behind that curiously repeated situation in the novels where the heroine finds herself, against her will, the confidante in a love affair that concerns her all too closely. *Sense and Sensibility* provides the most obvious case, but there is poor Fanny Price, too, and Anne Elliot watching the Musgrove sisters compete for Captain Wentworth, and listening to his sister's comments on the progress of the affair. Even Emma knows a near touch of tragedy when Harriet artlessly confides in her that she loves Mr. Knightley and imagines her love returned.

This is not, of course, to suggest that Jane Austen harped on this painful theme because she had suffered a similar experience. She need not have been in love with Tom Fowle, as her sister was, though it does seem a possibility not to be ignored. She may, quite simply, have been jealous of Cassandra's love for him. It would have been a very human reaction. For the first time, she would have found herself taking second place in the beloved sister's affections. It must have been very lonely, all of a sudden, in the shared bedroom at Steventon.

The first result of this, in my view, was *Lady Susan*, a kind of literary exercise, a study at once in evil and in the novel in letters. It was never to see the light of day in Jane Austen's lifetime. Cassandra did not mention it in her chronology of her sister's books, but left the untitled manuscript to her niece Fanny Knatchbull. James Edward Austen-Leigh published it, with his title and Lady Knatchbull's permission, as an addition to the second edition of his *Memoir* of his aunt in 1871. That is almost all that we know about this undated fair copy, except that two of the sheets are watermarked 1805. But the *Memoir* refers to a family tradition that it was "an early production", while the authors of the *Life* say it was written about the same time as *Elinor and Marianne*, which they attribute to 1795.

There were probably two good reasons for the use of the old-fashioned letter form in *Lady Susan*. The first was that by using letters for her study of a brilliant, unscrupulous woman, Jane Austen was putting her anti-heroine at one remove from the reader. She was implying, as Richardson did in his books, that she was merely the "editor", not the creator of her adventuress. Why did she do this? In my view, because Lady Susan is the only one of her characters who is quite evidently, and to a surprisingly large extent, drawn from life—or rather, from two lives.

Which brings us to the other, and probably less conscious reason for Jane Austen's use of the letter form. If Eliza de Feuillide was half so faithful a correspondent with Steventon as she was with her Cousin Philadelphia, Jane Austen must have had a perfect goldmine of raw material ready to hand. One has only to compare a few of Lady Susan's letters with Eliza's (preserved in the *Austen Papers*) to be aware of the resemblance. And Eliza would certainly have written regularly to Steventon because she did not like to lose touch with her "beaux". It is her word, and it gives an immediate clue to Jane Austen's feelings about her. In the novels, it is the vulgar characters who talk about beaux, the Miss Steeles, and Emma Watson's underbred sisters. Gay, worldly Eliza must have failed some half-conscious test of her Cousin Jane's, and at this time of psychological low-water her letters may have provided the same kind of springboard into fantasy that contemporary novels had previously supplied.

But though the style of Lady Susan's letters is like Eliza's, her character is not. Eliza de Feuillide may have been a lightweight, but within her limits she seems to have been a good mother and a good wife. Lady Susan is nothing of the kind. For her character, Jane Austen had almost certainly gone back to the stories the Lloyd girls could tell about their mother and aunts' sufferings at the hands of the unnatural Lady Craven. Lady Susan's heartless treatment of her daughter Frederica is crucial to the plot of this hard, brilliant book. A widow with one daughter, Lady Susan has to leave her friends the Manwarings, with whom she has stayed since the death of her husband, because of the justified rage of Mrs. Manwaring. As if having an affair with Mr. Manwaring was not enough, Lady Susan has also contrived to snatch Mrs. Manwaring's sister's young man, not for herself but for her daughter, who detests him. Penniless, Lady Susan then

44

goes to stay with her brother-in-law, Mr. Vernon, and his wife, against whom she has plotted in the past. They are therefore armed against her wiles, but just the same she has soon charmed Mr. Vernon into believing her more sinned against than sinning. Worse still, she entertains herself by making Mrs. Vernon's brother Reginald fall in love with her, despite all that he knows about her. The skilfully varied letters that fly to and fro between the characters show Lady Susan successful up to the very end, when an unlucky meeting between Reginald and Mrs. Manwaring betrays everything and leaves him free to marry Frederica.

Lady Susan shows no signs of the audience participation that was so characteristic of the *Juvenilia*. This was no shared family joke, but a private investigation of the problem of evil. Its heroine may be an adulteress but it is an almost heavily moral book. I imagine that the same could almost certainly be said of the original *Elinor and Marianne*. Here again we have the suggestion of a literary exercise, a cold-blooded study of the effects of over-caution and over-enthusiasm on the heroines' careers. By the time she revised it, Jane Austen had her favourite audience back, and we have no way of knowing how much of the comedy was written in then. I think the first version was probably a serious attempt by the author to analyse the springs and bases of human behaviour. They were always to fascinate her, but at this point, just for a little while, they failed to amuse. She had learned, before she was twenty, that loneliness is the human condition.

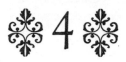

4

1795 HAD BEEN A YEAR OF CHEQUERED EXPERIENCE, BUT 1796 opened gaily with the first letter of Jane Austen's that has been preserved. It was, naturally, to Cassandra, who was staying with her fiancé's family at Kintbury, in Berkshire, and, appropriately enough, it described an affair of Jane Austen's own. "Imagine to yourself everything most profligate and shocking in the way of dancing and sitting down together." She had been amusing herself by an outrageous flirtation with her friend Mrs. Lefroy's nephew, Tom Lefroy from Ireland. He was "a very gentlemanlike, good-looking, pleasant young man, I assure you," and "has but *one* fault . . . his morning coat is a great deal too light." So, by the sound of it, were Jane Austen's feelings about him.

Her Victorian relatives were to defend Jane Austen with rather touching vehemence against old Mrs. Mitford's remark that she was "the prettiest, silliest, most affected, husband-hunting butterfly she ever remembers". It is true, as Edward Austen-Leigh points out, that by the time Jane Austen was old enough to hunt husbands, Mrs. Mitford had left the district, but it is also true that the old lady still had friends there. I like to think that this report may have been superficially correct, though basically false. If we take it in conjunction with Jane Austen's own letters we can see that what was intended as criticism was in fact high praise. It shows how successfully Jane Austen had embarked on her double life. Young ladies were supposed to be pretty, and silly, and on the catch for husbands. Jane Austen had decided to conform. And as "an artist can do nothing slovenly", she was, naturally, the prettiest and silliest of them all.

The letters give her away. Laughter will keep breaking through. In the next one to Cassandra, she reports that she rather expects Tom Lefroy to propose to her. "I shall refuse him, however, unless he promises to give away his white coat." The young man, perhaps, as young men will, recognised that fatal undercurrent of laughter. He did not propose, but vanished back to Ireland, where he eventually became Lord Chief Justice, and remembered being in love with Jane Austen as a young man. "But it was a boy's love." There certainly seem to have been no broken hearts in the business. "At length the day is come on which I am to flirt my last with Tom Lefroy, and when you receive this it will be all over. My tears flow as I write at the melancholy idea." And without so much as stopping to dry her eyes, or mop up a non-existent blot on her paper, Jane Austen went on with her light-hearted account of family doings.

It must have been a happy year, despite Tom Fowle's departure for the West Indies. When Cassandra had returned from her farewell visit to Kintbury, Jane set off by way of London to stay with their prosperous brother Edward, who was settled with his wife and children at a house called Rowling in Kent, which combined the virtues of belonging to her family, the Bridges, and being in comfortable visiting range of his adopted parents, the Knights of Godmersham. Writing from Cork Street on the way to Kent, Jane Austen begins, "Here I am once more in this scene of dissipation and vice, and I begin already to find my morals corrupted." Edward and Frank were with her, and they were all going to Astley's. Her next letter, dated from Rowling, shows her well acquainted with the place and people. It was obviously not her first visit. But it presented her with a problem by which she was often to be plagued, that of transport. Young ladies did not travel alone, still less in public vehicles. That is why General Tilney's behaviour in sending the seventeen-year-old Catherine Morland seventy miles across country by herself was so monstrous.

At twenty Jane Austen was dependent on her brothers' plans for her conveyance home, and naturally her convenience must give way to theirs. "Tomorrow I shall be just like Camilla in Mr. Dubster's summer-house; for my Lionel will have taken away the ladder by which I came here." She was referring to Fanny Burney's *Camilla*, which was published that year, and to which she subscribed. She had other problems. "I am in great distress—I cannot determine whether I shall give Richis[1] half a guinea or only five shillings when I go away. Counsel me, amiable Miss Austen, and tell me which will be the most." On allowances of twenty pounds a year, the Miss Austens could never afford to be lavish, and the curious use of "most" instead of "best" probably shows how this rankled, specially among those rich relatives in Kent.

[1] Presumably a Rowling servant.

47

But life in Kent was always entertaining, with calls, and balls, and plenty of people to laugh about. "Miss Fletcher and I were very thick, but I am the thinnest of the two." And, on what might, if the author were not Jane Austen, have been a more serious note, "We went by Bifrons, and I contemplated with a melancholy pleasure, the abode of him, on whom I once fondly doted." Mrs. Mitford's "butterfly" must have been remembering a flirtation with one of the five suitable sons of the Rev. Mr. Taylor, who lived there. It is a reminder of how little we know about her youth.

But the problem of how to get home was to become acute. Frank, who might have accompanied her, received his sailing orders for the frigate *Triton* and had to leave forthwith. Henry's plans, as usual, were uncertain. If Jane could not accompany Frank, Edward would take her to Greenwich and, "My father will be so good as to fetch home his prodigal daughter from town, I hope, unless he wishes me to walk the hospitals, enter at the temple, or mount guard at St. James." Unfortunately, Jane's arrangements depended on a friend of Henry's, Miss Pearson, to whom he seems to have been briefly engaged at about this time. Miss Pearson was also in Kent, being driven out by Henry, and there was a plan for her to go back to Hampshire with Jane and be introduced to the family. Writing about this, Jane sounded a warning note: "If Miss Pearson should return with me, pray be careful not to expect too much beauty. I will not pretend to say that on a *first view*, she quite answered the opinion I had formed of her — My mother I am sure will be disappointed, if she does not take great care."

We do not know whether Miss Pearson did go back to Steventon that autumn, but by November Eliza de Feuillide was writing Philadelphia Walter to say that, "Henry Austen has been in town: he looks thin and ill. I hear his late intended is a most intolerable flirt, and reckoned to give herself great airs. The person who mentioned this to me says she is a pretty wicked looking girl with bright black eyes which pierce through and through." Eliza was by no means an impartial observer. She had been a widow for two years now, and her letters to Philadelphia Walter show her debating the question of remarriage. Should she abandon "dear liberty, and yet dearer flirtation"? She had been visiting a relative and entertaining eleven beaux, but Philadelphia obviously thought she was about to engage herself to James Austen, whose wife had now been dead for more than a year. Eliza was undecided. There was a Lord S— in the picture too. "But it does not signify, I shall certainly escape both peer and parson."

She was right. In her next letter to Philadelphia she had to report the surprising news that James had engaged himself to his sisters' friend Mary

Lloyd, "who is not either rich or handsome, but very sensible and good-humoured". Eliza seems to have been a little out of touch with the realities of life in Hampshire, for so far back as September Jane Austen had been writing Cassandra from Kent to ask "which of the Marys will carry the day with my brother James". By Christmas, Mary Harrison (the other Mary) was out of the running, and James and Mary Lloyd were married in January, 1797.

Meanwhile Jane Austen had got home that autumn without falling "a sacrifice to the arts of some fat woman who would make me drunk with small beer". She was doubtless able to watch the progress of James's second courtship for herself. If Miss Pearson in fact went back with her, Jane may at the same time have been watching the dissolution of Henry's engagement. And she herself was doubtless back in the pleasant Steventon routine, trimming up her caps for the monthly balls at Basingstoke, or for those given by their neighbours in the country, where she acted to the life the part of the pretty, silly young girl.

And all the time, upstairs in the dressing-room with its common-looking carpet, Jane's piano, and the oval glass between the windows, the pretty, silly girl was hard at work on *First Impressions*, with Cassandra once more as critic and confidante. Their niece Anna, James's daughter, who lived with them until her father's remarriage, remembered later in life that she heard her two aunts reading the book aloud, with gales of laughter, and had threatened to betray the well-kept secret by picking up the names of the characters and repeating them downstairs.

Unfortunately, no copy of this early version of *Pride and Prejudice* survives. It is a great loss. All we know about *First Impressions* is that it was the basis of *Pride and Prejudice* and that, when the veil of secrecy was lifted, it was an immense, and must have been an encouraging, success with the Austen family. And no wonder. The title, as well as common sense, tells us that the main plot of the book must have been the same as that of *Pride and Prejudice*, with Elizabeth and Darcy disliking each other at first, then warming into love and marriage.

Like *Elinor and Marianne*, *First Impressions* is the story of the problems encountered by two sisters on their way to matrimony. But the problems are more interesting ones. In *Elinor and Marianne* (our *Sense and Sensibility*), the main handicap of the two girls is their lack of money. In *First Impressions* the lack of money is compounded by the quite appalling vulgarity of Jane and Elizabeth Bennet's mother and younger sisters. One longs to know whether, in revising *First Impressions*, Jane Austen sharpened or softened her effects here. It is a temptation to credit the lines one likes least to the early version; for instance Darcy's gratuitous rudeness about Elizabeth at their first meeting, and Mr. Bennet's remark about Mary at the Netherfield ball. But of course it is quite unjustifiable. All we know for sure is that, like *Elinor and Marianne* it could be, and has been, described as a wish-fulfilment story in which two sisters marry and live happily ever afterwards. It was also, judging by those betraying gales of laughter from the upstairs room, highly entertaining.

And yet its writing must have been interrupted by a disaster that struck the diminished family in the spring of 1797. Instead of Tom Fowle, who was expected home, came a letter breaking the news that he had died of yellow fever in the West Indies. Lord Craven was later to make bad worse by saying that if he had known of the engagement he would never have taken his kinsman to so unhealthy a spot. For the present, Eliza de Feuillide wrote to her Cousin Philadelphia that, "Jane says that her sister behaves with a degree of resolution and propriety which no common mind could evince in so trying a situation."

It is tempting to recognise a graver note in the last chapters of *Pride and Prejudice*, and explain it by Cassandra's bereavement. At least, Jane Austen cannot have stopped working on the book for long, as we have Cassandra's authority for the fact that the first version was finished in August. It did not long remain a secret from the rest of the family. By November 1st, Mr. Austen was writing to Cadell, a well-established London publisher, offering him "a manuscript novel, comprising 3 volumes, about the length of Miss Burney's *Evelina*". It has been argued that the reference to *Evelina* was fatal to the book's chances. Although it was nearly twenty years since Fanny Burney's first novel had been an instantaneous success, publishers must still have been receiving optimistic imitations by "young ladies". One can hardly blame Cadell, though one must pity him, for rejecting the offer of *First Impressions* by return of post. At least, in fairness to him, it must be remembered that he had not seen the manuscript. All he had to go on was a letter from an unknown country clergyman. We ought to be grateful to him. The one thing of which we can be sure is that if *First Impressions* had been accepted and published in 1797, *Pride and Prejudice*, as we know it, would never have been written. It is a sobering thought.

There are no letters of Jane Austen's for 1797. Perhaps Cassandra burnt them, as too personal, or, more likely, the two sisters stayed together through the first anguish of Cassandra's bereavement. We know from the *Life* that Mrs. Austen and her two daughters paid a visit to Bath in November, probably to stay with the Leigh Perrots, and doubtless to marriage to a frivolous cousin ten years his senior, but it seems likely that it was a painful time for them all. Tom Fowle had only died that spring, and Cassandra must have been thinking of the wedding that would never take place. And if Jane had consciously used Eliza's letters as a model for Lady Susan's, she can hardly have failed to be disconcerted when her favourite brother married the original. She probably sighed, and, one hopes, smiled, and put *Lady Susan* "on the shelf" like a later book. Fortitude was always to be one of the great virtues for Jane Austen. I have no doubt that she behaved perfectly, and watched Cassandra do likewise, but she must have been laying down a stock of deep-felt experience, which was to show itself in the silent endurance of many of her heroines. Man must work, she might well have said, and woman must not weep. She demonstrated the value of this precept in the stories of Elinor, and Fanny, and Anne.

Henry's own story seems to have had a happy ending. Eliza, who had always been a careful mother to her poor little backward boy, proved a good wife, and, later on, Jane's letters record happy visits to them in London. Cassandra was certainly visiting them by 1800, for a letter of Jane's refers to her comments on a Mrs. Marriott who had been a witness at the wedding. If Eliza Austen sat for the portrait of Mary Crawford as well as that of Lady Susan, a comment of their creator's is much to the point. "Impartiality would not have denied to Miss Crawford's nature, that participation of the general nature of women, which would lead her to adopt the opinions of the man she loved and respected, as her own." Henry and Eliza's story is that of Edmund Bertram and Mary Crawford, but with a happy ending. Only James's wife Mary never forgot her husband's earlier flirtation with Eliza and later refused to let her step-daughter Anna visit the Henry Austens in London.

That cannot have been an altogether happy winter at Steventon, but still there was the farmer with his plough, "meaning to have spring again", and still there was the social pretence to be kept up, and work to be done. We know from Cassandra's note that *Susan* was begun in 1797, so presumably Jane Austen had already settled to the working habit by which she started a new book while revising the old one. With Marianne to suffer for, and Susan (our Catherine Morland) to laugh at, there must have been plenty of occupation in the upstairs dressing-room. Presumably Anna Austen was now living with her father and stepmother, so there was also more privacy. Unfortunately, Anna and Mary Austen never got on very well, but then Mary was to prove the most difficult of the sisters-in-law, and it is perhaps not surprising that Anna, confided to her care at the age of four, should have grown up something of a problem child, to be described later by her Aunt Jane as "quite an Anna with variations".

Jane Austen's letters begin again, on a sober note, in April 1798, when she wrote to condole with their cousin, Philadelphia Walter, on the death of her father. A very proper letter, this one must have been a comfort to Jane Austen's Victorian relatives: "The goodness which made him valuable on earth, will make him blessed in heaven." And then, on a more characteristic note of realism, "This comfort [of knowing him to be in heaven] must be heightened by the consideration of the little enjoyment he was able to receive from this world for some time past." A tragedy closer to home at this time was the death, in a carriage accident, of Lady Williams, the Austen's cousin Jane Cooper, who had gone to school with Cassandra and Jane. No letter of Jane Austen's on this occasion survives, but she was not to use a carriage accident in her novels until her last work of all, *Sanditon*, written in 1817, when she was herself dying.

A more cheerful letter, dated in October 1798, shows that the visits to Kent continued. Edward Austen's adopted father, Mr. Knight, had died in 1794. In 1797, Edward had agreed, after a high-flown exchange of letters with his adoptive mother, to move into the big house at Godmersham, while she settled in dowager style nearby. If life at Rowling had been easy, life at Godmersham was luxurious. This autumn visit was the Austens' first since the move. All four of them went, but Cassandra (who was Edward's favourite sister as Jane was Henry's) stayed behind when the others left in October. Edward's wife Elizabeth had just produced one of the eleven children she was to bear in seventeen years, and there were "patients, little and great" to be looked after. The Austen sisters were always in demand when it came to sick-nursing.

Mrs. Austen, too, had been suffering from one of her ailments, and Jane wrote a comfortable letter to Cassandra from the Bull and George, Dartford, to report a successful first day's journey. It had been marred by one crisis. Her writing and dressing boxes had been accidentally put into the wrong chaise and had been retrieved three miles on their way to the West Indies. "No part of my property could have been such a prize before," wrote Jane, "for in my writing-box was all my worldly wealth, £7, and my dear Harry's deputation." It did not occur to her to mention which, if any, of her irreplaceable manuscripts had nearly been shipped off to the West Indies. Her "dear Harry" was one of their neighbours, the Digweed brothers, who figure a good deal in the correspondence of these years, and the "deputation" was his permission to shoot over the grounds

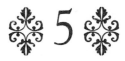

BY THE WINTER OF 1798, LIFE AT STEVENTON RECTORY HAD changed enormously. Cassandra had taken over the housekeeping by now, and Jane wrote to her in Kent to boast, semi-comically as usual, about her own prowess as substitute in her absence. "I am very grand indeed . . . I carry about the keys of the wine and closet, and twice since I began this letter have had orders to give in the kitchen." She talked knowledgeably about ragout veal, haricot mutton and the killing of pigs, and when Mr. Lyford, their Basingstoke surgeon, came to see their mother was "not ashamed at asking him to sit down to table, for we had some pease-soup, a spare-rib, and a pudding". It sounds, for those days, a significantly frugal regime, but she was probably glad of Mr. Lyford's company, for an earlier letter had reported, "My father and I dined by ourselves. How strange!" The rectory must have seemed very large and empty, with even Cassandra away.

Jane Austen had other things on her mind besides the loneliness of a daughter at home. Her next letter reports a meeting with Mrs. Lefroy, who never mentioned her nephew's name. "And I was too proud to make any enquiries." Luckily Mr. Austen asked about Tom Lefroy, and thus Jane learned that he had gone to London on his way to Ireland. The "boy's love" was apparently over, and perhaps this defection was the reason for Jane's lack of spirits. It is one thing to decide not to accept a proposal, and quite another not to receive it. There may have been more to the affair than the light tone of the 1796 letters suggests, and moreover, according to the authors of the *Life*, by 1798 Tom Lefroy was tacitly engaged to someone else, whom he married the following year. Years later, when she was dying, Jane Austen was to write with bracing sympathy to her niece

Fanny, who was in a similar situation. "Why should you be living in dread of his marrying somebody else?— (Yet, how natural!)—You did not choose to have him yourself; why not allow him to take comfort where he can?" But it was natural for Fanny to mind, and Jane Austen knew all about it.

She had her distractions, that autumn of 1798. A young clergyman, identified as Samuel Blackall of Emmanuel College, Cambridge, had been staying with the Lefroys and had written a rather Collinsish letter, which Mrs. Lefroy showed to Jane, and Jane quoted to Cassandra. "I am very sorry to hear of Mrs. Austen's illness," Mr. Blackall had written. "It would give me particular pleasure to have an opportunity of improving my acquaintance with that family—with a hope of creating to myself a nearer interest. But at present I cannot indulge any expectation of it."

"This is rational enough," commented Jane, "there is less love and more sense in it than sometimes appeared before . . . it is therefore most probable that our indifference will soon be mutual, unless his regard, which appeared to spring from knowing nothing of me at first, is best supported by never seeing me." Jane Austen was perhaps beginning to learn that young men do not much like the suspicion of feminine laughter. It is pleasant to know that she had the last laugh, in 1813, when the Reverend Mr. Blackall married a Miss Lewis. "I should very much like to know what sort of a woman she is. He was a piece of perfection, noisy perfection himself which I always recollect with regard . . . I would wish Miss Lewis to be of a silent turn and rather ignorant, but naturally intelligent and wishing to learn—fond of cold veal pies, green tea in the afternoon, and a green window blind at night."

Tom Lefroy, and Mr. Blackall, and who knows how many others, taught Jane Austen a lesson from which she profited in drawing one type of heroine. Catherine Morland "was heartily ashamed of her ignorance. A misplaced shame. Where people wish to attach, they should always be ignorant. To come with a well-informed mind, is to come with an inability of administering to the vanity of others, which a sensible person would always wish to avoid. A woman especially, if she have the misfortune of knowing anything, should conceal it as well as she can."

This is Jane Austen's most overt comment on the classic predicament of the intelligent female, and it is comforting to think that although she lets Catherine Morland and Fanny Price win their heroes, at last, by the sheer weight of their devotion, she still gets her, and our, greatest pleasure out of the witty heroines who give as good as they get. Elizabeth Bennet and Emma may possibly sometimes seem pert (Victorian readers certainly thought so) but at least they never seem stupid, and one cannot help feeling that their marriages stand a better chance of success, for instance, than Henry Tilney's with his doting Catherine. Did he manage to educate her before the two of them degenerated into a Mr. and Mrs. Bennet? And, similarly, when Fanny realised how much more intelligent she was than her beloved Edmund, had she the sense to keep quiet about it?

Life at Steventon was quiet enough, with Cassandra's visit in Kent prolonging itself like the endless war that was beginning to affect the cost of living. In November 1798 Jane wrote, "There is to be a ball at Basing-stoke next Thursday. Our assemblies have very kindly declined ever since we laid down the carriage, so that dis-convenience and disinclination to go have kept pace together." To give up one's carriage was a drastic move, although, in fact, the Austen girls went right on going to balls, no doubt "taken up" in the carriages of their friends.

Their brother James kept his carriage, and it is possible that about now the Austen girls were beginning to feel the difference made by his occupation of Deane. Mr. Austen had made the same kind of sacrifice, in giving him this living, that Mr. Morland offered to his son James when he engaged himself to Isabella Thorpe. But the living that Isabella scorned brought in about four hundred pounds a year, where James Austen had married for the first time on an income of three hundred pounds, including an allowance from his wife's parents, which was continued after her death. The curacy of Deane was worth fifty pounds, and the increase in James's income meant a proportionate diminution of his father's. It was, per-haps, beginning to strike the Austen sisters that he and his difficult Mary were leading a rather more luxurious life than the family at Steventon.

Charles, the youngest of the Austens, had been commissioned as lieutenant in December 1797, so, with the exception of poor George, all the boys must have been pretty well self-sufficient by now, but to counter that Mr. Austen had given up taking pupils, so that the family of four were living on the income from Steventon, plus a tiny income of Mrs. Austen's, which she later estimated as a hundred and sixteen pounds a year, and the interest on a thousand pounds which Tom Fowle had left to Cassandra. The farming of the glebe must have been more important than ever, and the name of John Bond, who managed the farm, appears a good deal in the letters of this period. The rise in prices for farm products must have been the Austens' only cushion against the general inflation of wartime, and John Bond was Mr. Austen's William Larkins, and as indispensable as the latter was to Mr. Knightley. After reporting her solitary dinner with her father, Jane Austen went on to say, "He and John Bond are now very happy together, for I have just heard the heavy step of the latter along the passage." Was Mr. Austen beginning to feel his position as one man among three women? Perhaps he was one of those men who find serious conversation with women difficult, and with their daughters almost impossible. This would go far to explain the dearth of references to him in Jane Austen's letters.

By 1798, Tysoe Saul Hancock's gloomy prediction, years earlier, had acquired its first hint of truth. "I fear George will find it easier to get a family than to provide for them," he had written. So far, the successful launching in life of all the sons but his own godson, George, seemed to have proved him wrong, but there had been no room for saving in the budget of that active family at Steventon Rectory and, as a result, there can have been little or no possibility of dowries for the daughters. Tom Fowle need not have gone to the West Indies, Tom Lefroy might have stayed, Mr. Blackall might well have tried to create a "nearer interest" if there had only been some money to offset that dangerous hint of mockery.

On the other hand, the gift of laughter must have been an enormous comfort in those quiet days at the rectory. It was probably very much easier to bear with Mary Austen when one had Isabella Thorpe growing in one's mind. And life was not all minor economies like Irish linen at three and six a yard. There were balls, still, and books to buy, though Jane Austen did not much approve of her father's purchase of their friend Egerton Brydges' new book, *Arthur Fitzalbini*. "There is very little story, and what there is told in a strange, unconnected way. There are many characters introduced, apparently merely to be delineated." With three novels of her own finished (counting *Lady Susan*), she was beginning to criticise like a professional.

It was not only books that she criticised. Both Elizabeth and Mary Austen had recently had babies and she had a sharp comparison to make. "Mary does not manage matters in such a way as to make me want to lay in myself. She is not tidy enough in her appearance ... Elizabeth was really a pretty object with her nice clean cap put on so tidily and her dress so uniformly white and orderly." Criticising her least favourite sister-in-law, Jane Austen must temporarily have forgotten the contrast she herself often drew between the luxuries of Kent and the austerities of Hampshire. "People get so horridly poor and economical in this part of the world, that I have no patience with them — Kent is the only place for happiness, everybody is rich there." Elizabeth, of course, was Edward's wife, and doubtless had a large staff at Godmersham to see to it that her cap was clean and her dress "uniformly white and orderly".

In Hampshire, one economised. "I took the liberty a few days ago of asking your black velvet bonnet to lend me its cawl, which it very readily did, and by which I have been enabled to give a considerable improvement of dignity to my cap, which was before too nidgetty to please me." Jane meant to wear it at Thursday's Basingstoke ball, for which she was to stay at Manydown with the Misses Bigg, who doubtless sent their carriage for her. Later, she changed her mind about the trimmings of the cap. In the end it "makes me look more like Lady Conyngham now than it did before, which is all that one lives for now". Lady Conyngham, the handsome daughter of a rich London shopkeeper, had married an Irish peer and was later to oust Lady Hertford as George IV's mistress. Jane Austen was evidently not above reading the gossip columns of newspapers and magazines.

There was news of the sailor brothers. Frank wrote cheerfully from Cadiz, and Charles "begins to feel the dignity of ill-usage". He meant to write to their cousin by marriage, Sir Thomas Williams, about his prospects, while Mr. Austen would write to Admiral Gambier (one of the Lords of the Admiralty) who "must already have received so much satisfaction from his acquaintance and patronage of Frank, that he will be delighted I dare say to have another of the family introduced to him". Those were the days when promotion in the Navy, as elsewhere, went largely by patronage, and luckily for the Austens, they had just enough "connection" to under-write Francis's and Charles's obvious competence at their job.

Jane Austen had actually walked the mile and a half to Deane by herself. "I do not know that I ever did such a thing in my life before." It was the day after her twenty-third birthday and she may have been beginning to think of herself as an old maid. The same letter painted an austere picture of their quiet family life. "We dine now at half after three, and have done dinner I suppose before you begin — We drink tea at half after six — I am afraid you will despise us — My father reads Cowper to us in the evening, to which I listen when I can." But then, were things so much more frivolous in Kent? "How do you spend your evenings? — I guess that Elizabeth works, that you read to her and that Edward goes to sleep."

Life at Steventon would be brightened by the opening of a circulating library announced in "a very civil note from Mrs. Martin" to Jane Austen. She must have been known in the district as the most bookish member of the family. "My mother finds the money — Mary subscribes too, which I am glad of, but hardly expected — As an inducement to subscribe Mrs. Martin tells us that her collection is not to consist only of novels, but of every kind of literature, etc. etc. — She might have spared this pretension to *our* family, who are great novel-readers and are not ashamed of being so — but it was necessary I suppose to the self-consequence of half her subscribers."

The remark is a useful reminder that, according to Cassandra, the first version of *Northanger Abbey* was written "about the years 1797 and 1798". While Mr. Austen read aloud Cowper, Jane Austen probably retired quietly into her own world and consoled herself for Cassandra's absence with the adventures of Susan, who was to become Catherine Morland. Perhaps the day they received Mrs. Martin's "civil note" she sat down and wrote the first draft of her famous defence of the novel: "Only a novel . . . Only *Cecilia*, or *Camilla*, or *Belinda* . . . only some work in which the greatest powers of the mind are displayed, in which the most thorough knowledge of human nature, the happiest delineation of its varieties, the liveliest effusions of wit and humour are conveyed to the world in the best chosen language."

Obviously this passage was changed in a later revision, since Maria Edgeworth's *Belinda* was not published until 1801, but all the evidence suggests that the revision of *Susan* was very much less drastic than that of *First Impressions* and *Elinor and Marianne*. If it were not for Cassandra's authority to the contrary, one would naturally asume that *Northanger Abbey* (or *Susan*) was the logical successor to the *Juvenilia*. This, of course, would mean that it was written directly after *Lady Susan*, an absurdity which thoroughly confirms Cassandra's dating. Jane Austen did not in the least mind using the same names over again, but she would surely never have given the same one to two heroines running.

But though the lack of revision makes *Northanger Abbey* sometimes seem like an earlier work than *Sense and Sensibility* or *Pride and Prejudice*, there is an obvious and remarkable development in the treatment of the heroine. The days of wish-fulfilment books about two sisters are over. In the first two novels, the action is seen and understood largely through the intelligence of the heroines, although, as always, Jane Austen shows consummate artistry in the way she slides in and out of their minds. But in *Northanger Abbey* she has taken a step back from her heroine and is trying a new method, or rather one that she had not used since the last of the *Juvenilia*, the unfinished story of another Catherine. It is curious that biographers have tended to use Catherine Morland's early experiences as illustrative of Jane Austen's own, for of all the heroines, she is the one from whom Jane Austen, and therefore the reader, seems most remote. The whole comic opening puts her in her place as a spoof heroine; she is never provided with a real confidante, for Isabella Thorpe is a parody of the breed, and Eleanor Tilney hardly comes alive to take her place. In fact, Henry Tilney is the nearest thing she has to a confidante, and the scene where he finds her in his dead mother's bedroom and gently exposes the absurdity of her ideas goes far to explain, and make possible, their eventual marriage.

But then, Catherine is very far, in fact, from being the goose she appears at first. As always, Jane Austen is handling her story on many different levels at once, and we gradually realise that Catherine, for all her absurdities, is well endowed with what her contemporaries would have called "bottom" and we might call character. Like Anne Elliot, she is not afraid to step forward and take her own line when she feels it necessary. It may be partly infatuation that makes her run after the Tilneys when John Thorpe has given them a false message on her behalf, but it is also good manners. And, in the end, as several critics have pointed out, Jane Austen vindicates even her folly at Northanger Abbey. She suspected General Tilney of being a villain for all the wrong reasons, but he finally proved himself just that by turning her out, if not into the snow, like the heroine of a Victorian melodrama, but still under comparable circumstances. And again Catherine behaves with creditable composure. The seventeen-year-old girl who left home for the first time to go to Bath, and who imagined so many horrors at Northanger Abbey, has grown up fast. The lonely journey "had no terrors for her", and—one of Jane Austen's deliciously realistic notes—"Her youth, civil manners and liberal pay, procured her all the attention that a traveller like herself could require." If Eleanor had not thought to lend her some money, Jane Austen suggests, the journey would have been a very different affair, and herein lies the worst of General Tilney's behaviour. Jane Austen has often been attacked for her emphasis on economic motives, and this sentence seems to me to be a *locus classicus* for the defence. Of course she recognised the importance of money; anyone who does not is either saint or fool, and she was neither. But she kept it, always, in its place. Her heroines will not marry for money, but they often cannot marry without it, and Catherine's youth and civil manners might not have been enough to ensure her good treatment, if they had not been reinforced by her lavish tipping.

In its final version, *Northanger Abbey* is both a better and a more enjoyable book than its near contemporary, *Sense and Sensibility,*

Instead of Johnsonian moralising, it gives us the glint of irony; instead of dull Edward Ferrars, we get perhaps Jane Austen's most engaging hero, Henry Tilney, the only one, in my view, into whom she put anything much of herself. Heroes, of course, are obviously a problem for a female author, as heroines are for a male one. In fact, the authoress's position is the more difficult, since, in society as at present constituted, the male is expected to be the protagonist. Jane Austen varied her approach to this crucial problem from book to book. Edward Ferrars and Colonel Brandon are little more than lay figures, while Darcy has something of the young girl's dream hero about him. He anticipates Charlotte Brontë's saturnine Rochester and all his tribe of descendants. With Henry Tilney Jane Austen tried something new. She gave him her own intelligence and opinions, and then, incorrigibly, laughed at him for them, as in the discussions of the picturesque and the use of language. He is the only man in her books who speaks with her voice, for Edmund Bertram is a lay figure again, while Knightley is a most interesting and satisfactory development of Darcy, the Rochester figure, into a sensible man, and Wentworth obviously owes much to the beloved sailor brothers, and something, perhaps, to the unknown, romantic figure in her own life.

Henry Tilney is one of the liveliest and most convincing men ever created by a woman, and it is no wonder if many (male) critics think him thrown away on his Catherine. Jane Austen first created him in her early twenties, when she was still unreconciled to the problems of the intelligent woman in a world dominated by men. It is significant that it is in *Northanger Abbey* that she sings the mock-praises of ignorance. "A woman, especially, if she have the misfortune of knowing anything, should conceal it as well as she can." In *First Impressions*, she had poured her intelligence into her heroine, allowed her to challenge the hero in the battle of wits, and of the sexes, and actually to come to terms with him at last, like Millamant in *The Way of the World*. In *Northanger Abbey* she reversed the process. Henry Tilney's was the intelligent, educated mind; Catherine's the untrained intelligence. One of the great pleasures of the book is the sight of Catherine succumbing to Henry's quality (as well as to his good looks), and then seeing him fall in love with her love for him.

The book also has some of Jane Austen's happiest comic scenes and characters. Mrs. Allen and the odious Thorpes are sketched, but more light-heartedly, by the master hand that drew Mrs. Norris and the Bates. Perhaps, with this book, she had resumed her old habit of family reading aloud. At all events, its composition was undoubtedly interrupted by a piece of good news the Austens received on Christmas Eve of 1798. Writing exultantly to Cassandra, Jane was able to report that their father had received a favourable answer to his letter to Admiral Gambier about Frank and Charles. It is a remarkable comment on the efficiency of both post and civil service at the end of the eighteenth century. On December 18th Jane had said, "My Father will write to Admiral Gambier." By the 24th, she could write to report the receipt of a friendly and encouraging answer, and go on, "There! I may now finish my letter and go and hang myself, for I am sure I can neither write not do anything which will not appear insipid to you after this." Having thus reminded us of how very much the Austens cared about each other, Jane did, of course, go on to describe her visit to Manydown, and the ball, which "was very thin, but by no means unpleasant ... Mr. Calland ... stood every now and then behind Catherine and me to be talked to and abused for not dancing. We teased him, however, into it at last." No doubt, having finished her letter to Cassandra, Jane Austen picked up another small piece of paper and added a touch or two to her picture of the Thorpes.

It is pleasant to know that even at the advanced age of twenty-three, Jane Austen had found herself capable of dancing twenty dances without any fatigue. "From my slender enjoyment of the Ashford balls (as assemblies for dancing) I had not thought myself equal to it, but in cold weather and with few couples I fancy I could just as well dance for a week together as for half an hour." Hampshire clearly had one advantage over rich Kent. It was full of old friends.

In Kent, Cassandra, too, had been to a ball and had actually supped with Prince William of Gloucester, son of the secret marriage of one of King George III's disreputable brothers. This meeting had shocked a Kent connection of theirs. Mrs. Cage, who had, according to Jane Austen, "all those kind of foolish and incomprehensible feelings which would make her fancy herself uncomfortable in such a party". Characteristically, Jane Austen goes on, "I love her, however, in spite of all her nonsense." For Jane Austen, laughter never precluded love, but merely kept it healthy. Her attitude here, and in a later letter, is the worldly, realistic one of the eighteenth century. In 1801 she reported that Eliza Fowle had met her husband's kinsman Lord Craven (who had provided that fatal job for Tom Fowle) and "found his manners very pleasing indeed. The little flaw of having a mistress now living with him at Ashdown Park, seems to be the only surprising circumstance about him." It is no wonder that Jane Austen's novels sometimes shocked the Victorians. She took for granted things they preferred to ignore.

But there were much more important events for the Austen girls, that winter of 1798, than encounters with minor royalty, or tarnished nobility. Admiral Gambier had wasted no time. By December 28th, Jane Austen could report triumphantly that "Frank is made". He was now a Commander, and appointed to H.M. Sloop *Petterel*, while Charles's wish had also been granted and he had been removed to a frigate. Best of all, it meant that they could expect Charles home for a visit, and indeed Jane hoped he would arrive in time for Lady Dorchester's ball, but, "Charles never came. Naughty Charles! I suppose he could not get superseded in time." As usual, Jane Austen was taken to the ball by friends, but does not seem to have enjoyed it overmuch. "One of my gayest actions was sitting down two dances in preference to having Lord Bolton's eldest son for my partner, who danced too ill to be endured."

"I do not think I was much in request," reports Jane the realist. "People were rather apt not to ask me till they could not help it." There may, perhaps, have been a connection between this discovery, her brother James's decision, reported in the same letter, to give dinner parties, and a family plan to go to Brighton in the summer. Were the Austens making serious attempts, with family dinners and holidays, to find husbands for their daughters? If so, Jane's reaction was predictable. "I dread the idea of going to Brighton as much as you do," she wrote, "but am not without hopes that something may happen to prevent it." So far as we know, something did. What we do not know is whether Brighton was written into *First Impressions* as the scene of Lydia Bennet's disastrous visit before or after this episode. There was a military camp there at this time, as well as the Prince of Wales's set, and E. M. Forster must have missed Jane Austen's reaction to the proposed visit when he wrote his curiously unpleasant review of the *Letters*. "Lydia Bennet is all pervading: balls, officers, giggling, dresses, officers, balls, fill sheet after sheet until every one except Kitty grows weary . . . The young girl dances and her eyes sparkle duly, but they are observant and hard; officers, dances, officers, giggling, balls." Jane Austen's eyes were always observant, but were they ever hard?

In fact, Jane Austen was plagued a good deal about this time by eye trouble and some critics have used this to explain the dearth of descriptions in her books. It was a weakness that afflicted her all her adult life, and her niece Caroline Austen tells us that she used to play at cup-and-ball, "when she suffered from weak eyes and could not work or read for long together". If she was, in fact, short-sighted it would certainly help to account for the rather generalised nature of some of her descriptions, "the white glare of Bath" in *Persuasion* or the "something white and womanish" in *Sanditon*. She seems to have had expert advice about her eyes, later in life, but never wore the primitive spectacles of her time, and it is no wonder if the fine needlework and careful copying of which she did so much strained her eyes. We have no idea of what the Austen family budget for "working candles" was, but it was almost certainly a frugal one, and it is safe to assume that once dusk fell their lighting was, to put it mildly, inadequate. There would be no retiring to the peaceful dressing-room upstairs once it was dark; the family would gather together round what light there was. It is one of the reasons for the prevalent habit of reading aloud, which undoubtedly had such a beneficial effect on Jane Austen's style. If modern authors read aloud more, and heard their work read, they might write more tidily. Jane Austen herself read aloud admirably and one of her nieces said her rendering of *Evelina* was as good as a play.

The small batch of letters for 1798 and 1799 contains news of the Austen girls' best friends. On the way home from Lady Dorchester's ball, Jane had spent a happy couple of nights with James and Mary at Deane, sharing a bed with their dear friend Martha Lloyd, Mary's sister. "The bed did exceedingly well for us, both to lie awake in and talk till two o'clock and to sleep in the rest of the night. I love Martha better than ever . . ." In the same letter, Jane speaks of Catherine Bigg, who "con-gratulated me last night on Frank's promotion, as if she really felt the joy she talked of". Like Emma, the Austen girls amused themselves in "making matches" for their friends and relations. This letter ends on a similar note: "My father and mother made the same match for you last night, and are very much pleased with it. *He* is a beauty of my mother's." Marriage was incontrovertibly the business of young ladies, as well as, possibly, their pleasure. Critics who attack Jane Austen for making it the main subject of her novels are simply failing to take into account the hard facts of her time. Writing today, would she, I wonder, have enjoyed herself as much describing her heroines' attempts to become Prime Ministers or efficient principals of women's colleges?

❧ 6 ❧

In May 1799, Cassandra's long visit to Godmersham was over at last. She must have returned to Steventon in company with Edward, Elizabeth and their children, and the Edward Austens promptly took Mrs. Austen and Jane off to Bath with them, along with their two eldest children, while Cassandra minded the others. Maiden aunts had their uses. Edward was to take the waters at Bath, since he was either the least robust of the brothers or the only one with leisure and money enough to indulge a penchant for "stomach complaints, faintnesses, and sicknesses". His sister's tone, when she writes about his health, or lack of it, tends towards the same dryness she uses of their mother. "She would tell you herself that she has a very dreadful cold in her head at present; but I have not much compassion for colds in the head without fever or sore throat." As for Jane, she must finally have taken advice about her eyes, for she reports that she finds no difficulty in "doing" them in their lodgings.

In Bath there were the Leigh Perrots to be visited. "My uncle is quite surprised at my hearing from you so often." There were also a great many commissions to be executed for family and friends at home. The letters are full of bonnets and fruit trimmings, patterns of lace and problems about shoes. On what might be a graver note, Jane reports meeting an old acquaintance: "Dr. Hall in such very deep mourning that either his mother, his wife, or himself must be dead." She was not old enough yet to find death dreadful.

She also met a "very young man, just entered of Oxford", who, "wears spectacles, and has heard that *Evelina* was written by Dr. Johnson". Perhaps in the great Doctor's honour, she tried a sentence in the style of

Mrs. Piozzi[1] in her next letter. "I had some thoughts of writing the whole of my letter in her style, but I believe I shall not." Did thoughts of Henry Tilney, who was so "nice" in his views of style help to dissuade her? She was thinking about other types of style too and had decided that "it is more natural to have flowers grow out of the head than fruit." And then, back to her writing, she urged Cassandra not to let Martha Lloyd read *First Impressions* again. "She is very cunning, but I saw through her design; she means to publish it from memory, and one more perusal must enable her to do it." There is always an unmistakable note of confidence when Jane Austen speaks of *First Impressions*.

Writing and its mechanics went on being a preoccupation. "I do not know what is the matter with me today, but I cannot write quietly; I am always wandering away into some exclamation or other." And, in the next paragraph, "We walked to Weston one evening last week, and liked it very much. Liked *what* very much? Weston? No, *walking* to Weston. I have not expressed myself properly, but I hope you will understand me." She may not have polished and repolished her letters as she did her novels, but they show the same passionate search for the precise word, the exact effect. It was all invaluable writing practice. As she herself said, on a frivolous occasion, "An artist cannot do anything slovenly."

Their summer plans were still not settled. "I should like to make a compromise with Adlestrop, Harden, and Bookham that Martha's spending the summer at Steventon should be considered as our respective visits to them all." The Brighton plan had been abandoned in favour of a round of family visits to which Jane and Cassandra apparently looked forward with almost as little enthusiasm. There were Leigh connections living at all three places, but in fact their summer was to be worse than they could have expected. In August, Mrs. Austen's sister-in-law, Jane Leigh Perrot, was accused of shoplifting in Bath. It appears to have been an attempt at blackmail by an unscrupulous shopkeeper, who took it for granted that the Leigh Perrots would pay hush money rather than risk prosecution and the chance, under the barbarous law of the day, of Mrs. Leigh Perrot's being sentenced to death, if found guilty, with a probable commutation into transportation to Australia. It is impossible not to respect the Leigh Perrots for the line they took. Denying the absurd charge absolutely, they refused to compound in any way, and Mrs. Leigh Perrot was committed for trial at the next Assizes. Since these did not take place until the following spring, she spent the winter in lodgings attached to Ilchester gaol. Her devoted husband stayed there with her, and she

[1] As Mrs. Thrale, Mrs. Piozzi had been a close friend of Dr. Johnson.

hoped to have James Austen, who was generally assumed to be their heir, to support her at her trial, describing him as "a perfect son to me in affection and his firm friendship all through this trying business". Unluckily, James's horse fell with him and he broke his leg just before the Assizes, so that neither he nor his wife Mary could be there. Mrs. Austen, whose own health must have been precarious as usual, wrote offering her the company of Cassandra and Jane, but this was declined. "To have two young creatures gazed at in a public court would cut one to the very heart." James's was to prove an unlucky accident for the Austens.

Mrs. Leigh Perrot, having kept her ailing husband going through the anxious months of waiting with sympathy and James's Powders,[1] was supported at the trial by her own cousin, Penelope Cholmeley, and was honourably acquitted by a jury after seven and a half minutes' deliberation. "The frightful expense I cannot estimate," she wrote. "What a comfort that we have no children." And, also to her cousin, Penelope's brother, "Your sister I know has a heart warm to every affectionate tie—indeed *she* well proved her friendship. Others talked, and wrote of it, perhaps felt it—but it was a distant glow, or rather a little spark which required more trouble to blow up than the thing was worth." Mrs. Austen made a mistake when she let James's accident or her perennial ill health keep her from her sister-in-law's side, but it was a respectable mistake. It is obvious from her daughter's letters that none of the family really liked Jane Leigh Perrot, and the fact that she and her husband were rich already, and had expectations of more, may have acted as a kind of high-minded, backhanded argument against going.

No letters of Jane Austen's for this period of crisis survive, so we do not know what she and Cassandra thought about being offered as gaol companions to their unpopular aunt. It is curious to think of the Dickensian chapters Jane Austen would have been equipped to write if Mrs. Leigh Perrot had accepted the offer, but it seems unlikely that she would have written them. She did, in fact, go round a gaol in Canterbury later on, with her brother Edward, who was a visiting magistrate, and wrote about it to Cassandra, but she knew her province, and kept to it. Only *Sanditon*, apart from the *Juvenilia*, is capable of comprehending a prison scene, and *Sanditon* is unfinished.

By the time that Jane Austen's letters take up again, cheerfully, in October 1800, the family drama had been long played out, and the Leigh Perrots had resumed their comfortable, self-contained life, divided between Bath and their house, Scarlets, in Berkshire. Apparently, relations

[1] That well-known contemporary nostrum.

70

with the Austens were as friendly as ever, but the Leigh Perrots did not forget easily.

Edward Austen had been visiting his parents in the autumn of 1800 and had taken Cassandra home with him to Godmersham. He had left Jane with the reasonably pleasant task of distributing his "charity" to the poor of the district. It was not, in fact, exactly Jane's line. In an earlier letter she had admitted her own shortcomings as a visitor of the poor. "I called yesterday on Betty Londe, who enquired particularly after you, and said she seemed to miss you very much, because you used to call in upon her very often. This was an oblique reproach at me, which I am sorry to have merited, and from which I will profit." And again, without enthusiasm: "Of my charities to the poor since I came home you shall have a faithful account."

It was a curious situation and, with luck, one that Jane Austen was equipped to find amusing. Edward's adoptive father, Thomas Knight, had given his real father the living of Steventon. Now, as Mr. Knight's heir, Edward was lord of the manor and was presumably doing his best, through his sisters, to make up for Mr. Austen's constrained deficiencies in the charitable line. It does not seem to have occurred to him until a much later date that he might do something more positive about his family's straitened circumstances. When his sisters went to Godmersham they tended to get "presents" of money both from Edward and from his adoptive mother, old Mrs. Knight, of whom they were very fond. They were delighted to get these presents: "Her very agreeable present will make my circumstances quite easy," but there is all the difference in the world between presents, however lavish, and an assured increase of income, however small. It is impossible, in this connection, not to remember the superb discussion between the Dashwoods about what John Dashwood had promised to do for his mother and half-sisters. After much deliberation they came down at last in favour of the odd present. "Whatever I may give them occasionally will be of far greater assistance than a yearly allowance, because they would only enlarge their style of living if they felt sure of a larger income, and would not be sixpence the richer for it at the end of the year ... A present of fifty pounds, now and then, will prevent their ever being distressed for money."

Of course the Dashwoods are very far from being the Edward Austens. They are merely one more instance of how Jane Austen took the painful grit of experience and transmuted it into her pearl. But this and other passages in the novels serve to illustrate the quite unusual family solidarity of the Austens. Ever since the days of the *Juvenilia*, they had been used to what Caroline Austen later described as Jane's habit of "imagining for her neighbours impossible contingencies, by relating in prose or verse some trifling incident, coloured to her own fancy". And they were intelligent enough to recognise the all-important colouring of fancy. Jane did not need to tell them that "it was her desire to create, not to reproduce." Reporting this, in the *Memoir*, her nephew adds a charming remark of hers: "Besides, I am too proud of my gentlemen to admit that they were only Mr. A or Colonel B."

Anyway, Jane Austen could use episodes like this one, lightly based on family events or characters, without the slightest fear that the family would take offence. "They were all pleasant in their own family," said Caroline Austen ". . . I have thought since, after having seen more of other households, *wonderfully*, as the family talk had much of spirit and vivacity, and it was never troubled by disagreements as it was not their habit to argue with each other." And the author of the *Memoir* came near to apologising for what Americans would call the "closeness" of the Austen family.

> There was so much that was agreeable and attractive in this family party that its members may be excused if they were inclined to live somewhat too exclusively within it. They might see in each other much to love and esteem, and something to admire. The family talk had abundance of spirit and vivacity, and was never troubled by disagreements even in little matters, for it was not their habit to dispute or argue with each other: above all, there was strong family affection and firm union, never to be broken but by death.

It is important to remember this background of family solidarity against which Jane Austen wrote. She could count on the audience she most cared about. If they were with her—and clearly they always were—everything else was comparatively unimportant. It would take more than Cadell's brusque refusal of *First Impressions* to stop her writing, so long as she had the family for audience. And similarly she could ignore the problem of people who would see themselves as characters (or caricatures) in her books, so long as Henry took no exception to hints of himself in Henry Crawford, or his wife in Mary, and Edward never thought of being John Dashwood. They must, indeed, have been a remarkable family.

But affluence was still confined to Kent. Cassandra and Jane made the best of their straitened circumstances in those days of rising prices. Other people fared worse. In October 1800, Jane reported that Mrs. Martin, who had started the circulating library in 1798, had "totally failed in her business, and had very lately an execution in her house". Luckily for Mrs. Martin, "Her own brother and Mr. Rider are the principal creditors, and they have seized her effects in order to prevent other people's doing it." But it can have been no pleasure to Mrs. Martin, while the failure of the local lending library would hardly have been an encouraging circumstance to a so far unpublished author.

On the surface, the Austens appeared to be managing fairly well in that eighth year of the war with France. They were discussing improvements in the garden, ordering glass from London and tables to be made locally, though it is true that these may have been a present from Edward. "They are both covered with green baize," said Jane, "and send their best love." Cassandra had ordered the glasses in London along with other family errands, and Edward had been buying useful presents for the relatives he had just left. James's wife Mary was "delighted about the mangle . . . You will thank Edward for it on their behalf." And life continued pleasant. There had been a ball at Basingstoke and three different friends had invited Jane to go with them. "With three different methods of going, I must have been more at the ball than anybody else." But the long war was beginning to take its toll. "There was a scarcity of men in general—a still greater scarcity of any that were good for much . . . There was commonly a couple of ladies standing up together." Jane had danced with Catherine Bigg as well as with Stephen Terry, Thomas Chute and James Digweed.

Charles, on H.M.S. *Endymion* now, was waiting for orders, and Jane was busy making shirts for him, but the end of her letter strikes a couple of notes of warning. Old Mrs. Lloyd was not looking well, and, serious for the Austens, the farm had cleared only three hundred pounds in the last year. Mr. Austen's conferences with John Bond cannot have been so profitable as Mr. Knightley's with William Larkins. Another of this series of letters reports one of those bits of raw material that Jane Austen did not think fit to use. A friend of theirs who had already made an unfortunate marriage had now shot himself in the leg. Jane's sympathy was mainly for his family. "*One* most material comfort however they have; the assurance of it's being really an accidental wound . . . Such a wound could not have been received in a duel."

At Steventon, life went on as usual. The Austens were thinking of going to Dawlish next summer, and a storm had blown down several of their and their neighbour's elm trees, but had done no other damage. "We grieve therefore in some comfort." The next letter teases Cassandra: "James Digweed . . . must be in love with you . . . from his supposing

73

that the two elms fell from their grief at your absence. Was not it a gallant idea?"

They had heard from Frank, who had distinguished himself in the eastern Mediterranean, and Charles had visited them while waiting for the *Endymion* to sail "danced the whole evening" at a ball where, says Jane Austen, "I believe I drank too much wine . . . I know not how else to account for the shaking of my hand today." None of her heroines, after the *Juvenilia*, ever did this.

A few days later, Jane was writing from Ibthorp, where she was visiting Martha Lloyd and "spending my time very pleasantly". A Mrs. Stent, who lived with Martha's mother, was unconsciously sitting for the portrait of Miss Bates. "I have been here ever since a quarter after three on Thursday last, by the Shrewsbury Clock, which I am fortunately enabled absolutely to ascertain, because Mrs. Stent once lived at Shrewsbury, or at least at Tewkesbury." And again, "Mrs. Stent gives us quite as much of her company as we wish for." A later reference to the unfortunate Mrs. Stent, in 1805, shows Jane Austen gradually mellowing towards that loving portrait of Miss Bates. "Poor Mrs. Stent! it has been her lot to be always in the way; but we must be merciful, for perhaps in time we may come to be Mrs. Stents ourselves, unequal to anything and unwelcome to everybody."

But that was in 1805, when Jane Austen was rising thirty. In November, 1800, Martha and Jane were full of cheerful plans. Martha was to accompany Jane back to Steventon. "Our plan," said Jane, "is to have a nice black frost for walking to Whitechurch, and there throw ourselves into a postchaise, one upon the other, our heads hanging out at one door, and our feet at the opposite." They sound just like the heroines of *Love and Friendship*. In fact, they were actually going to travel by themselves. Jane was just twenty-five and Martha probably older.

Cheerfulness ended when they got to Steventon. In Jane's absence, Mr. and Mrs. Austen had suddenly decided that the time had come for him to retire. Cassandra was still at Godmersham, so Jane's visit to Martha had left their parents alone. In the echoing solitude of the old rectory, they had come to their drastic decision. According to family tradition, Mrs. Austen announced the plan without preparation or preamble. "Well, girls, it is all settled. We have decided to leave Steventon . . . and go to live at Bath." Totally unprepared—after all they had recently been buying furniture and discussing improvements to the garden—Jane fainted. She had lived at Steventon all her life.

We do not know the precise grounds for the Austens' sudden decision.

Mrs. Austen may have found the burden of housekeeping too great, with both daughters away, and the rambling empty house to run. And Mr. Austen was rising seventy and may well have been beginning to find the combined management of parish and glebe too much. John Bond was getting on too, and the farm had done badly that year. It is easy to imagine a gloomy conversation over the account books and then the sudden decision to move.

There may have been other reasons. Mrs. Austen's health seems to have been rather worse than usual, which would help to explain the choice of Bath. The Leigh Perrots, on the other hand, thought the Austens wanted to remove Jane from Steventon because of a growing attachment between her and one of the three Digweed brothers at Steventon Manor, perhaps her "dear Harry" whose deputation she nearly lost, or perhaps William Francis, the entry of whose birth follows hers in the Steventon parish register. Or it may have been the third brother, James, despite his pretty thought about Cassandra and the elms. There may even have been a double flirtation going on, for a later letter of Jane's teases Cassandra about James Digweed's visit to Kent while she was at Godmersham. What is hard to understand is why the Austens would not have approved of such a match. Two of the Digweeds married quite soon afterwards, James in 1803 and Harry in 1808, but William Francis seems to have remained single, so anyone who likes can imagine him as wearing the willow for Jane.

Another possibility is that young Harris Bigg Wither, six years her junior, was showing too much interest in Jane, but I think it altogether more likely that no one was showing enough. Cassandra was almost twenty-eight, and Jane just twenty-five, and they must have made a fairly formidable combination. There may have been method in the way the family split them up by separate visits to Edward, but still it would not do. If Jane dismissed the young men she met at balls as not "good for much", what did they think of Jane? And if there was a dangerous hint of laughter about her when she went to balls alone, what in the world can she and Cassandra have been like together? Even the best of good manners cannot quite hide the delicious complicity of a shared joke.

The Austens had tried James's dinner parties, had meditated visits to Brighton or to Dawlish, now they were to try the more desperate expedient of a move to Bath, no doubt on the principle Jane Austen herself enunciated in *Northanger Abbey*, that "if adventures will not befall a young lady in her own village, she must seek them abroad." If Jane recognised this unacknowledged matrimonial consideration as a reason for the move, it would go far to explain her distress. She may have written about the husband hunt, but she never approved of it. Besides, she was already on record as disliking Bath, and all her roots were in Steventon.

It must have been a bad time for her, and, inevitably, her letter to Cassandra announcing the proposed move has been destroyed. But she believed in fortitude. The first surviving letter is dated January 3rd, 1801, less than a month after the bad news had broken. It shows her determined to be cheerful, though straining at it a little. "We plan having a steady cook, and a young giddy housemaid, with a sedate, middle-aged man, who is to undertake the double office of husband to the former and sweetheart to the latter—No children of course to be allowed on either side." They were hard at it discussing different districts of Bath, and plans in general for the move, which was to be followed by a visit to the sea somewhere in the west country. Jane's heart was set on going with Cassandra to stay with the Leigh Perrots and look for a house. "*Your* going I consider as indispensably necessary, and I shall not like being left behind; there is no place here or hereabouts that I shall want to be staying at ..." This seems to dispose at once of the James Austens and the Biggs at Manydown. Jane Austen was apparently not prepared for the kind of compromise by which her own Anne Elliot left her beloved Kellynch Hall not for Bath at once but for a visit to her sister at Uppercross. But then, Anne Elliot and her kind of fortitude were far in the future. In the present, Jane Austen was doing her best to seem resigned, but her real feelings would break through. "I get more and more reconciled to our removal ... For a time we shall now possess many of the advantages which I have often thought of with envy in the wives of sailors or soldiers." It takes a moment to recognise the stinging irony of this.

The arrangements went on. James was to take over the living at Steventon as his father's *locum tenens*, and the Austens hoped to have six hundred pounds a year to live on in Bath. The curacy of Deane was now to be disposed of, and Mr. Austen was thinking of offering it to James Digweed, but, said Jane, "Unless he is in love with Miss Lyford, I think he had better not be settled exactly in this neighbourhood, and unless he is very much in love with her indeed, he is not likely to think a salary of £50 equal in value or efficacy to one of £75."

Jane Austen did not seem to take her own suggestion about James Digweed and Miss Lyford very seriously, for she went on to say that he might reconsider the living at Deane if Cassandra was "to be considered as one of the fixtures of the house!" But in fact James Digweed did refuse the curacy, and did marry Mary Susannah Lyford in 1803. As for James Austen, his sister's tone about him and his wife becomes increasingly dry as this series of letters continues. The process of handing over does not seem to have gone smoothly, except, perhaps, for James and Mary. "The brown mare, which as well as the black was to devolve on James at our removal, has not had patience to wait for that, and has settled herself even now at Deane . . . everything else I suppose will be seized by degrees in the same manner." It does sound a little as if Mrs. Norris was at work.

James, apparently did not need or did not want the glebe, which was to be let to a neighbour, Mr. Holder, who was prepared to take John Bond with it. Jane was disappointed, as Harry Digweed had intended to offer him the position of superintendent at Steventon Manor. It was now that James Digweed was in Kent, near Cassandra. "Why did not J.D. make his proposals to you? I suppose he went to see the Cathedral, that he might know how he should like to be married in it." This is probably Austen-nonsense, like a remark about their old friend and patroness, Mrs. Knight. "I am happy to hear of Mrs. Knight's amendment, whatever might be her complaint. I cannot think so ill of her however in spite of your insinuations, as to suspect her of having lain-in—I do not think she would be betrayed beyond an *accident* at the utmost." Cassandra obviously wrote Austen-nonsense too. Unfortunately none of her letters to Jane survives, and only a few others, notably the moving ones she wrote to their niece Fanny after her sister's death. But exchanges like this one about Mrs. Knight serve as a useful reminder of how close and private the correspondence between the sisters was. No doubt they made a point of putting in passages suitable for reading aloud, as Jane urged her niece Fanny to do, later, when Fanny was writing to her about her own love affairs. We know that Jane did not show Fanny's letters even to Cassandra, and it is therefore safe to assume that the sisters' letters were shown to no one. Jane Austen did not write, like Pope or Byron, with one eye half-fixed on posterity, and critics who forget this are in danger of looking very silly. She could write nonsense about Mrs. Knight's imaginary pregnancy or Mrs. Hall's dead baby because she was writing to Cassandra, who would understand. Nobody else, in this context, matters.

Letters were all very well, but, with this family crisis at the boil, Jane Austen actually admitted to missing Cassandra, though in characteristic style. "Neither my affection for you nor for letter-writing can stand out against a Kentish visit. For a three months' absence I can be a very loving relation and a very excellent correspondent, but beyond that I degenerate into negligence and indifference." Luckily, Cassandra was already

77

planning her return home by way of a visit to Henry and Eliza, now settled in Upper Berkeley Street. A mention of Charles and Frank serves as a reminder of how long it took to communicate with the Navy. They had both been in the Mediterranean, and Charles, writing from Lisbon on his way home, did not know whether Frank had yet had news of the promotion to Post Captain that he had received the year before. Both brothers were shortly expected in England and would be able to pay visits to Steventon, "while Steventon is ours". Meanwhile, the Austens were busy with farewell visits. They had been to see some Dysons. "The house seemed to have all the comforts of little children, dirt and litter. Mr. Dyson as usual looked wild, and Mrs. Dyson as usual looked big." Jane Austen felt more and more strongly, as she grew older, about the drain of constant child-bearing on her married friends. Probably, without being aware of it, she was becoming less and less marriageable herself. Might she even, at this point, have agreed with her Cousin Eliza's views on "dear liberty"? Probably not, since her liberty, such as it was, merely tied her to her parents, and, through them, to Bath.

As so often, she was to be disappointed in that wish of hers about visiting Bath with Cassandra. In vain was her plan of "disordering my stomach with Bath buns", so as to be less of an expense to her rich and frugal Aunt Leigh Perrot. All their plans changed in the course of the winter, and in the end Jane and her mother went to Bath alone, to visit the Leigh Perrots in Paragon Buildings, while Cassandra stayed with Martha Lloyd at Ibthorp and Mr. Austen visited relatives in Kent and London.

Inevitably, the letters from Bath are full of houses with rising damp, or tiny rooms, or both. It took some time for the Austens to find what they wanted, but in the meantime the Leigh Perrots were being very kind, and Mrs. Austen's health had improved. Jane, on the other hand, was sleeping badly, and so was Cassandra. "I hope you improve in sleeping — I think you must, because I fall off." Although it was just the end of the season at Bath, and they were only in time for the last two, ill-attended balls, there were plenty of people to be observed. Life in Bath stopped Jane writing, but it provided her lavishly with material for the future. After her first ball she was able to report that, "I am proud to say that I have a very good eye at an adulteress." She had no doubt met Mrs. Rushworth for the first time. There were other characters to be observed. "Mrs. Badcock and two young women were of the same party, except when Mrs. Badcock thought herself obliged to leave them to run round the room after her drunken husband. His avoidance, and her pursuit with the probable intoxication of both, was an amusing scene." It would not have amused Fanny Price, still less Jane Austen's Victorian kinsmen. Quoting this letter, Lord Brabourne quietly cuts the word adulteress, though he leaves in the intoxicated Badcocks.

There was a continuing source of irritation in the news from Steventon, where the valuation and sale of the family's effects was continuing. Because of the expense and risk of moving furniture, everything the family possessed, except, oddly enough, their beds, was being sold, a good deal of it, at a valuation, to James. Jane had wanted James to take their father's five hundred books "at a venture at half a guinea a volume", but shrewd James waited for the valuation and got the lot for seventy pounds. "The whole world is in a conspiracy to enrich one part of our family at the expense of another," said Jane. The tables that had been brand new, and sent their love to Cassandra, in November, had fetched only eleven guineas, and one must hope that it was not Mary Austen who got Jane's piano for eight. Jane, too, had sold her books. "Ten shillings for Dodsley's *Poems* however please me to the quick and I do not care how often I sell them for as much." We can only imagine what she really felt on parting with the books she had collected since childhood. The news of the move had been something to faint about.

Meanwhile, in Bath, she threw herself with a slightly unconvincing gusto into the elderly but extensive social life of her aunt and uncle, describing parties, "not quite so stupid as the two preceding ones", calls, people, and, of course, clothes. She actually went out driving by herself with a married Mr. Evelyn in "a very bewitching phaeton and four", and made friends despite herself with a Mrs. Chamberlayne—"We shake hands whenever we meet." They had gone for a walk together, too, which receives a would-be comic description. It is not often that Jane Austen fails in this line, and the failure is undoubtedly indicative of her real state of mind at this time. She did her best to sound cheerful for Cassandra's benefit, but her best was not quite good enough, except when she had something really heart-warming to describe, like their brother Charles's return home. "He has received £30 for his share of the privateer and expects more—but of what avail is it to take prizes if he lays out the produce in presents to his sisters. He has been buying gold chains and topaze crosses for us; he must be well scolded." The gift was probably as timely in Jane Austen's life as a similar one was to be in Fanny Price's, and fraught with fewer complications.

❦ 7 ❦

No letters of Jane Austen's survive for the period between May 1801 and September 1804, which probably means that a great deal happened to her, not much of it good. We have Eliza Austen's authority for the fact that the family spent the summer of 1801 in Devon. In the autumn they were back in Bath, settled at last in Number 4, Sidney Gardens, one of the possible positions Jane had rather ironically described to Cassandra. "It would be very pleasant to be near Sidney Gardens!—We might go into the labyrinth every day." Sidney Gardens was a kind of Bath Vauxhall, providing firework displays and other such delights. The Austens' house faced the gardens, so they doubtless got the full benefit of these displays, but on the other hand it had the signal virtue, from the point of view of an active walker like Jane Austen, of being on the outskirts of the town. If she could find a Mrs. Chamberlayne, or, better still, Cassandra for company, she could indulge herself freely in the activity she and Elizabeth Bennet both enjoyed.

The Austens spent their summers at the seaside during this period, and it was probably on one of these visits that Jane Austen met the young man Cassandra was to describe, years later, to their niece Caroline. He was,

A gentleman whom they had met one summer when they were by the sea—I think she said in Devonshire; I don't think she named the place, and I am sure she did not say Lyme, for that I should have remembered—that he seemed greatly attracted by my Aunt Jane—I suppose it was an intercourse of some weeks—and that when they had to part . . . he was urgent to know where they would be the next summer, implying or perhaps saying that he should be there also, wherever it might be. I can only say that the impression left on Aunt Cassandra was that he had fallen in love with her sister, and was quite in earnest. Soon afterwards they heard of his death ... I am sure she thought he was worthy of her sister, from the way in which she recalled his memory, and also that she did not doubt, either, that he would have been a successful suitor.

There are conflicting versions of this story. Caroline's older half-sister, Anna Lefroy, assigned it to 1798 or 1799 when, according to her, Jane Austen visited Devonshire with her parents and met a Mr. Blackall, a clergyman, who promised to come to Steventon, but died before he could do so. There is obviously some confusion here with Mrs. Lefroy senior's friend Mr. Blackall. Since Mrs. Lefroy senior died in 1804 and Anna did not marry her son until 1814 there was plenty of time for such confusion to arise. It seems likely that Anna simply mixed up two stories she had heard about her aunt's past, and Caroline's dating certainly seems the more probable.

Yet another variant of the story sets the scene of the unlucky romance in Switzerland, suggesting that the Austens went there in 1802 when the brief peace with France made European travel possible. In this version, the young man was a naval officer who met them at Chamonix and left them briefly with the intention of rejoining them, instead of which they received news of his sudden death. This story is wildly unlikely. The Austens' diminished income would hardly have allowed of trips to Switzerland, even if Mrs. Austen's health had, and anyway they were in Dawlish in the summer of 1802.

In whatever form, it is a sad little story, and an odd one in that it parallels Cassandra's own experience so closely. Is it possible that the charming young man had, in fact, behaved like Tom Lefroy and Mr. Blackall and who knows how many others before him, become frightened of those quietly intelligent sisters, and simply disappeared? And that, remembering the episode many years later, Cassandra supplied her beloved sister with her own more tragic and, from a contemporary point of view, more respectable ending to the affair?

This, of course, is pure conjecture. What is certain is that we must, selfishly, be grateful to the young man for dying, or disappearing, whichever he did. If Jane Austen had settled down, either in 1799 or in the early 1800s to marriage and the inevitable string of babies, her first three novels would probably have been lost, and her last three would certainly never have been written. But if, as Cassandra suggested, she really loved the young man, it must have been a bleak time for Jane Austen, however she lost him. With her first three books still unpublished, the fact that she was laying down experience for the creation of Anne Elliot would have been small consolation. When the letters begin again, there are several references to the plight of the impoverished old maid or widow. There is "poor Mrs. Stent! . . . always in the way", and, of another widow of their acquaintance, "at her age, perhaps, one may be as friendless oneself, and in similar circumstances quite as captious". Jane Austen believed in facing facts, and, the fact was that the impoverished spinsters of her day were in even worse case than widows, lacking the status that marriage conferred.

It was doubtless because she had such a clear eye for the bleak realities of her situation, and Cassandra's, that Jane Austen involved herself in a surprising episode in the winter of 1802. She and Cassandra had gone back to Steventon to stay with James and Mary, and gone on from there to visit the Biggs at Manydown. The Biggs are not, in fact, mentioned by name in Caroline Austen's story of this episode, but they are the only people who fit the facts as recounted. At all events, the two sisters returned to Steventon, in their hosts' carriage, much sooner than they were expected, and James and Mary, watching, presumably, from a window, saw them say a hurried farewell, with many tears, to their hostesses, before they came into the house and insisted that they must go back to Bath at once. It was not at all convenient for James to accompany them, as it involved both Sunday travelling and missing his own Sunday duty, but for once Jane and Cassandra were firm. James yielded, and took them home, learning, in due course, that Jane had actually accepted an offer of marriage from Harris Bigg Wither the night before, thought again, and refused him in the morning. It was a drastic action for a young woman of her day, but probably an extremely sensible one. Jane Austen was twenty-seven and Harris twenty-two at the time. He married two years later. For her, it was probably the last flicker of romance. In her books, twenty-seven is the climacteric year, the one when Anne Elliot recovers her bloom and her lost lover, and Charlotte Lucas catches Mr. Collins. As for Jane herself, from now on, as Mrs. Austen perceptively said, she and Cassandra "were wedded to each other". It was a happy marriage, and a productive one. "I have got my own darling child from London," said Jane Austen in 1813, on receiving her first copy of *Pride and Prejudice*.

By now it will be evident that critics of Jane Austen who claim that she had little or no experience in matters of the heart have simply not studied her life. The only thing that probably never happened to her was a totally satisfactory proposal, and this, it is true, is something at which she tends to boggle, fobbing the reader off with summary and hearsay. But whether this is from lack of experience, or from her own intense feeling of the privacy of such an episode, it would be hard to say. Her hand with the early stages of courtship is masterly. Darcy falling insensibly in love with Elizabeth while she goes right on disliking him, and rather fancies herself in love with Wickham, is as good as Elizabeth's gradual slide into love for Darcy, and the delicate comedy of it is summed up in Elizabeth's final comment to her beloved sister Jane, who has asked when, in fact, she began to love Darcy. "It has been coming on so gradually," replies Elizabeth, "that I hardly know when it began. But I believe I must date it from my first seeing his beautiful grounds at Pemberley." Perhaps the most delightful thing about this characteristic Jane Austen remark is that critics as eminent as Sir Walter Scott have taken Elizabeth Bennet at her word and dismissed her as a fortune-hunter.

Jane Austen had watched two brothers marry once, and another one twice. She must have studied the development of Cassandra's engagement to Tom Fowle with an almost painful intensity. There was not much she did not know about the ways of men with women, and vice versa. She had also been almost too close to several marriages, and was to be closer still. She had plenty of chance to study the effect of Mary on her brother James, and the happier situation of Edward and his Elizabeth. When she refused Harris Bigg Wither after what must have been a sleepless night, she knew exactly what she was doing. She was condemning herself to a lifetime as a second-class citizen, an object of contemptuous humour, an old maid. She was also condemning herself to write *Emma*, *Mansfield Park* and *Persuasion*, and we must be grateful to her, and to Cassandra, who undoubtedly made it possible. If there had been no Cassandra, I imagine there would have been no sleepless night, and a large family of extremely intelligent little Bigg Withers.

As it was, characteristically, Jane Austen must have taken a deep breath, called up her considerable reserves of fortitude and gone on playing the part of the daughter at home in Bath. A painful distraction was her mother's serious illness which took place at some time during these silent years. Mrs. Austen came near to death, recovered, and celebrated the event in a set of very passable comic verses, in which she gives the credit equally to her doctor, her husband's prayers, and her daughters' devoted nursing.

Another anxiety at this time was the visit Henry and Eliza Austen paid to France in the hopes of recovering the de Feuillide estates. Henry had left the army by 1801, and he and Eliza were living, according to Eliza's cousin, Philadelphia Walter, "quite in style in Upper Berkeley Street". Eliza's backward child, little Hastings, died that year, which must, one would think, have considerably weakened any claim on the de Feuillide estates. But according to family tradition, Henry and Eliza went to France after the Peace of Amiens in 1802 and stayed on until war broke out again in 1803, when Napoleon took the unprecedented step of ordering the internment of all British subjects then in France. Many unfortunates who had hurried back to the gaieties of Paris found themselves incarcerated for the very considerable duration of the war. Quick-witted Eliza got the two of them safely home by taking entire charge of their journey. Her French was so good that they got to the coast unsuspected, but they had had no success about the estates.

The Peace of Amiens had affected the sailor brothers too. Francis Austen had been put on half pay, and was probably relieved when war broke out again, as all thinking people were sure it would, in 1803. He went back to work at once, raising a corps of sea fencibles (a sort of sea version of the more recent British Home Guard) to defend the shores of Kent from the invasion threatened by Napoleon. His headquarters were at Ramsgate, and Jane must have visited him during this period, since Sir Egerton Brydges mentions meeting her there. Frank got engaged about this time, and returned to Ramsgate in 1806 to marry there, but by then he was back at sea, and had just missed Trafalgar. His match with Mary Gibson ended a fond hope of Cassandra's and Jane's that he would marry their friend Martha Lloyd, who had suffered a "disappointment" as so many young women did and do. In fact, Frank's wife Mary was to be a favourite sister-in-law and, many years later, after her death, he actually did marry Martha Lloyd. But by then Jane was dead too.

In 1803 she may have been visibly unhappy. Perhaps in an attempt to cheer her up, her father made a second and, on the face of it, more successful attempt to get one of her books published. This time it was *Susan* (our *Northanger Abbey*), which was sold outright to Messrs. Crosby & Cox for the vast sum of ten pounds. It probably did seem vast to Jane Austen compared with her allowance of twenty pounds a year. Since there are no letters for this period we do not know what she did with the money, but must hope that it was something satisfactory, for having bought the book and advertised it once, Crosby apparently lost heart and did no more about it. It must have been an exacerbating experience for its author, and it would probably have been little comfort to her to know that modern critics would argue that it was possibly the very quality of the book that caused its suppression. The Gothic romances it satirised were still best-sellers, and Crosby may have decided not to foul his own nest by publishing this splendid mockery of them.

But the slow, bitter disappointment of his failure to publish *Susan* was in the future. For the moment, the sale may have helped to start Jane Austen writing again. Change of scene is always a problem for an author, and, for her, moving from Steventon to Bath was probably as drastic as for a modern author to cross the Atlantic. At all events, she seems to have written nothing for the first few years at Bath. The next thing she started, the untitled fragment that is known as *The Watsons*, is on paper water-marked 1803, and we have the authority of a great-neice that it was begun in 1804. Jane Austen was writing again, but she was not writing happily. *The Watsons* is her most cold-blooded and least humorous attempt at studying the realities of the husband hunt. Its heroine, Emma Watson, is one of a large, impecunious family and has had the apparent luck of being adopted by a wealthy, widowed aunt. But the adoption has been informal and before the story opens the rich widow has married again—this time an Irish adventurer. The story begins with Emma back at home, penniless like her sisters, but with higher standards, to make what she can of her life. And what can she make but a good marriage?

Through her lips, Jane Austen makes perhaps her clearest statement about the husband hunt. "To be so bent on marriage—to pursue a man merely for the sake of situation—is a sort of thing that shocks me; I cannot understand it. Poverty is a great evil, but to a woman of education and feeling it ought not, it cannot be the greatest—I would rather be a teacher at a school (and I can think of nothing worse) than marry a man I did not like." In 1804, those were strong words. The fragment of *The Watsons* shows opportunity opening before Emma. The local aristocrat, Lord Osborne, takes a fancy to her and so, inevitably, does his admirably drawn toad-eater, Tom Musgrave, but we have the authority of the Austen family for the fact that in the end she married neither of them, choosing instead the respectable clergyman whose little nephew she had befriended. A husband may not have been Jane Austen's recipe for herself, but she always provided them for her heroines.

The author of the *Memoir*, a worthy son to James and Mary Austen, thought his aunt had abandoned *The Watsons* because she found she had set her scene in too low a class of society. This is, quite obviously, absurd, and would have amused Jane Austen very much. She enjoyed dealing with the fringe situations between aristocracy and middle class, and was superbly equipped to do so. The misunderstandings, affronts and absurdities involved were meat and drink to her, as they would be to Henry James, and, in rather different terms, to many modern novelists. The scene where the foppish young aristocrats come to call just as the Watsons' vulgar servants are producing the knife-box for their unfashionably early dinner is masterly of its kind.

But on the whole there is something slightly flat about *The Watsons*, which may simply mean that it lacks the hard revision and final polish that Jane Austen liked to give to her books, but may well indicate her own state of mind when she wrote it. At all events she was doomed to be interrupted. The first break was a pleasant one, their summer visit to the sea, which took them, in 1804, to Lyme Regis. The Henry Austens went too, and then took Cassandra on to Weymouth with them, leaving Jane and her parents at Lyme, but soon afterwards an urgent summons sent Cassandra hurrying to Ibthorp, where Martha Lloyd's mother was dangerously ill. One letter from Jane to Cassandra survives. "I endeavour as far as I can to supply your place and be useful, and keep things in order. I detect dirt in the water-decanter as fast as I can and give the cook physic which she throws off her stomach." She is thinking about words again. Their servant "has a great many more than all the cardinal virtues (for the cardinal virtues in themselves have been so often possessed that they are no longer worth having)." If there was one thing Jane Austen detested, it was an overworked phrase.

This letter also has a couple of interesting sidelights on the Austen family life. A friend of theirs had shown Mrs. Austen a letter Cassandra had written her, and Jane Austen comments, in parenthesis, "which by the bye in your place I should not like". It is another reminder that letters, for Jane and Cassandra, were a private affair. In this one, Jane mentions visiting a Miss Armstrong. "Like other young ladies she is considerably genteeler than her parents. Mrs. Armstrong sat darning a pair of stockings the whole of my visit. But I do not mention this at home, lest a warning should act as an example." One cannot help feeling a little sorry for Mrs. Austen, and remembering the old days at Steventon when she used to do the mending in the family parlour because there was so much of it to do.

They were enjoying Lyme. Jane Austen bathed and found it so delightful that she stayed in rather too long. She also walked on the Cobb, no doubt storing up impressions, consciously or otherwise, for one of the most famous scenes in her books. It is pleasant to think that the unusually romantic description of Lyme in *Persuasion* reflected a halycon period in her own life. "A very strange stranger it must be, who does not see charms in the immediate environs of Lyme, to make him wish to know it better." When she speaks of "green chasms between romantic rocks", it is possible, for once, to think of her as the contemporary of Coleridge and Wordsworth.

Mrs. Lloyd recovered, and presumably all four Austens were back in Bath when they received the news that Jane's dear friend Mrs. Lefroy had been killed by a fall from her horse. It happened on December 16th, Jane's birthday, and four years later Jane commemorated the disaster in stiff, heartrending verses:

> But come, fond Fancy, thou indulgent power;
> Hope is desponding, chill, severe, to thee:
> Bless thou this little portion of an hour;
> Let me behold her as she used to be.

Three years younger than Coleridge, and five than Wordsworth, she was still writing the verse of the eighteenth century.

But the stiff lines are eloquent of real grief. She had lost a very dear friend. Next month, she lost her father. Mr. Austen died after an illness of only forty-eight hours on January 21st, 1805. Two letters from Jane Austen breaking the news to Frank have survived. She had to write twice, because the first letter was sent to an out-of-date address. Both letters are models of their kind. She thought of everything that Frank would need to know, and gave him all the comfort she could. The illness had been short; their father had suffered as little as possible; their mother was bearing up. Oddly, there is no mention of Cassandra in either letter. She was probably away.

They had moved by now to a house in Green Park Buildings, and Jane told Frank that though James had pressed them to come back to Steventon with him, she thought they would stay there for the three months for which the house was rented. But of course they were faced with the immemorial problem of widows and orphans. Mr. Austen's income from Steventon Rectory died with him. The living devolved on James, and Mrs. Austen and her two daughters were left with a combined income of two hundred and ten pounds. Mr. Austen had started his children well in life, but he had not been able to save for them. In fact, even the annual two hundred and ten pounds was partly Cassandra's, the interest on the thousand pounds left her by Tom Fowle.

Though they say everything that should be said, there is something a little stiff about Jane Austen's letters on her father's death. It lends substance to the comment of some critics that her books never show happy, established marriages, or functioning parents. There is certainly some truth in this rather general accusation. So far as really satisfactory marriages are concerned, only the Crofts and the Harvilles leap to the mind, and they are both, significantly, naval, and in *Persuasion*, the last and mellowest of Jane Austen's completed books. When she wanted to describe a satisfactory marriage, Jane Austen seems instinctively to have turned to those of her sailor brothers. But there is absolutely nothing to suggest that Mr. and Mrs. Austen senior were not a happy couple. It seems more likely that they were, if anything, too contented with each other. What had probably, and painfully, happened to Jane was that she had recognised the fact that she had outgrown them. She could take Cassandra with her, but when their mother read *Pride and Prejudice* aloud, she spoiled it. We do not know at what point in her life Jane looked at the "handsome proctor" with his fine head of white hair, and found him wanting, but she probably did so. As for their mother, a tone of affectionate impatience had crept into the letters quite early on, but then daughters do outgrow their mothers.

And, in fact, functioning parents are the last thing one wants in the kind of gay, romantic novel that Jane Austen's books appear to be. If Mrs. Woodhouse had survived, Emma would have been less spoiled, and if sensible Mrs. Morland had taken her daughter to Bath, she would have seen to it that none of those delicious adventures happened. But it remains significant that when Catherine returns home with a broken heart, her mother fails to recognise the condition. Jane Austen does seem to have thought of parents as makers of mistakes. Mr. Bennet lets Lydia go to Brighton against Elizabeth's advice; Sir Thomas Bertram leaves his daughters' moral training to their intolerable aunt. Only Mrs. Dashwood, learning by experience, "could be calm, could be even prudent, when the life of a child was at stake". And even here Jane Austen is making the point that if Mrs. Dashwood had been a little calmer and more prudent earlier on, she would have saved her children a great deal of trouble.

The problems of education, and of heredity, fascinated Jane Austen. She liked to trace things back to their roots, and was careful to provide Wickham with a spendthrift mother to explain his character, and to distinguish between the different kinds of education that made such different characters of the Ferrars brothers. She said that in *Mansfield Park* she was taking a new theme, ordination, but education would describe her subject as well, or better. The moral of that story seems to be

Steventon Rectory, where Jane Austen grew up. Drawn by her niece Anna, who later lived there. By courtesy of Miss Helen Lefroy   (*Photo J. Butler-Kearney*)

Godmersham Park, Kent, home of Jane Austen's brother Edward Knight

Silhouette showing the Reverend George Austen presenting his son Edward to his adoptive parents, Mr. and Mrs. Thomas Knight. By courtesy of Major Edward Knight
(*Photo J. Butler-Kearney*)

Jane Austen's cousin Eliza when she was Comtesse de Feuillide. From *Jane Austen, Her Homes and Her Friends* by M. C. Hill

Henry Austen after taking Orders. By courtesy of Major Edward Knight
(*Photo J. Butler-Kearney*)

Sidney Gardens, Bath. The Austens' first house there overlooked these pleasure gardens.
From *Bath, 1806*, by J. G. Nattes

Lyme Regis, which the Austens visited in 1804. Sketch by Turner
(Photo Courtauld Institute of Art)

Jane Austen, by her sister Cassandra
(*Photo National Portrait Gallery*)

Admiral Sir Francis Austen. By courtesy of
the Jane Austen Society
(*Photo J. Butler-Kearney*)

Captain (later Admiral) Charles
Austen as a young man. Note
the strong family likeness be-
tween the three youngest
Austens. By courtesy of the
Jane Austen Society
(*Photo J. Butler-Kearney*)

that there is nothing like a little good honest neglect for rearing children of character.

But *Mansfield Park* was far in the future. In the present, the problem was how the Austen ladies were to live. Luckily for them, they were not Dashwoods. A touching correspondence between the brothers (preserved in *Jane Austen's Sailor Brothers* by J. H. and E. C. Hubback) shows them all eager to do something for their bereaved womenfolk. In the end Edward gave his mother a hundred pounds a year. Frank wanted to do the same, but Mrs. Austen would only accept fifty from him. James gave the same amount, and Henry undertook to do so too, "so long as my present precarious income remains". Charles was still a mere commander of a sloop and was shortly to leave for seven years on the American station, during which he married and started a family, so that there was no chance of his being able to help for some considerable time. Henry, as usual, was optimistic. "I really think that my mother and sisters will be to the full as rich as ever." In fact, Jane Austen had earlier written that her father hoped to retire on an income of six hundred pounds. It takes the eye of hope indeed to look on the precariously subscribed four hundred and sixty pounds as equal to this. Edward and Frank undoubtedly paid up regularly, but it is difficult to be so sure about Henry. Significantly, there is no record of any offer of help from Mrs. Austen's rich brother, James Leigh Perrot, but years later, after Jane Austen's death and James Leigh Perrot's, his widow did help her sister-in-law.

At least, like her daughter, Mrs. Austen was a realist. She could not have reared eight children on a limited income otherwise. By April, the three of them had moved into furnished lodgings at 25, Gay Street in Bath with only one maid. Mrs. Lloyd was ill again, and Cassandra went to help nurse her. Her reports were not encouraging. "Poor woman!" wrote Jane in reply. "May her end be peaceful and easy as the exit we have witnessed . . . even the consciousness of existence I suppose was gone when you wrote." Jane Austen was learning about death. But the living were more important, and she wrote letters intended to amuse her sister. "The nonsense I have been writing in this and in my last letter, seems out of place at such a time; but I will not mind it, it will do you no harm, and nobody else will be attacked by it." Her niece Fanny was to do the same for her when she was dying.

Cassandra's next letter must have announced Mrs. Lloyd's death, and Jane's answer to it has been destroyed. The following one thanks Cassandra for a second letter with a "very comfortable" account of their bereaved friend Martha. She was alone now, since both her sisters were married, and it was already settled that she should throw in her lot with the three Austen ladies. "I am quite of your opinion as to the folly of concealing any longer our intended partnership with Martha, and whenever there has of late been an enquiry on the subject I have always been sincere." It was an arrangement that was to work out admirably for all of them. From then on, to all intents and purposes, Mrs. Austen had three daughters to share any burden that might have to be borne.

Meanwhile Mr. Austen had been dead three months and Jane and her mother were visiting again. "What request we are in! . . . I think we are just the kind of people and party to be treated about among our relations." Like Emma Woodhouse, Jane was arranging quiet evening parties for her solitary parent. She had a slight battle with herself about inviting the Leigh Perrots to one of them, but in the end decided that, "It was of the first consequence to avoid anything that might seem a slight to them." The Leigh Perrots were evidently difficult people to deal with, both socially and financially. "My aunt is in a great hurry to pay me for my cap, but cannot find in her heart to give me good money." It must have been trying as between a niece so poor and an aunt so rich.

There were cousins visiting Bath, on both sides of the family, and Jane spoke highly of one of them, George Cooke, a Leigh connection who "was very kind and talked sense to me every now and then in the intervals of his more animated fooleries with Miss Bendish". But, "there was a monstrous deal of stupid quizzing, and common-place nonsense talked, but scarcely any wit—all that bordered on it, or on sense came from my Cousin George, who altogether I like very well." George, son of Jane's godfather, was twenty-five at the time, and a Fellow of Corpus Christi. At twenty-nine, and in mourning twice over, Jane no doubt seemed a great deal older, and it is pleasant to think of her cousin recognising her quality and taking the trouble to talk sense to her.

A great advantage of having Martha settled with them was that now Cassandra and Jane could go to Kent together. The next surviving letter was written that August from Godmersham, where Jane was staying with Edward and Elizabeth, to Goodnestone, also in Kent, where Cassandra was staying with Elizabeth's widowed mother, Lady Bridges. Cassandra, who seems to have been the family nurse, had gone back to Goodnestone with Harriot Bridges, who had a cold. Jane was already demonstrating her virtues as an aunt, playing battledore-and-shuttlecock with her nephew William, and going for walks with "George and Henry to animate us by their races and merriment". She had heard from Frank, who "is in a great hurry to be married", and had "encouraged him in it". She had also found Cassandra's white mittens, which "were folded up within my clean nightcap, and send their duty to you". Elizabeth's hairdresser had charged Jane only two and six for cutting her hair: "He certainly respects either our youth or our poverty." A postscript enlarged on the theme. "I find on looking into my affairs, that instead of being very rich I am likely to be very poor, I cannot afford more than ten shillings for Sackree." Sackree was Elizabeth's maid. Tipping must always have been a problem to the Austen girls when they visited in Kent.

The next letter shows that Jane and Cassandra had changed places. Jane was at Goodnestone keeping Harriot Bridges company and Cassandra back at Godmersham. There were plans afoot for a joint excursion to Worthing, but Cassandra and Jane's part in it seemed uncertain. "We shall not be at Worthing so soon as we have been used to talk of, shall we? This will be no evil to us, and we are sure of my mother and Martha being happy together." No doubt Cassandra and Jane's visit to Kent was the usual three months or so, and the proposed meeting at Worthing would make their return to Bath easier.

Judging by the watermark on two of its pages, *Lady Susan* was fair-copied during 1805, but this is the only evidence there is of literary activity on Jane's part. She may still have been working on *The Watsons*, or she may have taken up the fair-copying of *Lady Susan* as a distraction after abandoning it. Obviously, this was a year of change and upheaval, with no time for much serious work. Settling down as a household of four women, instead of three women and a man, must inevitably have presented its problems, though, judging by the reference to Martha quoted above, these cannot have been too serious. Martha and Cassandra were in their thirties now, and Jane would be thirty in December. James's daughter, Caroline Austen was born this year. Many years later, she wrote a brief *Memoir* of her famous aunt. One remark of hers probably applies to about this time. "I believe my two aunts were not accounted very good dressers, and were thought to have taken to the garb of middle age unnecessarily soon—but they were particularly neat, and they held all untidy ways in great disesteem." We do not know how the family income of four hundred and sixty pounds was shared out, or whether Cassandra and Jane were still on twenty-pound allowances, but they probably had good reason for economy in dress.

There are no letters for 1806, but it was an eventful year. Frank came back from a cruise to the West Indies covered in glory, was thanked by

Parliament and married his Mary Gibson. He had probably already arranged with his mother that the two families should join forces that autumn in Southampton, a remarkably brave act on everybody's part, but one doubtless dictated by economic necessity. At least it freed the Austen ladies from Bath, which they left for good on July 2nd. One of Mrs. Austen's few surviving letters, written in April, gives a good idea of the life they were to leave. They had had James's daughter Anna staying with them, and, "I may well call this a gay week." There had been a ball, a concert where the famous Mrs. Billington sang, and a visit to the theatre.

But not even George Frederick Cooke as Macbeth could reconcile Jane Austen to life in Bath. Writing to Cassandra two years later, she spoke of their feelings of relief at getting away at last. "It will be two years tomorrow since we left Bath for Clifton, with what happy feelings of escape!" They had gone first to Clifton and then to stay with Mrs. Austen's cousin the Reverend Thomas Leigh, at his rectory of Adlestrop. The Leigh family was in a state of considerable upheaval at the time, since the Honourable Mary Leigh, life-heir to the Stoneleigh estates, had died on July 2nd. She had held the property under a rather curious will which left the succession in some doubt as between Thomas Leigh, his cousin James Leigh Perrot, and Thomas's nephew, the logical heir, James Henry Leigh.

Thomas had rather jumped the gun by moving straight into Stoneleigh Abbey on receiving the news of Mary Leigh's death in London, and some slightly acrimonious negotiations between the three possible heirs followed. But by August the heirs got together and began to work on what Jane Austen was to call, years later, "that vile compromise". Thomas Leigh, who was childless, was to succeed, with reversion to James Henry Leigh, while James Leigh Perrot waived his claim in consideration of a large sum of money and an annuity for himself and his wife. All this took some working out, and the "vile compromise" was not signed until November 1808. In the meanwhile, Thomas Leigh was master of Stoneleigh Abbey and took his cousins there with him when he moved in on August 5th. A surviving letter from Mrs. Austen senior reports: "The house is larger than I could have supposed ... I have proposed his [her cousin's] setting up *directing posts* at the angles." There were five and a half acres of garden, views of the Avon and a state bedchamber, with a high dark crimson velvet bed: "an *alarming* apartment just fit for a heroine". Had she been rereading *Northanger Abbey*? It is a letter that makes one feel more kindly towards Jane Austen's mother, particularly when she goes on to describe a fellow guest. "Poor Lady Saye and Sele[1] to be sure is rather tormenting, though sometimes amusing, and affords Jane many a good laugh."

One needs to remember this episode when considering a detestable letter that Jane Austen's favourite niece Fanny was to write, years later, to her younger sister. Fanny was Lady Knatchbull then, and very much aware of the importance of her position, and she felt she must apologise for her aunts. Her letter makes painful reading.

> Yes my love it is very true that Aunt Jane from various circumstances was not so *refined* as she ought to have been for her *talent*, and if she had lived 50 years later she would have been in many respects more suitable to *our* more refined tastes. They were not rich, and the people with whom they chiefly mixed, were not at all high bred ... and *they* of course though superior in *mental powers and cultivation* were on the same level so far as *refinement* goes—but I think in later life their inter-course with Mrs. Knight (who was very fond of and kind to them) improved them both and Aunt Jane was too clever not to put aside all possible signs of "common-ness" ... Both the aunts were brought up in the most complete ignorance of the world and its ways (I mean as to fashions &c) and if it had not been for Papa's marriage which brought them into Kent, and the kindness of Mrs. Knight, who used often to have one or the other of the sisters staying with her, they would have been, though not less clever and agreeable in themselves, very much below par as to good society and its ways.

So Lady Knatchbull. It is odd to think that among the letters that she did not make available to her nephew for his *Memoir* was one from Jane Austen dated September 1813, with a comment on two of Mrs. Knight's Knatchbull connections, for Fanny finally married a cousin. "They are very goodnatured you know and civil and all that—but are not particularly superfine." One must always remember the gap that existed between Kent and Hampshire. The Kent family probably knew little or nothing about the Leigh connection. Lady Knatchbull would have been amazed at the idea of her Aunt Jane getting "many a good laugh" out of "poor Lady Saye and Sele".

It is a remark of Mrs. Austen's for which we cannot be sufficiently grateful. After her daughter had died, and become famous, a terrible amount of nonsense was talked about how she never said an unkind thing, or laughed at the follies of others. It is, quite simply, impossible to

---

[1] A connection of the Leighs.

believe, and, luckily, we have her own mother's authority to the contrary. Jane Austen would undoubtedly have confessed, like her own Elizabeth Bennet, "Follies and nonsense, whims, and inconsistencies *do* divert me, I own, and I laugh at them whenever I can." Laughter was the sunshine that made Jane Austen's life bearable.

Jᴀɴᴇ Aᴜsᴛᴇɴ ᴡᴀs ᴡᴇʟʟ ᴀᴄQᴜᴀɪɴᴛᴇᴅ ᴡɪᴛʜ ᴛʜᴇ ᴍᴇᴄʜᴀɴɪᴄs ᴏꜰ the country house life of her day. Stoneleigh Abbey was merely one of the larger houses that she visited, and she could undoubtedly have written volumes, had she so wished, about the subtle distinctions between different styles and levels of living. She could easily have expatiated on the complexities of the servants' hall, and talked knowledgeably about butlers, and footmen, and grooms of the chambers. But these were the kind of excessive "particulars of right hand and left" against which she would, later in life, warn her niece Anna. Servants, when they appear in her books, are always used for more than to open doors, or to serve meals. Lady Bertram actually thinks of sending her own maid to help Fanny Price dress for her first ball, but, characteristically, sends her too late. Sir Thomas, on the other hand, though angry with Fanny for her refusal of Henry Crawford, remembers to tell a housemaid to light the fire that her Aunt Norris prohibited.

But in the main, Jane Austen's servants are like the invisible hands of the fairy tale. We will never know what the footman thought who let a furious Emma out of the carriage in which Mr. Elton had proposed to her, nor whether the housekeeper at Pemberley approved of Elizabeth Bennet. Jane Austen has been accused of snobbery because of this omission, but it is merely another instance of her extraordinary sense of artistic proportion. There is no room, on her tiny piece of ivory, for what the butler saw. And, of course, she was writing for an audience who would take servants just as much for granted as she did herself. The "servant problem" with all its manifold snobberies, is largely a twentieth-century phenomenon.

Meanwhile, that summer of 1806 provided plenty of varied country house experience. The Austen ladies were between homes, safely away, at last, from Bath, but not yet settled in Southampton. After the usual long visit at Stoneleigh Abbey, they went on to visit more cousins, the Coopers at Hamstall-Ridware, where Edward Cooper was rector. He was the son of Mrs. Austen's sister Jane, who had caught diphtheria from the children, years before, and died of it. Jane does not seem to have thought very highly of his sermons, of which he published at least three volumes, but then her standards were high.

Martha Lloyd must have been engaged in her own round of visits, but by the autumn the three Austens were settled at last in Southampton. Frank Austen was temporarily without a ship and he and his new wife Mary joined forces with the Austen ladies, first in lodgings, then in a house in Castle Square. They were all hard up together and lived very quietly, but must have made a success of their odd household, since Mary (known as Mrs. F. A. to distinguish her from James's less agreeable Mary) was always a much-loved sister-in-law. Just the same, the stresses and strains of a household consisting of one man and four women (later five, when Martha joined them) must have been fascinating material for Jane Austen, and, an inevitable complication, Mary was soon pregnant.

But before this, Jane Austen's letters have taken up again. In January 1807, Cassandra was visiting the Edward Austens at Godmersham and Jane was busy at home with "the torments of rice pudding and apple dumplings", caused by a visit from James and Mary Austen. Mary had invited Jane to go back to Steventon with them but, "I need not give my answer." More practically, Mary had also invited Mrs. Austen to come to them when the other Mary was due to be confined, which Mrs. Austen "seems half inclined to do". Jane herself had had whooping cough and been disgusted by Madame de Genlis' book *Alphonsine*: "It has indelicacies which disgrace a pen hitherto so pure; and we changed it for the *Female Quixote*, which now makes our evening amusement; to me a very high one as I find the work quite equal to what I remembered it!" Charlotte Lennox's skit on the novel had been written as early as 1752, and its heroine who supposed "romances were real pictures of life", and "drew all her notions and expectations from them", serves as a useful reminder that *Northanger Abbey* was not the only book to mock contemporary fictional absurdities; it was just the best.

On a more mundane note, Mrs. Austen had been surprised and pleased to find herself beginning the new year, 1807, with thirty pounds more in hand than the year before, "and when she has written her answer to my aunt, which you know always hangs a little upon her mind, she will be above the world entirely." The aunt in question is, of course, Jane Leigh Perrot, and it does seem possible that the reference is to some kind of financial help from the rich Leigh Perrots to the poor Austens. We do know that Mrs. Leigh Perrot was giving Mrs. Austen a hundred pounds a year in 1821.

Frank, still without a ship, was poor too, and though he and his mother both felt they could manage their present expenses, they could not face "much increase of house-rent". Frank felt that four hundred pounds a year must be his limit. But even in lodgings, there were naval friends of his to visit and to be visited by. Jane Austen has one of her realistic comments on one party. "They will not come often, I dare say. They live in a hand-some style and are rich, and she seemed to like to be rich, and we gave her to understand that we were far from being so; she will soon feel therefore that we are not worth her acquaintance."

Jane was missing Cassandra, whose return, as so often, had been delayed. "It is no use to lament," she wrote. "I never heard that even Queen Mary's lamentation did her any good, and I could not therefore expect benefit from mine." Martha was still away, too, but there were pleasures for the little party in planning improvements to the house and garden in Castle Square into which they were to move in March. Lord Lansdowne was proving a co-operative landlord and Jane wanted a syringa for the garden "for the sake of Cowper's line". No doubt she got her "syringa ivory pure".

They had been visited by the little daughter of friends, who "is now talking away at my side and examining the treasures of my writing-desk drawer". It is a charming picture of Jane Austen writing her letter to Cassandra while the little girl played with the contents of the invaluable writing-desk. If Jane could entertain a child while she wrote a letter, it begins to seem less amazing that she managed to write the later novels in the busy atmosphere of the family living-room at Chawton. She had little privacy in her life, and plenty of practice in concentration.

She has an interesting comment on her child visitor. "What is become of all the shyness in the world? — Moral as well as natural diseases disappear in the course of time, and new ones take their place. Shyness and the sweating sickness have given way to confidence and paralytic complaints." The Bertram sisters were to suffer from no "natural shyness", but Fanny Price must have been old-fashioned, perhaps more like Jane Austen herself, who goes on to describe little Catherine as "a nice, natural, open-hearted, affectionate girl, with all the ready civility which one sees in the best children of the present day—so unlike anything that I was at her age that I am often all astonishment and shame." There may have been some truth in that comment of Philadelphia Walter's, years before, that the young Jane was "very prim ... whimsical and affected". Jane had no doubt simply been shy with her older cousin.

Jane herself was well known in the family for her way with children. She had been an aunt since she was seventeen and had had plenty of opportunities to exercise her talent for dealing with the young on their own terms. Caroline Austen remembered that her aunt's "charm to children was great sweetness of manner—she seemed to love you and you loved her naturally in return". And, again, *Everything* she could make amusing to a child." She used to tell them "the most delightful stories chiefly of fairyland, and her fairies had all characters of their own". Imagine Mrs. Norris as the wicked fairy at the christening. It was no wonder that "as a very little girl", Caroline was always "creeping up to her [aunt], and following her". And it is dismally characteristic of Caroline's mother, James's wife Mary, that she told little Caroline privately that she "must not be troublesome to my aunt". Did Mary Austen add jealousy to her other disagreeable qualities?

At Southampton, there were visitors who presented greater problems than nice little Catherine. Incidentally, Henry Tilney would not have approved of Jane Austen's use of that word "nice", and perhaps the slipshod usage is an indication of the distraction the child was causing. Another visitor had called in vain. A friend of Frank's wife Mary had paid her a visit when they were out, and, oddly, had left no address at which her call could be returned. After some puzzlement over this curious behaviour, the Austens decided that she must be staying with the Miss Pearson who had once been engaged to Henry. The brief episode was at least ten years dead, but apparently it still made visiting between the two families impossible. "What an unluckiness," appropriately Jane Austen quotes Fanny Burney's Madame Duval.

Where visiting was possible, it was not necessarily a pleasure. James was expected again, and either Cassandra's scissors missed a passage, or Jane was more outspoken than usual. "I am sorry and angry that his visits should not give one more pleasure; the company of so good and so clever a man ought to be gratifying in itself—but his chat seems all forced, his opinions on many points too much copied from his wife's, and his time here is spent I think in walking about the house and banging the doors, or ringing the bell for a glass of water." James and Mary sound more and more like Mr. and Mrs. John Dashwood.

Cassandra's visit in Kent went on and on, and Martha too was still only promising to come to them. Apparently she had not yet joined the party in Southampton, for Jane promised to tell Cassandra "what she thinks of Mary" when she did. Mary's confinement was getting nearer, and she asked, through Jane, for advice on various points from Elizabeth Austen, expert mother of ten. Frank was still at home and making himself useful about arrangements for the house into which they would move before the baby was born. "Frank has got a very bad cough, for an Austen — but it does not disable him from making very nice fringe for the drawing-room curtains." They sound an agreeable household, with a hint of the Harvilles, and it is possible that Jane, with her gift of imagination, was better equipped than Cassandra or Martha to smooth the transition into the unusual ménage.

Other people had been inheriting money. A connection, John Austen, had succeeded to the estates of a cousin: "Such ill-gotten wealth can never prosper!" There was a good deal of rather wry joking between Jane and Cassandra about the legacies they never got: "Legacies are very wholesome diet." Jane Leigh Perrot had written that Elliston, the actor, had just succeeded to a considerable fortune on the death of an uncle. And Jane Leigh Perrot herself was "in good humour and cheerful spirits . . . The long negotiation between them and Adlestrop so happily over indeed, what can have power to vex her materially?" It is odd that this reference to the Leigh family settlement should be so different from Jane's later remark about the "vile compromise". Perhaps the Austens were not yet aware of the exact terms of the settlement. Anyway, as so often, there was money about, and none of it coming their way.

Cassandra's return was delayed once again, but at least Martha seems to have got there in time to help with the move into the commodious house in Castle Square. "We hear that we are envied our house by many people," said Jane, "and that the garden is the best in the town." There are no letters after this one until the summer of 1808, so we do not know whether Cassandra was back for the birth of little Mary Jane Austen in April, or whether Mrs. Austen did pack up and go to stay with James and his Mary till it was all over.

Frank had taken command of H.M.S. *St. Albans* the month his child was born, and left for the Cape of Good Hope on convoy duty, not to return until the following year. The feminine household must have been a quiet one. Meanwhile Charles was still on the American station, enforcing the unpopular British blockade that was to lead, in the end, to war with the United States. In May of 1807 he married Frances Palmer, daughter of the Attorney-General of Bermuda, and she seems, like Mrs. Croft, to have spent most of her time on board ship with him. They were far from well off, so this was doubtless from economy as much as from choice. Meanwhile, his letters were providing Jane with the West Indian background for *Mansfield Park*. Always meticulous about accuracy of detail, she would know all about how the long war and consequent worsening of relations between Great Britain and the United States would affect Sir Thomas Bertram's property in Antigua.

In the autumn of 1807 Mrs Austen and her daughters paid a visit to Chawton House, part of Edward's Hampshire estate, where, presumably, he and his family were staying. Next spring they visited the James Austens at Steventon and then went on to stay with the Fowles at Kintbury. In June, Jane was writing from Godmersham to Cassandra, who was back with their mother in Castle Square. Jane had been staying with Henry and Eliza on her way to Kent. They were living comfortably in Brompton now, since Henry had changed careers and was a partner in a firm of bankers. Austen, Maunde and Tilson, Bankers, of 10, Henrietta Street, Covent Garden, had connections with Austen, Gray and Vincent of Alton, Hampshire, which were ultimately to prove disastrous, but for the moment Henry was enjoying the "considerable share of riches and honours" that Eliza had predicted before she married him.

A later reference in Jane's letters suggests that Eliza was still leading the fashionable life she enjoyed. Elizabeth Austen's maid Sackree had also been in London on her way back from taking one of the Edward Austens' sons to school. She and Jane "saw the ladies go to Court on the 4th". June 4th was the King's birthday and always ceremonially observed. Young ladies like Maria Edgeworth's Belinda ordered special (and very expensive) dresses for the occasion, and no doubt Jane and Sackree watched and admired as Eliza put the finishing touches to her toilette. Sackree "had the advantage indeed of me in being in the Palace". Presumably Sackree was taken along as lady's maid. Jane Austen must have heard all about the splendid occasion, but, not having been there herself, she never sent a heroine to court. She left the experience, offstage, for Sir William Lucas and Sir Walter Elliot. If she troubled to describe Eliza's birthday dress to Cassandra, the letter has not survived, but very likely she did not. Their own dress was a constant, and practical interest, but in her letters, as in her books, she spends little time on the description of frills and furbelows in general.

She had travelled from Brompton to Godmersham in the James Austens' carriage. They had been staying at the Bath Hotel in London, "which, by-the-bye, had been found most uncomfortable quarters — very dirty, very noisy, and very ill-provided". This sounds like a quotation from Mary. Doubtless partly because of lack of space in the carriage and partly because she did not get on very well with her stepmother, Anna Austen, James's daughter by his first wife, had been left behind to stay with her grandmother in Castle Square. As it was, James had had to take the public coach, leaving Mary and Jane to travel down in his carriage with the two children, James Edward (author of the *Memoir*) and Caroline. Jane felt rather badly about this. "As James has no horse, I must feel in their carriage that I am taking his place. We were rather crowded yesterday, though it does not become me to say so, as I and my boa were of the party, and it is not to be supposed but that a child of three years of age was fidgety."

Jane was finding it odd "to be at Godmersham without you", and odder still to have such a great place as the yellow room all to herself. She had found Edward looking well, but could not say the same of Elizabeth, who was expecting her eleventh child. "I cannot praise Elizabeth's looks, but they are probably affected by a cold." Neither Elizabeth nor her eldest daughter, fifteen-year-old Fanny, would admit that she was "fatigued by her attendance on the children", but there were ten of them, after all, and Jane resolved that when Elizabeth's sister Louisa left she would at least try to take her place in hearing the little girls read.

Jane, too, had a cold and admitted to feeling "rather languid and solitary". The company on this visit was clearly not so much to her taste as it had been on the previous one when Cassandra had accompanied her, and Elizabeth's older sister, Harriot Bridges had been there. Harriot had married a Mr. Moore in the meantime and Cassandra and Jane seem to have had their doubts about him. "I will not pretend in one meeting to *dislike* him, whatever Mary may say, but I can honestly assure her that I saw nothing in him to admire." The Moores had a little girl by now, and, "Harriot's fondness for her seems just what is amiable and natural, and not foolish."

Jane Austen has been accused of disliking children, but what, in fact, she very reasonably disliked were spoiled children, like the little Middletons. When she comments on James Edward Austen's behaviour at table: "He was almost too happy, his happiness at least made him too talkative," she reminds us of Elinor Dashwood: "I confess . . . that while I am at Barton Park, I never think of tame and quiet children with any abhorrence." It is doubtful whether the ten young Austens of Godmersham were always, or often, "tame and quiet". A later letter reports that, "Mary finds the children less troublesome than she expected, and independent of *them*, there is certainly not much to try the patience or hurt the spirits at Godmersham." An observant aunt, Jane has comments for her sister on the growth and development of Edward's children, and a perceptive remark on their relations with their visiting cousins, James and Mary's two children, Edward "is very happy here . . . but I believe the little girl will be glad to go home — her cousins are too much for her." Caroline was sitting for the portrait of Fanny Price. "I have tried to give James pleasure by telling him of his daughter's taste, but if he felt, he did not express it — *I* rejoice in it very sincerely." Here, too, is a hint for the Bertram family's unawareness of Fanny. And it is surely more than a coincidence that in the same letter Jane is debating the relative merits of a silver knife and a brooch as a present for Frank's Mary. Fanny Price, whose uncle had given her ten pounds for her trip to Portsmouth, was to find that "wealth is luxurious and daring". Some of the money was used to join a circulating library, and some to buy a little silver knife for her sister.

Jane had had a letter from Edward's adoptive mother, old Mrs. Knight, "containing the usual fee, and all the usual kindness", and was to spend a few days with her. "Her very agreeable present will make my circumstances quite easy." The visit, when it happened, was an extremely lively one, with a constant stream of other guests, so that it was "a matter of wonder to me, that Mrs. K. and I should ever have been ten minutes alone . . . Yet we had time to say a little of everything." Mrs. Knight obviously liked Cassandra and Jane and was loved in return. "I cannot help regretting," said Jane, "that now, when I feel enough her equal to relish her society, I see so little" of her.

Back at Godmersham, Jane wrote letters full of family news. Frank was expected home shortly in the *St. Albans* . . . Mrs. Austen was to visit the James Austens on their return to Steventon and, "You and I and Martha shall have a snug fortnight while my mother is at Steventon." There was gossip to report, too. "Mr. Waller is dead I see — I cannot grieve about it, nor perhaps can his widow very much." Jane would not pretend to feelings she did not have. There was also "a sad story about Mrs. Powlett", who had eloped with a viscount and thus no doubt provided another of those tiny grains of material Jane Austen was unconsciously collecting for her next book, *Mansfield Park*.

Talking of books, James was reading Scott's new poem aloud in the evenings. "Ought I to be very much pleased with *Marmion*? — as yet I am not." Perhaps James was better at sermons than at Scott. As for Jane, she was suffering from the usual problems about getting home. "But till I have a travelling purse of my own, I must submit to such things." She had refused an invitation from Edward and Elizabeth to stay on until the autumn because she and Cassandra were hoping for a visit from their friends the Misses Bigg. For some reason this visit must be kept a secret from James and Mary. It would have been like the James Austens to be still remembering that unlucky night's engagement with the Bigg girls' brother Harris, and the day James had to miss his Sunday duty as a result.

Jane, on the other hand, was much looking forward to Alethea and Catherine Bigg's visit, which would more than compensate for the comparative austerity of life in Castle Square after the luxury of Godmersham.

> In another week I shall be at home—and then, my having been at Godmersham will seem like a dream, as my visit at Brompton seems already. The orange wine will want our care soon—But in the mean-time for elegance and ease and luxury—; the Hattons and Milles dine here today—and I shall eat ice and drink French wine, and be above vulgar economy. Luckily the pleasures of friendship, of un-reserved conversation, of similarity of taste and opinions, will make good amends for orange wine.

Jane Austen always had her priorities right. Perhaps she was already brooding about the plight of Fanny Price when Henry Crawford proposed to her and the world of wealth was suddenly at her feet.

Something of the kind may just possibly have happened to Jane herself in the course of this visit. Writing to Cassandra in October when she, in her turn, was staying at Godmersham, Jane said, "I wish you may be able to accept Lady Bridges' invitation, though *I* could not her son Edward's." Edward Bridges was a clergymen four years younger than Jane Austen and certainly had marriage in mind. In November, Jane wrote, "Your news of Edward Bridges was *quite* news . . . I wish him happy with all my heart, and hope his choice may turn out according to his own expectations, and beyond those of his family . . . As to money, that will come you may be sure, because they cannot do without it." From the tone of this it does rather sound as if Jane was reassuring Cassandra about her own feelings. Edward Bridges may have been like Captain Benwick who moved swiftly from a romantic friendship with Anne Elliot into marriage with Louisa Musgrove. If he did, in fact, propose to the thirty-two-year-old Aunt Jane, she cannot have settled quite so firmly into the appearance and manner of spinsterhood as the family's later recollections suggest.

Cassandra had gone to Godmersham to be with her sister-in-law for the birth of her eleventh child, and the first of this batch of Jane's letters is in answer to one reporting the birth of little John. It is a cheerful letter, describing the sociabilities of Southampton. They had had unexpected callers, "and our labour was not a great deal shorter than poor Elizabeth's, for it was past eleven before we were delivered". The arrangement with the Frank Austens showed signs of coming to an end. Frank and Mary were in Yarmouth now, "and with fish almost for nothing, and plenty of engagements and plenty of each other, must be very happy." Mrs. Austen had heard that houses could be rented for as little as a hundred and thirty pounds at Alton and was seriously thinking of moving there. The house in Castle Square would doubtless be too expensive for the diminished party.

Martha was away visiting, and Jane Austen and her mother were entertaining each other by reading aloud the *Letters of Espriella*. "The man describes well, but is horribly anti-English. He deserves to be the foreigner he assumes." Southey, who wrote these pretended letters from a young Spanish visitor to England, would no doubt have thought Jane Austen's comment high praise. She was always a passionate English-woman. Her next letter congratulates Edward on completing his thirtieth year and is full of the usual cheerful gossip: "The Miss Ms were as civil and as silly as usual." There had been a fire in Southampton and Jane admitted that, "One could not but feel uncomfortable, and I began to think of what I should do, if it came to the worst." She doubtless made extremely sensible plans, but luckily they were not needed. The fire engines soon had the fire under control, though not before there had been panic and looting. It was an experience that would have found its way swiftly into a novel by Fanny Burney or Maria Edgeworth, or, of course, Charlotte Brontë, but was useless as raw material to Jane Austen.

She was much more interested in the character of their niece Fanny, Edward's eldest daughter, who was now fifteen. "I am greatly pleased with your account of Fanny; I found her in the summer just what you describe, almost another sister—and could not have supposed that a niece would ever have been so much to me." There were nephews, too, to be discussed. Martha had returned to Southampton by way of Winchester, where she had three boys to take out from the College. They were Edward and George Austen, sons of Edward senior, and her own nephew, William Fowle, her sister Eliza's son. Jane was able to report to Cassandra that Edward Austen's manners were excellent and that George reminded Martha of his Uncle Henry.

Their friend Catherine Bigg was to be married that month, to a clergyman called Herbert Hill, and this apparently secret engagement may be the explanation of the odd silence that had had to be maintained about the Bigg sisters' visit to Southampton that summer. It was to be the last one before Catherine's marriage. She remained a close friend, and Jane Austen was to visit her and her husband at Streatham. He was Southey's uncle, but there are no letters of Jane's from Streatham, so one can only conjecture about possible meetings with Southey or even with Wordsworth or Coleridge. Jane Austen liked to illuminate her characters by comments on their favourite writers, but she has only one reference to the authors of *Lyrical Ballads*, which had appeared in 1798. Sir Edward Denham, in *Sanditon*, thinks that Wordsworth has "the true soul" of poetry. But praise from Sir Edward is not to be confused with praise from Miss Austen.

Jane's letter of October 7th ends on a note of unconscious irony. "We must turn our black pelisses into new, for velvet is to be very much worn this winter." On the eighth, Elizabeth Austen died suddenly. Eleven children had been too many, and Jane had been right to be anxious about her looks in the summer. At Southampton, they had the first news from James's wife Mary, who had written Martha a quick note on her way to collect the Austen boys from school at Winchester. Cassandra's letter arrived next day. "And with much melancholy anxiety was it expected. We have felt, we do feel, for you all." There is no doubt about the genuineness of the feeling. Jane wrote again a few days later. "Edward's loss is terrible, and must be felt as such." And, of little Lizzy Austen, "One's heart aches for a dejected mind of eight years old." Always practical, Jane was sending Cassandra her mourning. The black velvet was indeed to be in use. More important, she was concerned for her nephews, Edward and George Austen, who had been removed from school by their Aunt Mary and taken back to Steventon. Jane was not happy about this arrangement, though she made the best of it. "They will have more means of exercise and amusement there than they could have with us, but I own myself disappointed by the arrangement—I should have loved to have them with me at such a time. I shall write to Edward by this post."

The result of her leter was immediate. On the twenty-fourth she was able to report that Edward and George had arrived two days before. Edward was fourteen and George almost thirteen, and their aunt was doing her best to keep them occupied. There was cup-and-ball, for which she had such a talent, "spillikins, paper ships, riddles, conundrums, and cards ... watching the flow and ebb of the river, and now and then a stroll out". Later she took them boating and let them go over a seventy-four-gun ship at Northam. No doubt an aunt who could tell such entrancing fairy stories to her nieces, could also distract her nephews, in their grief, with real-life stories of the adventures of their sailor uncles.

It was probably a relief to her to be so busy entertaining them, for this death had hit her hard. It shows in her style. She may have busied herself with bilbocatch and ordering black pantaloons for the boys, but she thought all the time about the stricken household at Godmersham. "I see your mournful party in my mind's eye under every varying circumstance of the day ... poor Edward, restless in misery, going from one room to the other, and perhaps not seldom upstairs, to see all that remains of his Elizabeth." And, of the funeral that would put an end at least to this misery: "Glad shall I be to hear that it is over." There are times when it is not convenient to have too much imagination.

Edward's tragedy, and perhaps the support Cassandra had been to him through it, had turned his thoughts to his mother and sisters. By the time Jane wrote to tell of her nephews' arrival, Mrs. Austen had had a letter from their father offering her a choice of two of the various houses he owned. One was near to his own at Godmersham, the other on his other estate at Chawton in Hampshire. Perhaps he hoped that his mother and the two invaluable aunts would settle near him and help with the education of his eleven motherless children. If so, it was handsome of him to offer the alternative, which his mother, characteristically, accepted. She had not visited Kent for years, and she was not going there now. The house that had been occupied by Edward's steward at Chawton was gratefully accepted, and one can only wonder that the offer had not been made sooner.

9

WHILE CASSANDRA STAYED WITH THE MOTHERLESS FAMILY IN Kent, plans for the move to Chawton went on apace. Mrs. Austen was relieved to hear that the house had six bedrooms, besides garrets which could be made into rooms for Edward's manservant when he came to stay, and perhaps for one of their own. With no rent to pay, the little family could plan a slight relaxation of their stringent economy. It sounds, too, from a comment by Jane on a disagreeable letter they had had from Aunt Jane Leigh Perrot as if they were perhaps getting some help, though of a grudging kind, from that quarter. Unfortunately, Henry was involved in the arrangements about this, and Henry does seem to have had a talent for making muddles, though in the nicest possible way.

There was a by-election for the county of Hampshire that autumn, and Thomas Heathcote, brother-in-law of the Bigg sisters, was standing. Jane Austen wrote knowledgeably about it. Alethea Bigg had written asking for her interest, "which I conclude means Edward's," said Jane, and asked for it. Mr. Heathcote had been returned for Bletchingley in the election of 1807, but now seemed to have come to some private arrangement with the sitting member for Hampshire, Mr. Thistlewaite, who preferred not to stand again, "acknowledging himself still smarting under the payment of late electioneering costs". Such arrangements were mere routine in those pre-Reform days, and it was an expensive business to get into Parliament, but Mr. Heathcote managed it, and sat for Hampshire, first as Mr. and then as Sir Thomas Heathcote, until 1820.

With easier times ahead, the little party seem to have lived an unusually social life that autumn. Jane planned to take Martha to the Southampton theatre for the first time, and also to go to "as many balls as possible, that

I may have a good bargain". She and Martha had been to one of the Southampton Assemblies and found perhaps thirty couples of dancers, but, "The melancholy part was, to see so many young women standing by without partners, and each of them with two ugly naked shoulders!" After this comment on the new fashions, Jane went on, "It was the same room in which we danced fifteen years ago! — I thought it all over — and in spite of the shame of being so much older, felt with thankfulness that I was quite as happy now as then." She may have been beginning to discover the advantages of cheerfully admitted spinsterhood, of having outgrown the anguish of a partnerless Catherine Morland, suffering "the discredit of wanting a partner". In fact, she reported with wry amusement that she had actually been asked to dance, apparently by a French émigré, who "seems so little at home in the English language that I believe that his black eyes may be the best of him".

There were marriages to report, and to speculate about. Mr. Sloper had married a governess (and of somebody's natural children at that), and Lady Sondes's "match surprises but does not offend me . . . I consider everybody as having a right to marry once in their lives for love, if they can." The Godmersham family had decided that Jane must marry the batchelor Rector of Chawton, Mr. Papillon, and Jane retaliated by pretending to think that Cassandra would soon receive a proposal from Edward's brother-in-law, Sir Brook Bridges, whose wife had died in 1806. This reiterated joke about possible marriages was very probably part Austen-nonsense, part a necessary defence against the implied ignominy of spinsterhood. Jane sent a message to Mrs. Knight. "She may depend upon it, I will marry Mr. Papillon, whatever may be his reluctance or my own — I owe her much more than such a trifling sacrifice." The kind hopes of their friends may have been becoming hard to bear.

A chance reference in the same letter suggests Jane Austen's best defence against what Henry Tilney called the "neighbourhood of voluntary spies". She had met someone named Emma, which was worth an exclamation mark, no doubt in reference to Emma Watson, rather than Emma Woodhouse. There might be small pin-pricks, and some greater ones, but there was always the secret consolation of the double life. Everything was possible material for Jane Austen, who felt like an author even if she was still an unpublished one. The Watsons' circumstances were worse than the Austens', although Jane had a slight financial blow to report. The Leigh Perrots had settled a hundred pounds a year on James, to compensate him for highmindedly refusing to commit the contemporary sin of pluralism by accepting another living. Mary had sent

Mrs. Austen her sister-in-law's letter on the occasion and, "Nothing can be more affectionate than my aunt's language in making the present, and likewise in expressing her hope of their being much more together in future." It sounds as if the Leigh Perrots had decided to forget and forgive at least James for that enforced neglect at the time of the trial. Jane Austen adds, "My expectations for my mother do not rise with this event." She later reported that they had calculated James's income as "eleven hundred pounds, curate paid". The world went right on enriching one part of the Austen family at the expense of the other.

They had a visit from Frank and Mary, probably to collect little Mary Jane, who had been staying at Castle Square, but, Jane wrote, "The *St. Albans* perhaps may soon be off to bring home what may remain by this time of our poor army." She was referring to Sir John Moore's long, terrible retreat through Spain that ended with his death at Corunna. And she was nearly right about Frank. In fact he was active in the disembarkation in England of the battered remnant of Moore's army. She was close, too, in her speculations, in this same letter, about a possible Regency. George III had been mad, off and on, for years, but his son did not actually become Prince Regent until 1811.

Writing to her sister, Jane was more concerned with family news. They had heard by roundabout means that Charles and Frances were well at Bermuda. "You may guess in what extravagant terms of praise Earle Harwood speaks of him. He is looked up to by everyone in America." Earle Harwood was the young man who had made the unfortunate marriage and then shot himself accidentally in the leg. His praise must have been a little too extravagant for Jane's taste, judging by the little glint of irony in her tone. There was good news, too, of Eliza Austen, who had been unwell, but was now recovered, and of her husband, whose bank was flourishing, as banks do in time of war.

There were plans about silver and china for Chawton, and, "Yes, yes, we *will* have a pianoforte, as good a one as can be got for thirty guineas, and I will practise country dances, that we may have some amusement for our nephews and nieces." The piano Jane Austen had had to sell when they moved to Bath was to be replaced at last. The nephews and nieces were growing up. Fanny was to take her dead mother's place at Godmersham when Cassandra's long visit ended, and Anna had been to her first ball, a private one at Manydown. It "was a smaller thing than I expected, but it seems to have made Anna very happy. At her age," says Jane Austen, "it would not have done for *me*."

There were books to be discussed. "We are now in *Margiana*, [by Mrs

Sykes], and like it very well indeed. We are just going to set off for Northumberland to be shut up in Widdrington Tower, where there must be two or three sets of victims already immured under a very fine villain." Jane Austen had the gift of enjoyment, but she could also be critical. "We have got *Ida of Athens* by Miss Owenson, which must be very clever, because it was written as the authoress says, in three months." Jane Austen, that meticulous polisher, might well have added that, like Anna's ball, "It would not have done for *me*." Their cousin, Edward Cooper, had a third volume of sermons out, "which we are to like better than the two others," and Jane was looking forward somewhat dubiously to Hannah More's *Coelebs in Search of a Wife*. "I do not like the Evangelicals – Of course I shall be delighted, when I read it, like other people, but till I do I dislike it." Years later, in her *Personal Aspects of Jane Austen*, Mary Augusta Austen-Leigh was to quote a contemporary's opinion. "Miss Austen had on all the subjects of enduring religious feeling the deepest and strongest convictions, but a contact with loud and noisy exponents of the then popular religious phase made her reticent almost to a fault."

It is impossible, at this remove, to tell just what that reticence hid. Certainly Jane's letters to Cassandra on the death of Elizabeth Austen show more than mechanical religious feeling. "May the Almighty sustain you all", and, "Tell Edward that we feel for him and pray for him." But, while remembering the virtues of the departed, "her solid principles, her true devotion", Jane Austen has no phrase, as in her letter on her father's death, about Elizabeth's being "blessed in heaven".

On the other hand, a comment on the death of Sir John Moore has brought her under a fire of angry criticism ever since. "I wish Sir John had united something of the Christian with the hero in his death." This does seem to be one of the rare occasions when Jane Austen, that splendid realist, failed to "clear her mind of cant".[1] Sir John, dying on the field of battle, was preoccupied with the duty he had left unfinished, and with thoughts of friends at home, and the reports of his death omit any reference to God or a life to come. For once, it is fair to say, Jane Austen's imagination failed her, but then, how could she know what it would be like to die under such circumstances? It is even possible that she did not want to know, since it could so easily happen, at any moment, to either Frank or Charles. The strong, selective spirit that limited her field of work, may have operated in the same way on her sympathies. When she could not afford to feel sympathy, she did not let herself imagine too deeply. It

[1] Boswell: *Life of Dr. Johnson*.

would account for this remark and for a few others, like that curiously heartless one about Mrs. Hall and her dead baby.

But I think there was more to it than that. After July 1809 there are no letters extant for almost two years. We know from the letters written in the spring of 1809 that extensive family visiting was planned for that summer, before they moved to Chawton. They were at Godmersham that spring and one would have expected that both aunts would pay frequent visits to Edward's motherless household; but, in fact, Jane did not go there again for four years. Cassandra, however, almost certainly did. There must have been letters for this period, and they must heve been committed by Cassandra to that lamentable bonfire.

Why did she do this? What was the matter? There may have been practical problems about the move to Chawton, although once he had made up his mind to house his mother and sisters, Edward seems to have been lavish in the way of alterations and enlargements. But the trouble was probably at a deeper level. A recent psychological study (in *Work, Creativity, Social Justice* by Professor Elliott Jaques) has suggested that artists tend, even more than ordinary people, to go through an emotional crisis in their middle years, and, indeed, that they have a higher than average mortality rate at this time of life.

In 1808, Jane Austen was only thirty-two, but it is easy to see why her crisis should have come early. For her, the problem of the artist was compounded by that of the woman. As a woman of her time she could be said to be a failure. She was poor, and unmarried, and could look forward, apparently, to nothing but decline and fall. Worst of all, and no doubt worse still, because it would be almost impossible to admit, was the fact that she, Cassandra and their friend Martha were bound, for her lifetime, to old Mrs. Austen. Those tell-tale occasional remarks in the letters about how snug they will be while Mrs. Austen is off visiting are a total giveaway here.

There was no possible escape, even if they had been so heartless as to consider it, which Jane Austen, with her strong sense of family duty, would never have done. Aristocrats, like the Ladies of Llangollen might possibly set up housekeeping together and survive socially, though it was touch and go with them, but for young women of the middle classes it was, simply, impossible. Besides, there would have been no money. The Austen brothers might subsidise the respectable household of mother and sisters, but they would never have supported a breakaway.

Was it in a spirit of optimism or despair that Jane Austen made, in 1809, one more attempt at getting published? She did it herself, rather than getting Henry to act for her, as she was to do later. She wrote, under the assumed name of Mrs. Ashton Dennis, to Crosby, the publisher who had accepted *Susan* back in 1803. Why had the book never been published, she asked, since "early publication was stipulated for at the time of sale". If the publishers had lost their copy, she would undertake to provide another one. Should they not answer her letter, she would feel free to attempt publication elsewhere. It was a firm letter, and got a firm answer. Richard Crosby wrote by return to say that they had indeed bought *Susan* outright for ten pounds cash, "but there was not any time stipulated for its publication, neither are we bound to publish it". He went on to threaten proceedings if she published elsewhere, and offer her the manuscript back for the ten pounds it had fetched.

It must have been a bitterly disappointing letter, and Jane Austen clearly did not feel able to venture half her annual allowance (if she was in fact still getting twenty pounds) on such a chimera. Silence falls on *Susan* until 1816. And only one more letter of Jane Austen's remains before silence falls on her too. It is in verse, congratulating Frank on the birth of a son, and ending with a happy description of Chawton:

> Our Chawton home, how much we find
> Already in it, to our mind;
> And how convinced, that when complete
> It will all other houses beat
> That ever have been made or mended,
> With rooms concise, or rooms distended.
> You'll find us very snug next year.

One can only hope that she was right. On the surface, the prospect certainly seemed fair enough. The rooms at Chawton may have been "concise" rather than "distended", but Edward was busy seeing to it that his mother and sisters would be comfortable there, and later family descriptions make it sound a delightful place, with its rambling outbuildings for children to play in, and old-fashioned garden. It still stands, now, as then, on a busy corner, but these days it is motor-coaches, loaded with tourists in search of Jane Austen, that crowd the way, not the stage-coaches that visiting nieces loved to hear sweep by in the night. In fact, people in carriages could look right in at the dining-room window, and the last glimpse we get of the Austen ladies before silence falls in 1809, is a chance remark by Mrs. Knight that an acquaintance of hers had seen "the Chawton party looking very comfortable at breakfast", from his post-chaise.

Mrs. Austen had entirely given over the housekeeping to her daughters by now, and Jane's duty was to make breakfast at nine o'clock. According to her niece Caroline Austen, this, and "the tea and sugar stores were under her charge—and the wine. And Cassandra did all the rest." Mrs. Austen, meanwhile, was indulging in her passion for gardening. Dressed in a green round smock like a labourer's, she was to keep at it in the Chawton garden almost until the end of her life. It is oddly reminiscent of that scarlet outfit she wore for the early years of her marriage, and then cut down into a riding habit for Frank. One cannot help liking Mrs. Austen, and regretting that she and her daughters had, somewhere, somehow, parted company in spirit, if not, unfortunately, in fact.

Life at Chawton, as reported, later, by the nieces, sounds quiet and pleasant. Jane played the piano before she made breakfast. According to Caroline she could never be induced to play in company, though "she played very pretty tunes, I thought". They were not a musical family and playing the piano may have been Jane's way of achieving privacy. Was she busy plotting her next book while she played the tunes that nieces were to dismiss, kindly, as pretty but rather simple? Or was she, for a while, wrestling with darker matters?

Certainly this interlude at the piano seems to have been her last private moment of the day. After breakfast the ladies sat "at work" in the drawing-room, perhaps doing the embroidery for which Jane was known, or perhaps, more prosaically, making clothes for the poor. After lunch, if the weather was fine, they would walk over to the Great House half a mile away, if one of the brothers was staying there, as they often were, with their families. If no one was there to be visited, they would stroll among the beech trees of Chawton Park, perhaps leaving old Mrs. Austen at home in her smock, hard at it in the garden.

Sometimes, but rarely, according to Caroline, they would go calling. They had no carriage, so that their range was inevitably limited to their immediate vicinity, which had not very much to offer. Again we have Caroline's authority. She was only five when her grandmother moved to Chawton, an easy morning's ride from her home at Steventon, but Anna Austen, her half-sister, was sixteen and they both helped their brother Edward with recollections for his *Memoir*, and obviously they were the members of the family best calculated to know what life was really like at Chawton.

It probably did not change much over the years. In the light of the letters, Caroline's description of them as on "friendly, but rather distant terms" with the neighbours rings true. The Austens did tend to be sufficient unto themselves. But Jane Austen "liked immensely" to hear about the neighbours. "They sometimes served for her amusement, but it was her own nonsense that gave zest to the gossip. She never turned *them* into ridicule . . . she never abused them or 'quizzed' them . . ."

A younger niece (perhaps Marianne Austen from Godmersham, who was eight in 1809) went further. "She was in fact one of the last people in society to be afraid of. I do not suppose she ever in her life said a sharp thing. She was naturally shy and not given to talk much in company, and people fancied, knowing that she was clever, that she was on the watch for good material for books from their conversation. Her intimate friends knew how groundless was the apprehension and that it wronged her." This, of course, refers to a later date, when Henry had betrayed the secret of her authorship, but she would presumably not have grown more shy with time. One can imagine her as one of those quiet people who only light up for a sympathetic listener. Anna, old enough at this time to notice, has a significant comment. Cassandra and Jane, she said, "were everything to each other. They seemed to lead a life to themselves within the general family life which was shared only by each other. I will not say their true, but their *full*, feelings and opinions were known only to themselves."

Anna also describes her aunt, presumably at about this time. "The figure tall and slight, but not drooping; well balanced, as was proved by her quick firm step. Her complexion of that rare sort which seems the particular property of light brunettes; a mottled skin, not fair but perfectly clear and healthy; the fine naturally curling hair, neither light nor dark; the bright hazel eyes to match, and the rather small, but well-shaped nose." Jane Austen, she said, was not regularly handsome, but attractive. According to Caroline Austen, "Aunt Jane's . . . was the first face that I can remember thinking pretty . . . Her face was rather round than long; she had a bright, but not a pink, colour, a clear brown complexion and very good hazel eyes. Her hair, a darkish brown, curled naturally in short curls round her face . . . She always wore a cap." And James Edward, drawing on both his sister and his half-sister's recollection for his *Memoir* sums it up. "In her person she was very attractive; her figure was rather tall and slender, her step light and firm, and her whole appearance expressive of health and animation."

The only certainly authentic picture of Jane Austen that survives is by Cassandra and, inevitably, does not do justice to its subject, making her look plump, prim and pop-eyed. It is, perhaps, possible to get a better idea of her real appearance by studying the portraits of the brothers older and younger than herself, Frank and Charles. They are remarkably alike, and remarkably like Cassandra's unsuccessful picture of Jane. Both their faces are handsome, firm and intelligent with the kind of piercing eyes one would expect equally in a succsesful Admiral of the Fleet, and an even more successful lady novelist.

But in 1809, at Chawton, Jane Austen was merely Aunt Jane, playing the piano before she made breakfast. What was she thinking of, protected, there, by the simple tunes she played and sang, by *The Soldier's Adieu* or *The Yellow-Haired Laddie*? I think she was going through a severe moral and religious crisis, during which the author of romantic comedy, of *Susan* and *First Impressions*, developed, painfully, into the grave moralist and extraordinary technician who could produce *Mansfield Park*.

The silence is absolute, and one can only speculate. But there are hints, here and there. In 1808, talking of Hannah More's *Coelebs in Search of a Wife*, Jane had said, flatly, "I do not like the Evengelicals." And, confirming this, is that remark of an acquaintance that "a contact with loud and noisy exponents of the then popular religious phase made her reticent almost to a fault". By 1814 she would be writing to her beloved niece Fanny, in a crisis of the latter's life, "I am by no means convinced that we ought not all to be Evangelicals, and am at least persuaded that they who are so from reason and feeling, must be happiest and safest." Cassandra has left us no way of knowing what moral gulfs, what cold loneliness lies between these two positions, but somewhere, I think, in the critical years of her mid-thirties, the light-hearted creator of *First Impressions* must have passed through a moral climacteric that turned her into the mature artist of *Mansfield Park*.

Which is not to say that *Mansfield Park* is an unqualified success. There is something very significant about Jane Austen's own reservation in her letter about the Evangelicals. She was "at least persuaded that they who are so from reason and feeling, must be happiest and safest". It leaves one wondering just what her own reason and feeling were telling her. We have no idea. In this passage, she sounds curiously like someone of our own times saying how much they would like to believe in God, if only they could. Possibly, during the silent first years at Chawton, she had found it difficult, at least in contemporary terms. She had lived all her life among clergymen, and may have known too much about them for her own moral comfort. It is impossible to forget that picture of James, "It makes me sad and angry . . ." In a fascinating essay on *Jane Austen and the Moralists* (reprinted in B. C. Southam's *Critical Essays on Jane Austen*), Professor Gilbert Ryle points out that Jane Austen's heroines "face their moral difficulties and solve their moral problems without recourse to religious faith or theological doctrines. Nor does it ever occur to them to seek the counsels of a clergyman." It is indeed hard to imagine Elizabeth Bennet turning to Mr. Collins for advice, or Emma to Mr. Elton. As for Edmund Bertram, the fledgling clergyman, significantly, it is he who turns to Fanny Price. Determined to yield to pressure, and act in *Lovers' Vows*, he comes to her for encouragement, and does not get it. "Give me your approbation, then, Fanny. I am not comfortable without it."

And Fanny, having compromised with him in a speech that suggests a moral novelist of our own time, Ivy Compton-Burnett, does not, when alone, burst into either prayer or tears. She sits down to consider her position morally and rationally, as, perhaps, Jane Austen had considered her own in the silent years of crisis. The result, for Fanny, was, for the time being, loneliness and misery. We have only the later books and letters as clues to how Jane Austen came out of her spiritual crisis, but I think this was the time when the laughter of youth turned into the double-visioned irony of maturity.

But all this was below the surface. Superficially, I am sure the double life went on as usual. Whatever Jane Austen thought or suffered, she continued to behave like an English lady, the daughter and sister of clergymen. She was to die, as she had lived, a good daughter of the Church, insisting on taking the sacrament, from her two clergymen brothers, while she was still conscious to receive it; and a passing remark about her nephew in 1813 shows how seriously she took the forms of religion. Perhaps she told Cassandra what she thought of its essence, but I doubt it. Even sharing a room with a beloved sister, the artist is inevitably alone. Perhaps she did not know herself; perhaps, always, in her books, she was trying to decide. In which case *Sanditon* suggests a dramatic new departure.

But that was still in the future. In the present, Jane Austen played the piano and made the breakfast and (incredibly) convinced her nieces that she never "said a sharp thing". Or was this, perhaps, the loving error of retrospection? At all events, the silent years at Chawton passed, with visits to the Great House and shopping excursions to the nearby town of Alton, and, most important of all, with Jane Austen, at some point, beginning to write again. She began, sensibly after the long silence, by revising her early work. She was always a passionate reviser and polisher, and, at this point, apparently, her hand lit on *Sense and Sensibility*, which had already been redrafted from her original *Elinor and Marianne*. If I am right in my assumption of a moral crisis over, *Sense and Sensibility*, the most moral of her early works, was a logical choice, and indeed this is an added confirmation of the theory. Otherwise, *Pride and Prejudice*, the family favourite, would have seemed the obvious choice for a new attempt at publication. But if Jane Austen wanted to try out her new, ironic view of life, her new detachment, what better vehicle than *Sense and Sensibility*, with its almost too obvious moral contrasts? If only she had left us her original version, much of this speculation would probably be unnecessary.

All we know is that by 1811, when the letters take up again, she had made a great stride forward. *Sense and Sensibility* was in the printer's hands and *Pride and Prejudice* was in the full swing of revision. The writer's block that had kept her frozen through the wandering years was dissolved. Presumably the moral crisis was over. She was thirty-five.

❧ 10 ❧

IT WAS APRIL 1811, AND JANE AUSTEN WAS STAYING WITH
Henry and Eliza, who had moved to a house in Sloane Street and were
still enjoying "riches and honours". Worldly Eliza was obviously an
admirable hostess. Where Edward, in Kent, tended to take it for granted
that his sisters came to merge themselves (and help) in the family life of
Godmersham, Eliza treated them as visitors, to be entertained. But then,
Eliza had no children now that Hastings[1] was dead, and Edward had
eleven. Anyway, Jane was enjoying herself. She was in touch with the
Cooke cousins and had visited the Liverpool Museum and the British
Gallery with Mary Cooke, "though my preference for men and women,
always inclines me to attend more to the company than the sight".
William Bullock's Liverpool Museum, now moved from Liverpool to
Number 22, Piccadilly, was a curious gallimaufray of natural history,
curios and antiquities, while the British Gallery was in fact the British
Institution for Promoting the Fine Arts, whose winter exhibitions of
contemporary painting were becoming increasingly popular.

As always on London visits, Jane had also gone shopping for muslin and
trimmings, bonnets and china. She needed straw hats and pelisses with
buttons that "seems expensive — *are* expensive, I might have said". Eliza
was arranging a busy social life and Jane was finding "all these little parties
very pleasant". There was to be a big party, too, with more than eighty
invitations, and professional musicians: "Fanny will listen to this." It is
always interesting, when reading Jane Austen's letters, to remember that
some portion of each one, at least, was intended to be read aloud to whichever members of the family Cassandra might be with.

[1] Her son by her first marriage.

There was news of the sailor brothers. Frank had been "superseded in the *Caledonia*" and Charles might be in England at last (after nearly seven years) in the course of a month. Their old patron Lord Gambier was giving up his command to Sir Edward Pellew and "some captain of his succeeds Frank", who had been Gambier's flag-captain in the *Caledonia*. It is a reminder of how careers in the Navy then depended on patronage. Admiral Gambier, who had got Frank his early promotion, had gone back to sea, been ennobled after the Copenhagen expedition and court-martialled after a fiasco in the Basque Roads in April, 1809. It had been an unlucky business. Gambier, a confirmed Methodist, had disapproved of the flotilla of fireships with which his subordinate, the flamboyant Lord Cochrane, proposed to destroy the French fleet. His support had been inadequate, the attempt a failure and Cochrane furious. Called a "canting and hypocritical Methodist" by his subordinate, Gambier insisted on a court martial, which was packed in his favour and gave him an honourable acquittal. He returned to his Channel Command until 1811, when he was finally superseded and, inevitably, Frank went with him. As we have no letters for the period of Gambier's court martial, we do not know what the Austens thought about it, though we can guess. Gambier was known for captaining a "praying ship" and Frank as "*the* officer who knelt in church".

Frank, in fact, had not been present at the Basque Roads affair, having sailed for China in H.M.S. *St. Albans* the month it happened. It was merely bad luck that he happened to be Gambier's flag-captain when he was superseded, and Henry, characteristically, was sure he would soon get another ship. Jane was less confident. "What will he do? And where will he live?" Life, for the self-supporting members of the Austen family was always precarious, but Frank was good at his job. That same July he took command of H.M.S. *Elephant* and served in her until 1814. He was to end his life as Sir Francis Austen, K.C.B., and Admiral of the Fleet.

His sister in Sloane Street had suffered a disappointment in "a very unlucky change of the play for this very night — *Hamlet* instead of *King John*". It seems an odd source of disappointment until one remembers that *King John* would have had the famous Mrs. Siddons as Constance. "I should particularly have liked seeing her in Constance, and could swear at her with little effort for disappointing me." As a result of one of Henry's muddles, Jane also missed Mrs. Siddons in *Macbeth* the following week.

But at this time Jane Austen had a talisman against all disappointment. *Sense and Sensibility* had been accepted for publication, and she was correcting proofs. "No indeed, I am never too busy to think of *Sense and*

Sensibility," she wrote to Cassandra. "I can no more forget it, than a mother can forget her sucking child; and I am much obliged to you for your enquiries. I have had two sheets to correct, but the last only brings us to Willoughby's first appearance. Mrs. Knight regrets in the most flattering manner that she must wait *till* May, but I have scarcely a hope of its being out in June." In fact, *Sense and Sensibility* was not advertised until October. Jane Austen had a great deal to learn about the facts of publishing.

Unfortunately, no record exists of why *Sense and Sensibility* was chosen for publication, or of how it came to be accepted. But it was published by Thomas Egerton of the Military Library, Whitehall, which at once suggests a connection with Henry, the ex-officer. Henry had indeed acted for his sister this time, as their father had in the earlier approach to Crosby. A later letter of Jane Austen's indicates that Henry actually put up (or at least guaranteed) the money for the printing of *Sense and Sensibility*. Writing of the second edition in November 1813, she says, "I suppose in the meantime I shall owe dear Henry a great deal of money for printing &c ..." Egerton had not been prepared to risk publishing at his own expense, and the book appeared as printed "For the Author" by C. Rowarth, and published by T. Egerton. It is true than an ingenious author might contrive to postpone paying for publication until the first profits were in, but it does not sound as if Jane and Henry managed this. According to family tradition, Jane was so uncertain of success that she set aside a contingency fund from her small resources, in case of failure. Considering that in her day it cost between one and two hundred pounds to produce an average edition of a two or three volume book, it is hard to imagine how she could have managed without Henry's help.

Publication at the author's expense was perfectly respectable in those days, with none of the modern stigma of "vanity publication". It had been used by Burns for his first volume of poems, and was to be used, later, by Browning for his. As late as 1890, an Authors' Society pamphlet recommended it for fiction or poetry.[1] It must be remembered that at this time publishing was still in a state of flux, with large and prosperous firms like Constable, Longman and Murray gradually developing out of the combined publisher-booksellers of the eighteenth century. John Murray the second, for instance, still referred to himself as a "publishing bookseller" when writing to Walter Scott, though the poet Campbell described him as "the only gentleman, except Constable, in the trade".

[1] S. Squire Sprigges: *The Methods of Publishing*. Published for the Society of Authors by Henry Glaisher, 85 Strand, W.C., 1890.

Modern author-publisher relations were in the future, and it is worth noting that the *Oxford English Dictionary*'s quotation for the use of the word "royalty" to describe "a payment made to an author, editor, or composer for each copy of a book ..." is dated 1880. In the early nineteenth century, various methods of publication were open to an aspiring author. He could still, as in the eighteenth century, publish by subscription, which had the advantage that he retained his copyright. Dr. Johnson and Pope, amongst many others, had solicited subscriptions for some of their work, though Dr. Johnson's experience with his *Shakespeare* demonstrated the hazards of this method. Having issued his proposals and received his subscriptions in 1756, he had to admit, nine years later, that he had "lost all the names and spent all the money" before it was finished. Wealthy authors might wait for their subscriptions until the book was actually printed; poor ones had to ask for some or all of the money in advance to cover their printing costs. It is not, perhaps, surprising that the method was falling into disrepute by the end of the century. But Fanny Burney, who sold the copyright of her first book, *Evelina*, for a total of thirty pounds, and got two hundred and fifty for her second, *Cecilia*, turned to subscription for her third, *Camilla*, and made three thousand. Jane Austen subscribed to *Camilla*, but subscription would not have suited her. It had to be done either by personal connection (and "puffing") or by newspaper advertising. And Jane Austen lived in the country, did not have a particularly wide or influential circle of acquaintance, and wished to remain anonymous.

Two other methods of publishing that preserved the author's control had been tried in the eighteenth century. In 1765, the Reverend John Trusler had initiated a "Literary Society" with the aim of printing direct, without recourse to a publisher, and thus achieving lower prices and larger circulations while retaining the author's copyright, but this co-operative venture seems to have had only a brief and qualified success. A limited start had also been made on publication in "Numbers", the serial method that was to make fortunes for Dickens and his mid-nineteenth-century contemporaries. In the late eighteenth century, William Dodd's *Commentary on the Bible* came out weekly in sixpenny parts, but it was, understandably, not in the same popular class as *Nicholas Nickleby*.

Individualists like Blake might engrave their own works, but the ordinary author needed a publisher to deal with printing, circulation and advertising. By the beginning of the nineteenth century, the wholesale book trade was developing, and the word "subscribing" which had meant a relationship between author and public had come to mean one between publisher and bookseller. But relations between author and publisher were still in a state of change.

With publication by subscription on the wane, there were three chief ways in which a publisher might agree to produce a book. If he was confident of its success, he preferred to buy the copyright outright. If he was not quite so confident, he might offer to pay all expenses and then share any final profit with the author, whose share seems to have varied from a third or half to as much as two thirds. Gibbon did well with two thirds of the profits for *The Decline and Fall of the Roman Empire*. This method, of course, would develop into the modern royalty system. A variant on it was Murray's publication of Byron's *Childe Harold*. He began by offering to print it at his own expense, and share the profits equally with Byron, leaving the question of the copyright to depend on the poem's success. He ended by paying six hundred pounds for the copyright, and clearing a handsome profit. But Murray was an unusual publisher.

Finally, a publisher who was dubious about a book's success might offer to publish on commission; that is to let the author pay the expenses and take the receipts, subject to a commission paid to the publisher for his handling of the book. Here, too, the author kept his copyright. It is worth remembering that under an Act of 1709, copyright only lasted for fourteen years from publication, with a further fourteen years if the author was alive at the end of the first. An Act of 1814 amended this to give the author twenty-eight years, or the term of his life, whichever was the longer.

There were obvious hazards for the author in all these methods of publication. Jane Austen sold *Susan* outright to Crosby for ten pounds, only to have it languish unpublished for thirteen years. The moral of this may have been that Crosby had not paid enough. *Sense and Sensibility* was published on commission, covered its expenses and made her a hundred and forty pounds for its first edition. This presumably encouraged Egerton to make an outright offer of a hundred and ten for the copyright of *Pride and Prejudice*. Jane Austen, who had asked for the very reasonable sum of a hundred and fifty, accepted this lower offer, largely, judging by her letter to Cassandra, to save Henry trouble. In fact, the hundred and ten did compare favourably with the thirty pounds Fanny Burney got for *Evelina* or the sixty that Goldsmith got for *The Vicar of Wakefield*. And there was another side to this outright sale. Publishers preferred it, and it gave them a much greater stake in a book's success.

James Lackington, the bookseller, in his *Memoirs*, urged authors to sell their copyright to a reliable publisher as the best way of getting fair treatment. The argument was simple. If a publisher had paid a good price for the copyright in the first place, he might not clear his expenses and begin to make a profit until the second, third or even fourth edition. It was therefore very much in his interest to do his best in the way of advertising and publicity generally. And these played a considerable part in early-nineteenth-century publishing. Out of a total expense of between one and two hundred pounds, twenty to twenty-five often went on advertising. Often, but not always. Histories of publishing houses of the period have their share of modern-sounding letters from authors complaining about lack of advertising. Lemprière, of the *Classical Dictionary*, complained to Cadell (the publisher who refused *First Impressions* unread) that he had not sufficiently advertised his translation of *Herodotus*, which, significantly, had been published by subscription. On the other hand, Murray, publishing *Childe Harold* at his own expense, actually irritated his noble author by his ingenious pre-publication pushing. Perhaps as a result, the small first edition of five hundred copies sold out in three days, and was followed by second and third editions totalling three thousand copies. Byron was mollified.

It is interesting that of all Jane Austen's books, only *Pride and Prejudice*, which Egerton bought outright, went into a third edition. He had more at stake, and may have made more effort. But his was not one of the large, prosperous publishing houses like Murray or Constable and it is possible that he could not afford to be generous, or, more important, to advertise and "puff" lavishly. William Lane, who ran the notorious Minerva Press, pandering to the contemporary taste for Gothic and sentimental trash, would resort to the gossip columns to promote his productions. Egerton, on the other hand, seems to have been content with the minimal formal advertising of Jane Austen's books, but he may have pushed *Pride and Prejudice* in other ways. At all events it went into a second edition in 1813 and a third in 1817. Egerton probably did not mention this to Jane Austen, who might reasonably have asked for more money on the publication of the second edition, though I doubt if she would have done so. But what she would most certainly have done was correct the badly set dialogue that she mentioned when writing to Cassandra on February 4th, 1813. "The greatest blunder in the printing that I have met with is in page 220, v. 3, where two speeches are made into one."[1] On the other hand, if Jane Austen learned of the second edition after the event, it might well have helped to account for her move to Murray.

[1] See note to page 343 of the Oxford edition.

Egerton must have made a pleasant profit on *Pride and Prejudice*, but he was still dubious about *Mansfield Park*, which was once more published on commission, at Jane Austen's expense. By this time she had earned and invested two hundred and fifty pounds, so that she had her contingency fund against disaster. We do not know exactly what she earned with *Mansfield Park*, but when Murray offered four hundred and fifty pounds for the combined copyrights of *Sense and Sensibility*, *Mansfield Park* and *Emma*, Henry told him that this was in fact less than the total his sister had made on *Mansfield Park* and the second edition of *Sense and Sensibility*. I think possibly Henry, who was ill at the time, may have been mistaken (or, characteristically, have exaggerated) here, for the note of her literary earnings that Jane Austen made in the last year of her life indicates a figure of three hundred and fifty pounds for the earnings to date on *Mansfield Park* and the second edition of *Sense and Sensibility* (see Appendix I).

Mansfield Park was so badly printed, and in so small an edition, that it is not surprising that Jane Austen should have considered a change of publisher. Egerton also apparently hesitated over a second edition, and this may have been the last straw. The next thing we know of is John Murray's offer of four hundred and fifty pounds for the combined copyrights of the three books in Jane Austen's control. "It will end in my publishing for myself I daresay," said Jane Austen.

It did. She kept the copyrights of *Sense and Sensibility*, *Mansfield Park* and *Emma*, and the ledgers of John Murray show that *Emma* and the second edition of *Mansfield Park* were published at her expense, with ten per cent commission to the publisher (see Appendix I). The results might be said to justify John Murray's caution. The figures for 1816 show that *Emma* made a profit of £221 6s. 4d. (that is after deduction of the expenses of publication and the publisher's commission), but at about the same time the second edition of *Mansfield Park* made a loss of £182 8s. 3d. Logically enough, the loss on the second book was set against the profit on the first, and in her summary of her earnings Jane Austen refers to £38 18s. for the first profits of *Emma*. One must assume that John Murray kept the odd penny.

Jane Austen's own figures show that she earned less than seven hundred pounds in her lifetime and there is no pretending that this does not compare miserably with the profits other people were making. Constable offered Walter Scott a thousand pounds for *Marmion* before he had seen it, and Longman offered Moore three thousand pounds for *Lalla Rookh* before the poet had written a line. This was poetry, it is true, and one must remember that the trash turned out by the Minerva Press, and similar panderers to the new reading class, had brought the novel into disrepute, but just the same Maria Edgeworth was earning between fifteen hundred and two thousand pounds a novel.

Jane Austen was right, later in her life, when she said that people were more apt to borrow and praise than to buy her novels. In her lifetime, she never touched the mass market, not even the all-important one of the libraries. This may have been largely her own fault, and on two counts. First, she was a great innovator. People nourished on the Gothics of Mrs. Radcliffe and her like would make a much easier transition to Walter Scott's vast romances than to Jane Austen's "little bit (two inches wide) of ivory". But equally important was her dislike of publicity. She would not be a "wild beast". If she was ever invited to the literary gatherings at John Murray's house in Albemarle Street, where Scott met Byron, she did not go. She was neither a lame peer nor a dramatic bankrupt. She was merely a quiet spinster who wrote supremely well. Perhaps if she had lived longer, and gone on writing, her sales would have built up steadily, as the word passed from cultivated person to person. As it is, a letter from Cassandra to John Murray of 1819 indicates that as Jane's literary executrix, she had received £479 1s. 2d. for *Northanger Abbey* and *Persuasion*, which had been published posthumously in December, 1817. But the figures from Murray's ledger are not altogether encouraging. The posthumous edition of *Northanger Abbey* and *Persuasion* in fact cleared £495 17s. 7d. by 1820, while *Emma* netted a total of £372 12s. 11d., and even the second edition of *Mansfield Park* finally cleared £118 18s. 4d., but by 1821 Murray must have felt that the books had had their day. The last figures for *Emma* and *Mansfield Park* are for "balance of copies sold at sale". The books had been remaindered.

Later, Cassandra and Henry (who presumably helped her as he had Jane) sold the copyrights of the five novels (excluding *Pride and Prejudice*) to Richard Bentley for two hundred and fifty pounds, for inclusion, in 1833, in his Standard Novels series. Later still, when they were out of copyright, George Routledge included *Pride and Prejudice* and *Sense and Sensibility* in his cut-price Railway Library (published at between one and two shillings a volume). But it was not until the publication of James Edward Austen-Leigh's *Memoir* of his aunt in 1870, and Lord Brabourne's edition of her *Letters* in 1884 that the "dear Aunt Jane" cult began, and with it the steady increase in the sales of her novels that has continued until today.

THAT SPRING OF 1811, JANE AUSTEN MUST HAVE BEEN HAPPY. Her metaphor of the sucking child is one that must have occurred, at one time or another, to most female authors. A first book is very like a first child, but with the advantage that when it appears the hard work is over. And when one considers that *Sense and Sensibility* had been in embryo, in one form or other, for well over ten years, one can understand how its proud author must have felt as she corrected sheet after sheet of proofs.

She was publishing anonymously, as "A Lady", but the secret of her authorship seems to have been a fairly open one, at least among the older members of the family. Fanny Knight knew; for an entry in her pocket-book for September 28th, 1811, reports a "letter from Aunt Cass. to beg we would not mention that Aunt Jane wrote *Sense and Sensibility*". The younger members of James's family, on the other hand, though they lived so much nearer, were kept in ignorance. Anna Austen had heard her aunts reading *Pride and Prejudice* aloud, years before, when it was *First Impressions*, but when she and her Aunt Jane were looking over new novels in the local library, she dismissed a copy of *Sense and Sensibility* as rubbish. Her half-brother James Edward only learned of his aunt's authorship when he was fifteen, in 1813, and sat down to write a set of congratulatory verses:

> No words can express, my dear Aunt, my surprise
> Or make you conceive how I opened my eyes . . .
> When I heard for the very first time in my life
> That I had the honour to have a relation
> Whose works were dispersed through the whole of the nation!

In 1811, Mrs. Knight, like the older members of the family, knew all about Jane Austen's writing, and seems to have given some advice about the financial affairs of the Dashwoods. "The incomes remain as they were, but I will get them altered if I can." Jane Austen had a passion for accurate detail, and did, in fact, make some small alterations in the description of the complicated Dashwood finances, but not until the second edition of *Sense and Sensibility*. Meanwhile, "I am very much gratified by Mrs. K.'s interest . . . I think she will like my Elinor, but cannot build on anything else." There is something touching about the way Jane Austen uses "my" of her heroines. To a great extent, they were her life.

On the surface, there was much else. "Our party went off extremely well." She went straight on to report the sixty-six guests ("considerably more than Eliza had expected") the musicians, the hot drawing-room, the friends and relations. Best of all, there was a Captain Simpson there who told her that Charles "was bringing the *Cleopatra* home, and that she was probably by this time in the Channel—but as Capt. S. was certainly in liquor, we must not quite depend on it." In fact, Jane rather hoped that Charles would not reach England until she was at home "and the Steventon party gone".

The James Austens had been staying with Mrs. Austen and Martha while Cassandra and Jane were away, and, "My mother and Martha both write with great satisfaction of Anna's behaviour. She is quite an Anna with variations—but she cannot have reached her last, for that is always the most flourishing and showy—she is at about her third or fourth which are generally simple and pretty." It is a charming instance of Jane Austen's knowledge both of music and human nature. Anna was always to be an "Anna with variations".

Jane had had a compliment of her own. One of the Knatchbulls had been at Eliza's party, and Cassandra, who was in Kent, had passed on his comment. " 'A pleasing looking young woman,' " Jane quoted it back. "That must do," she went on, "one cannot pretend to anything better now—thankful to have it continued a few years longer!" She turned at once to a more interesting subject. Mrs. Knight had been sleeping a little better, and Jane was glad of it, "But upon this occasion I wish she had another name, for the two nights jingle very much." Words fascinated her. A while before, she had made an acute remark about Fanny's admiration of her letters. "I am gratified by her having pleasure in what I write—but I wish the knowledge of my being exposed to her discerning criticism, may not hurt my style, by inducing too great a solicitude. I begin already to weigh my words and sentences more than I did, and am looking about for a sentiment, an illustration or a metaphor in every corner of the room." She was mocking herself, of course, as well as Fanny. Sentiments, illustrations and particularly metaphors were always her abhorrence, and it is one of the reasons why her books continue so readable. There is nothing so dead as an old-fashioned metaphor.

Writing to Kent, Jane Austen was thinking about the family there. They had a new governess. "Poor creature! I pity her, though they are my nieces." Cassandra and Jane had made firm friends with a previous Godmersham governess, Miss Sharpe, and Jane Austen obviously wrote with authority when she spoke of the Bertram girls' tyranny over a series of governesses.

She had been watching the Parliamentary reports for Edward's sake as he was much concerned over the Weald of Kent Canal Bill, and she could congratulate him, in some of her rather halting verses, on its postponement.

> Between session and session
> The First Prepossession
> May rouse up the Nation,
> And the villainous Bill
> May be forced to lie still
> Against wicked men's will.

It is characteristic of Jane Austen that, though she seems always to have been *au courant* with the affairs of the nation, she tends only to mention them when they affect the family. In those days when postage was paid by the recipient, one would not fill one's pages with information that could be culled from any newspaper.

By the end of May, Jane had visited Catherine Hill and her husband at Streatham and was home at Chawton, but Cassandra was still at Godmersham on one of those interminable visits. It was the Austen ladies' second spring at Chawton, and the garden had obviously flourished under Mrs. Austen's direction. "Our young peony at the foot of the fir-tree has just blown and looks very handsome, and the whole of the shrubbery border will soon be very gay with pinks and sweet-williams, in addition to the columbines already in bloom. The syringas, too, are coming out." It sounds the ideal, sweet-scented, old-fashioned garden, and Jane had doubtless had a hand in its planning, since there were syringas as at Castle Square.

There were complicated plans, as usual, for family visiting. Frank (still without a ship) would be visiting Steventon with his Mary, and Jane hoped for a visit from them on their way back, but if Martha was at home there would be problems of accommodation, as Frank and Mary now had three children and two maids. The house at Chawton was comfortable, but it was not large. As for their friend Miss Sharpe, from whom Jane hoped for a visit, it looked as if she would have to be put off until August. The family always came first.

Anna was staying with them when Jane wrote, and seems to have been something of a problem, for her aunt admitted to relief that she would not be at home for an engagement with the James Digweeds, who now lived at Chawton. "I think it always safest to keep her away from the family lest she should be doing too little or too much." The same letter contains one of Jane Austen's few admissions to suffering from what we would call "nerves". "We sat upstairs and had thunder and lightning as usual . . . Thank God! we have had no bad ones here. I thought myself in luck to have my uncomfortable feelings shared by the mistress of the house, as that procured blinds and candles." Jane Austen does not often thank God, so thunder and lightning probably affected her severely.

The next letter, among its references to Anna's gaieties and "pieces for the patchwork", has one of Jane Austen's glancing comments on world events. "How horrible it is to have so many people killed! — And what a blessing that one cares for none of them!" It sounds heartless enough, when one considers that it refers to the unusually bloody battle of Albuera, in which Wellington had defeated Soult on May 16th. But, as always, one must remember the kind of intellectual shorthand used between the two sisters. Jane Austen did not need to explain to Cassandra that she meant it was a mercy that none of their friends had been hurt. The Buffs, a Kentish regiment, had been involved, and with British casualties of seven thousand men it was indeed remarkable that none of their acquaintance had been killed.

They had had a visit from Henry and his banking partner, Mr. Tilson, and taken them for a walk to Chawton Park. "Mr. Tilson admired the trees very much, but grieved that they should not be turned into money." Another of Jane Austen's quietly ironic comments follows swiftly. Their mother had been sorry that Anna was away during her uncle's visit. "A distress which I could not share." Anna does seem to have been something of a problem, but Jane hoped that on her present visit she would have "plenty of the miscellaneous, unsettled sort of happiness which seems to suit her best". As for Henry, he was his engaging self, and would bring Cassandra and Martha home in his gig. "Should the weather be tolerable, I think you must have a delightful journey." The poor old King's death was expected once again, and they were planning to walk into

Alton to buy mourning. The Regency that Jane Austen had predicted in 1809 was finally established in 1811, but in fact George III was to live on until 1820.

Only one letter of Jane Austen's survives between June of 1811 and January of 1813. It was written to Martha Lloyd in November, 1812, and reported, among the usual selection of family news, that *Pride and Prejudice* had been sold to Egerton for a hundred and ten pounds. Later, Jane Austen must have bitterly regretted that outright sale, but for the moment, "Its being sold will I hope be a great saving of trouble to Henry, and therefore must be welcome to me."

Because of this gap in the letters, we have no way of knowing whether Jane Austen was aware that *Sense and Sensibility* had been favourably noticed in the *Critical Review* for February 1812, and the *British Critic* for May of the same year. "We think so favourably of this performance," said the latter, "that it is with some reluctance we decline inserting it among our principal articles." It was no wonder that Egerton was prepared to take a chance on *Pride and Prejudice*. Neither he nor Jane Austen could have known that Lady Bessborough was recommending *Sense and Sensibility* in a letter to Lord Granville Leveson-Gower as "a clever novel. They were full of it at Althorp, and though it ends stupidly I was much amused by it." If Lady Bessborough, sister of the famous Duchess of Devonshire and mother of the equally famous Lady Caroline Lamb was reading Jane Austen, then so was society.

Of all Jane Austen's novels, perhaps *Sense and Sensibility* has drawn the widest range of critical reaction. Some people find it intolerable, with Elinor a prig and Marianne a fool; others hail it as Jane Austen's romantic novel, with Marianne as the heroine and Elinor's one burst of real feeling aroused in that curious scene with Willoughby. Everyone agrees that the heroes are mere lay figures. Jane Austen mastered her unscrupulous charmers before she did her heroes. Wickham and Willoughby are in direct descent from the flighty Edward Stanley of *Catherine* in the *Juvenilia*, while Edward Ferrars and Colonel Brandon are not much better than the lifeless heroes of that period. The comic characters are admirably drawn, Mrs. Jennings in particular. Where the John Dashwoods and the Miss Steeles are flat, undeveloping caricatures, Mrs. Jennings lives and grows. The old bore who will embarrass a girl by talking about beaux becomes the kind-hearted hostess of Marianne's illness. Like all Jane Austen's novels, *Sense and Sensibility* can be read on many different levels, and will be a different book at each reading. But the fact remains that it is the most uneven. The moral theme is neither fully enough established nor well enough integrated with the plot, and the signs of revision are all too obviously there, as for instance in the otiose character, Margaret, who may once have acted as correspondent, but whose sole function as the book now stands is to keep her mother company when her sisters go to London. She is forgotten in many scenes. If, as I have suggested, Jane Austen began this revision when she was emerging from a psychological crisis, it is possible that she finally grew impatient and wanted to have done with it and turn to what had always been a greater favourite, *Pride and Prejudice*. If she hoped that Mrs. Knight would like her Elinor, she would not forgive anyone who did not love her Elizabeth.

It was a curious, though understandable, contradiction in Jane Austen's character that she passionately wished to remain anonymous and at the same time was just as passionately interested in what people thought of her books. It is particularly maddening, therefore, that there should be no letters for the time that *Sense and Sensibility* was published. Was she disappointed in its reception? Was that why Cassandra did not keep this batch of letters? Or were there other family problems for that year, which made it seem simpler, to Cassandra in her old age, to destroy all the letters, rather than go through the retrospective anguish of rereading them?

This is mere speculation. Luckily, two letters of Cassandra's survive to help fill in the background of this period. They were written to their cousin, Philadelphia Walter, who had corresponded with Eliza de Feuillide more than twenty years before, and who married at last in the summer of 1811. Cassandra's first letter, dated August 1811, is one of congratulation addressed to her as Mrs. Whitaker: "I think I cannot give you a better wish, than that you may be as happy as you deserve and that as a wife you may meet the reward you so well earned as a daughter." Cassandra's style does not seem to have developed in flexibility as her sister's did. She may once have been "the finest comic writer of the present age" but her later letters do little to confirm her sister's praise.

Writing to her cousin, Cassandra had a good budget of family news. Eliza Austen had been visiting them. "I think I never saw her in such good health before." And while Eliza was with them Charles and his family had actually returned at last from the West Indies. "After an absence from England of almost seven years you may guess the pleasure which having him amongst us again occasioned. He is grown a little older . . . but we had the pleasure of seeing him return in good health and unchanged in mind. His Bermudan wife is a very pleasing little woman, she is gentle and amiable in her manners and appears to make him very happy. They have two pretty little girls." But, "So expensive as everything in England is now, even the necessaries of life, I am afraid they will find themselves very, very poor." Jane, too, had been at home for this visit, which helps to explain why there is no letter of hers about it.

Cassandra's next letter, written in March of 1812, reports the usual family visiting and carries on the story of Charles. He had a ship at last, H.M.S. *Namur* at Sheerness, and Fanny and the children were "actually living with him on board. We had doubted whether such a scheme would prove practicable during the winter, but they have found their residence very tolerably comfortable and it is so much the cheapest home she could have that they are very right to put up with little inconveniences." The news from Kent was less good. Edward had been prevented from visiting them by old Mrs. Knight's illness and, writing of her motherless nephews and nieces there, Cassandra sounds a warning note. "I hope those young people will not have so much happiness in their youth as to unfit them for the rubs which they must meet with afterwards, but with so indulgent a father and so liberal a style of living I am aware there must be some danger of it."

Edward and his daughter Fanny stayed at Chawton House for three weeks that April, so there was probably daily visiting, with comfortable time for eighteen-year-old Fanny to get into close touch again with the aunt who had described her earlier as "almost another sister". But old Mrs. Knight's illness had been serious. She died that summer, and Cassandra and Jane, who had loved her, must have mourned her sincerely. Edward was now to take the name of Knight and henceforth he and his children were all Knights. "I must learn to make a better K," says Jane Austen, in one of the few letters to Martha Lloyd that have been preserved. That was in the autumn. In June, Jane and her mother had visited the James Austens at Steventon, and it is perhaps not surprising that Cassandra found it necessary to destroy any letters Jane may have written from there. Relations with James and Mary, never easy, were now complicated by the fact that Anna was eighteen, and more than ever a problem. Whatever happened during that visit, it was the last time Mrs. Austen left home, though she lived for another sixteen years.

According to the authors of the *Life*, Jane Austen had already been deep in her revision of *Pride and Prejudice* in April 1811, when *Sense and Sensibility* was in the printer's hands. No doubt by now she was well established in her Chawton habit of working in the family living-room, writing, according to a niece, on small scraps of paper that could be pushed quickly under the blotter when a handily creaking door announced the threat of a visitor. If original composition in such circumstances seems an

132

achievement, a close revision like that of *Sense and Sensibility* and *Pride and Prejudice* seems almost incredible. You cannot push a whole novel under the blotter, particularly if you have it dismembered on the table. I think this story, like the other charming one of her sitting quietly for a while at her work, then bursting into laughter and hurrying across the room to make a note, must be the happy later embroidery of her nieces.

She probably did write her books in the family sitting-room, for the bedroom she shared with Cassandra was tiny, and there were coal and candles to be considered, but I imagine that she wrote at the quiet time of the day when she could count on being undisturbed. Life, in those days, was lived to a rigid pattern, and callers would only arrive at the proper time. I suspect that Jane Austen planned her day's work, peacefully, at the piano before breakfast, while her hands found their way round the familiar notes, and that there was then some quiet bit of the day, later, when she could safely spread out *Sense and Sensibility* or *Pride and Prejudice* and lop and crop away to her heart's content. Granted her good manners and her intense feeling about privacy, the pieces of paper she pushed out of sight when guests called could just as well have been letters to Cassandra.

These letters take up again, on a cheerful note, in January 1813. For once, Cassandra was at Steventon rather than Godmersham, and Martha, who had been at the deathbed of an old friend in December, was there too. "Tell her that I hunt away the rogues every night from under her bed, they feel the difference of her being gone." The rogues in question were probably the dogs they kept at Chawton. One of the more absurd criticisms levelled at Jane Austen is that there are no animals in her books. In fact, dogs are used significantly, if without any great affection. Henry Tilney had "a large Newfoundland puppy and two or three terriers" at Woodston, which settled the question of where he really lived, while Charles Musgrove and Captain Wentworth had their sport spoiled by a young dog and therefore came home in time to join the walk to Winthrop. It does sound as if Jane Austen felt that dogs, like children, should not be spoiled. It is difficult not to agree with her.

The Austen ladies seem to have been active in establishing some kind of informal book club at Chawton, and Jane was enjoying the results. She had been reading Captain Pasley's *Essay on the Military Police and Institutions of the British Empire*. "I am as much in love with the author as ever I was with Clarkson[1] or Buchanan,[2] or even the two Mr. Smiths of the city — the first soldier I ever sighed for — but he does write with extraordinary

[1] Author of *Abolition of the African Slave Trade*, 1808, and *Life of William Penn*, 1813.
[2] Author of *Christian Researches in Asia*, 1811, and *Apology for Promoting Christianity in India*, 1813.

force and spirit." These references are a useful reminder that Jane Austen was not only a novel-reader. As for "the two Mr. Smiths of the city", Jane had tried to discuss their *Rejected Addresses* with Mrs. Digweed at a party. "Her answer was 'Oh dear yes, very much, very droll indeed – the opening of the house, and the striking up of the fiddles!' What she meant poor woman, who shall say?" Like Lady Saye and Sele before her, Mrs. Digweed had been worth a silent laugh to her courteous interlocutor.

The *Rejected Addresses* were probably worth more than a silent laugh to Jane Austen. Some of the Smith Brothers' parodies of contemporary poetry are brilliantly comic, and it is pleasant to think of Jane reading aloud their parody of Scott:

> Survey the shield, all bossy bright –
> These cuisses twain behold!
> Look on my form in armour dight
> Of steel inlaid with gold.
> My knees are stiff in iron buckles,
> Stiff spikes of steel protect my knuckles . . .

Or of Byron:

> Sated with home, of wife, of children tired,
> The restless soul is driven abroad to roam;
> Sated abroad, all seen, yet nought admired,
> The restless soul is driven to ramble home . . .

Or of her favourite, Crabbe:

> 'Tis sweet to view, from half-past five to six,
> Our long wax candles with short cotton wicks,
> Touched by the lamp lighter's Promethean art,
> Start into light, and make the lighter start.

The next letter is jubilant: "I have got my own darling child from London." *Pride and Prejudice* came out that January. "The advertisement is in our paper today for the first time 18s. He shall ask £1.1 for my two next and £1.8 for my stupidest of all." There is always that note of confidence when Jane Austen speaks of *Pride and Prejudice*, and how right she was. She never got £1.8 for her "stupidest of all", but *Emma* would sell at £1.4. Like *Sense and Sensibility*, *Pride and Prejudice* received two good reviews, one in the *British Critic* for February 1813, and the other in the *Critical Review* for March, and, also like *Sense and Sensibility*, it received acclaim in society. Annabella Milbanke, who was later, disastrously, to become Lady Byron, called it "the fashionable novel", and "a very superior work . . . It is not a crying book, but the interest is very strong, especially for Mr. Darcy." Did he remind her of Lord Byron?

Meanwhile, at Chawton, they were reading it aloud to an old protégée of theirs, Miss Benn. Of course they did not tell her who the author was, but, "She was amused, poor soul! – She really does seem to admire Elizabeth. I must confess," went on the happy author, "that I think her as delightful a creature as ever appeared in print, and how I shall be able to tolerate those who do not like *her* at least I do not know." There were not to be many such. When Jane next wrote she had received a letter full of praise from Cassandra, which was lucky as the second evening of reading aloud to Miss Benn had not gone so well, partly because old Mrs. Austen read too fast and could not make the characters "speak as they ought". They were in the second half of the first volume and one can imagine the author's silent anguish as she listened to her mother mangling the immortal Mr. Collins.

Did she know he was immortal? I suspect so. She has a comment of her own that suggests it:

> Upon the whole, however, I am quite vain enough and well satisfied enough. The work is rather too light, and bright, and sparkling; it wants shade; it wants to be stretched out here and there with a long chapter of sense, if it could be had; if not, of solemn specious nonsense, about something unconnected with the story; an essay on writing, a critique on Walter Scott, or the history of Bonaparte, or anything that would form a contrast, and bring the reader with increased delight to the playfulness and epigrammatism of the general style.

Most of this is Austen-nonsense, of course, and very significant at that. Jane Austen was laughing for pure pleasure. "I doubt your quite agreeing with me here," she goes on. "I know your starched notions."

In fact, she was artist and critic enough to recognise *Pride and Prejudice* as a masterpiece of its kind, and this is her polite way of saying so. It would be a brave critic who disagreed with her, though some have. Like *Sense and Sensibility*, and, as Macaulay would say, like Shakespeare's plays, *Pride and Prejudice* can be read at many levels. It is the most light-hearted and the most comic of Jane Austen's books, and yet it is, for many people, the most romantically interesting. It may not be a "crying book", but, as Jane Austen herself suggested, it would be a hardened character indeed who could resist being concerned with the fortunes of the entrancing Elizabeth Bennet. In her, the young Jane Austen had given full play to all the qualities she herself, in her double life, had learned to hide. Elizabeth Bennet is the suffragette, the women's liberation woman of her day. Like Emma Watson, she does not talk, she acts. She will not sit back and be quizzed by the men, but gives as good as she gets. Most women (and some men) love her for it. Elizabeth, said the anonymous reviewer in the *Critical Review*, "is in fact the Beatrice of the tale", and the parallel is as sound as it is complimentary. Jane Austen may have written a more interesting book than *Pride and Prejudice*, but she never wrote a more satisfactory one.

❖ 12 ❖

THE DOUBLE LIFE WENT ON THRIVINGLY. BY THE TIME THAT *Pride and Prejudice* was at the printer's, Jane Austen was hard at work on *Mansfield Park*, her first complete new book for more than ten years. The originals of *Sense and Sensibility* and *Pride and Prejudice* dated back into the late 1790s, while even *Susan*, still languishing with Crosby, had been finished and sold to him by 1803. *The Watsons* had been left unfinished, but at last, in 1813, Jane Austen could write, "Now I will try to write of something else, and it shall be a complete change of subject — ordination." In fact, she must already have been well started on *Mansfield Park*, for in a previous letter to Cassandra she had told her, "As soon as a whist party was formed, and a round table threatened, I made my mother an excuse and came away, leaving just as many for *their* round table as there were at Mrs. Grant's." The reference is to the scene in *Mansfield Park* where the diminished Bertram family dine with the Grants at the vicarage and Henry Crawford sits between Fanny and Lady Bertram at the round table and teaches them both speculation. As this episode is almost exactly half way through the second of *Mansfield Park*'s three volumes it is clear that Jane Austen's remark about ordination was by way of an afterthought; she was already well advanced in the book that was to bear unmistakable traces of the psychological crisis of the silent years.

She had worked herself back into the writing mood by revising her early books. Now, she was breaking new ground. But it was not new to her. *Mansfield Park* had been long in the incubation. Letters from her summer visit to Godmersham in 1808 had shown germinal ideas for the book. Perhaps she had, in fact, been planning it, based on the luxurious great house life at Godmersham, that last happy summer of Elizabeth

Austen's life, and had put it by for a while after her death. Certainly, as opposed to *Elinor and Marianne* and *First Impressions*, which seem to have been written fairly quickly and then polished and repolished, *Mansfield Park* must have gone through a prolonged period of gestation in its author's mind. The result is a book of great beauty and complexity, the final refutation of that extraordinary *Depreciation* of H. W. Garrod's. "A drab scenery the worse for use, a thin plot unfashionably cut, and by turning, re-lining and trimming made to do duty for five or six novels; a dozen or so stock characters—these are Miss Austen's materials." Of course, he meant to provoke, as, one must hope, he did in his objection to the phrase "great woman". He can hardly have been serious in suggesting that Jane Austen used the same plot for all her novels, unless he meant that the stories all end in a marriage or marriages, presumably intended to be happy. If this is what he meant, it is true of practically all the novels of the late eighteenth and early nineteenth century, with such obvious exceptions as *Tristram Shandy* and *Clarissa Harlowe* to prove the rule.

Sense and Sensibility and *Pride and Prejudice* were basically a young girl's brilliant experiments, and, as one might expect, in them the romantic theme is predominant, and the heroine the heart of the matter. *Mansfield Park* is the deliberate work of a mature artist. The first thing one notices is that the heroine has been moved away from the centre of the book, which is occupied instead by the moral issue with which Jane Austen was always, at one level, concerned. She had said she was writing about ordination, but as so often she did herself less than justice. The question of Edmund's ordination, like that of Fanny's determined adherence to her principles, first about the play and then about Henry Crawford's proposal, are both merely facets of the basic problem with which Jane Austen was concerned in this, her most serious book. It is, quite simply, the problem of good and evil. *Mansfield Park* is her *Pilgrim's Progress*, with Edmund and Fanny, the Christian hero and heroine, fighting their way through temptation towards a not very clearly defined goal. There is no Celestial City for them, just a happy marriage and the right work to do. The very fact that Jane Austen never talks in terms of easy answers and eternal salvation makes the moral struggles of her characters infinitely more interesting.

In defiance of the clues provided by the Crawfords' early behaviour, many critics have insisted that they are the true hero and heroine of *Mansfield Park*. This is proof, if any were needed, of the subtlety of Jane Austen's treatment. In fact, the Crawfords are the most dangerous characters in the book, because they are intelligent and yet corrupt. And, as always, Jane Austen is at pains to explain this. They have been badly brought up in the house of a vicious uncle. The ordered, stupid, selfish pattern of life at Mansfield Park is almost totally vulnerable to them. But not quite. Quiet, neglected, ailing, sometimes irritating, Fanny Price will not be beguiled by their charms; though, realist as always, Jane Austen points out that this is because she has her love for Edmund as talisman to support her in her decision of principle. Otherwise, although Henry Crawford would not have succeeded in seducing her, he would probably, Jane Austen suggests, have managed to marry her.

Fanny, timid, feeble, so unlike Jane Austen herself, is the touchstone of the book. She alone sees keenly and if we are to read the book as Jane Austen meant us to, we must accept her vision as true. In the vital, symbolic scene where they all go to Sotherton and the Bertrams and Crawfords lose themselves in a dangerous garden of delights, only Fanny sees things for what they are, and is aware of moral danger. After this, we should be prepared to accept her judgment about the play, which has caused so much critical anguish. Jane Austen loved plays: they had acted them when they were young at Steventon: she was bitterly disappointed when she missed seeing Mrs. Siddons in London. It is this play, in these circumstances, that Fanny recognises as morally dangerous, and we are supposed to feel that she is right.

But here, and with the question of Edmund's ordination, which comes to the fore at about the same time, lies the central weakness, in my view, of the book. Mrs. Inchbald's *Lover's Vows* was a rather vulgar, popular play, and perhaps it was not quite the thing to put it on when the head of the Bertram family was in danger at sea. Similarly, Edmund Bertram was a perfectly well brought up young man who intended going into the Church because there was a family living waiting for him. For some reason, Jane Austen loads these two strands of the book with more moral overtones than they can bear. It is at this point that the casual reader, looking round for relief, may well light on the Crawfords and think them ill-used. And because Jane Austen, according to the anonymous lady quoted in M. A. Austen-Leigh's *Personal Aspects of Jane Austen*, believed that "example and not 'direct preaching' was all that a novelist could afford to exhibit", she never quite succeeded in making her point.

Or was it because, in a sufficiently depressing world, she failed to convince herself on the moral issue? *Mansfield Park* is certainly her most serious attempt to come to grips with it, but it cannot be called an entire success. "Let other pens dwell on guilt and misery," she says at the end, with an almost perceptible shudder, and turns to one of her brisk, common-sense conclusions. She has been down into the depths, and has emerged intact, and with that double, ironic vision of hers sharpened in intensity, but it is a curious, disconcerting thought that of all the brilliantly drawn characters of *Mansfield Park*, it is Mrs. Norris, almost wholly bad, who first comes to mind. Was this, perhaps, catharsis on a personal level? Did Mrs. Norris represent everything that Jane Austen had found intolerable in James's Mary, and Aunt Jane Leigh Perrot, and all the host of other bustling, unintelligent women to whom she was exposed throughout her life?

If so, Mrs. Norris's creation probably made it easier for her author to bear with them, and Jane no doubt behaved perfectly during that unlucky second reading of *Pride and Prejudice*, when, one suspects, poor Miss Benn began to wriggle in her chair, or play with the contents of her reticule. And, for Miss Jane Austen, the author, there was real comfort coming, in the form of letters of high praise for *Pride and Prejudice* from Cassandra and Fanny. The latter, characteristically, had been a little more cautious to Cassandra than to Jane herself. Jane, the realist, saw it all. "To *me* it is of course all praise," she wrote Cassandra, "but the more exact truth she sends *you* is good enough."

A letter of February 1813 to Martha Lloyd, gives one of Jane Austen's comparatively rare comments on public events. The Prince Regent and his wife, the deplorable Princess Caroline of Brunswick, had been angrily separated for years, and in January 1813 the Princess had written to her husband protesting against her treatment, particularly with regard to their daughter, the next heir to the throne, Princess Charlotte. On receiving no reply to her letter, Princess Caroline gave it to the press, and Jane Austen comments, "I suppose all the world is sitting in judgment upon the Princess of Wales's letter. Poor woman, I shall support her as long as I can, because she is a woman, and because I hate her husband . . . I do not know what to do about it; but if I must give up the princess, I am resolved at least always to think that she would have been respectable, if the prince had behaved only tolerably by her at first." Jane Austen clearly knew the whole disastrous history of that marriage, from the moment when the Prince of Wales appointed his mistress as his new wife's lady-in-waiting; and had made up her mind about it. She was always one to go back to first causes.

Another letter to Martha, printed as an addendum by Chapman, and dated September 1814, must, I think, be two letters accidentally run together. The date and opening clearly belong to 1814, but the second half of the letter belongs just as obviously to 1812. Jane Austen is reporting

Henry's fears about war with America, which he and his friends think "certain, and as what is to ruin us". Jane herself is more hopeful. "If we *are* to be ruined, it cannot be helped — but I place my hope of better things on a claim to the protection of Heaven, as a religious nation, a nation in spite of much evil improving in religion, which I cannot believe the Americans to possess." This war broke out in 1812, and Henry and his friends proved right in their conjecture that the Americans could not be conquered, "We shall only be teaching them the skill in war which they may now want." "Mr. Madison's war" dragged to a close in 1814, although, due to the slowness of trans-Atlantic communication its last battle, a bloody one, was actually fought at New Orleans in January 1815.

Back in 1812, Henry's wife Eliza, the lively original of Lady Susan and Mary Crawford, was probably beginning to ail. She died after a long and painful illness in April 1813, and Henry went down to Chawton to be comforted. Jane went back to London with him, and her letter to Cassandra reports the journey cheerfully enough. Mercurial Henry does not seem to have needed too much comforting. In London, Jane was busy helping him close his Sloane Street house in preparation for moving to chambers over his bank at 10, Henrietta Street. At the moment the chambers were "all dirt and confusion, but in a very promising way", and so, apparently, was Henry, who took his sister to an exhibition by the Society of Painters in Oil and Water Colours where she found "a small portrait of Mrs. Bingley, excessively like her", but looked in vain for one of Mrs. Darcy. She rather hoped to find her at the British Academy. They were also going to an exhibition of Sir Joshua Reynolds's paintings at the British Institution in Pall Mall, but there was no picture of Mrs. Darcy anywhere. "I can only imagine that Mr. D. prizes any picture of her too much to like it should be exposed to the public eye." Though *Mansfield Park* must have been well advanced (it was published next May) it was for Elizabeth Bennet that Jane Austen looked, not for either Elinor Dashwood or Fanny Price.

Despite Henry's mourning, they had plenty of visitors. Jane was threatened with a meeting with Miss Burdett, probably a sister of Sir Francis Burdett, the famous Whig Member of Parliament and supporter of civil liberties, who had actually been sent briefly to the Tower in 1810 for breach of Parliamentary privilege. They seem odd acquaintances for a Tory Austen, but one must remember that Henry was also a banker, and Sir Francis had married a Miss Coutts, daughter of the famous banker. Jane "would like to see Miss Burdett very well, but that I am rather frightened by hearing that she wishes to be introduced to *me* — If I *am* a wild beast, I cannot help it. It is not my own fault." It was inevitable that Henry should betray the secret of his sister's authorship; but, in fact, she was never lionised like Scott, or Fanny Burney, or Maria Edgeworth. Her pleasures were simple and private ones. "I had great amusement among the pictures; and the driving about, the carriage being open, was very pleasant—I liked my solitary elegance very much, and was ready to laugh all the time, at my being where I was—I could not but feel that I had naturally small right to be parading about London in a barouche."

Henry, who obviously enjoyed giving such pleasures to his favourite sister, was going to drive her home, and visit James at Steventon, but his plans were uncertain as usual. "Whatever I may write or you may imagine we know it will be something different," said his sister. Meanwhile life at Chawton was lively too. The Charles Austens' little girls had been visiting there, and had been much improved in manners, and the Edward Austens, or rather, as one must now call them, the Knights, were staying at Chawton House while Godmersham was repainted. Fanny Knight's diary for 1813 speaks of constant meetings between the families and a "delicious morning" with her Aunt Jane.

Two of Jane Austen's few surviving letters to her brothers date from this year. They are both to Frank, who was captaining H.M.S. *Elephant* on convoy duty in the Baltic. Like all the best letter-writers, Jane Austen wrote differently to different correspondents, and these two to Frank are some of her most engaging letters. "God bless you—I hope you continue beautiful and brush your hair, but not all off." She congratulated him on his chance to see Sweden. "Gustavus-Vasa, and Charles 12th, and Christina, and Linnaeus—do their ghosts rise up before you?" And, like a good sister, she told him plenty of family news. They were seeing the Knights every day. "Edward is very well and enjoys himself as thoroughly as any Hampshire-born Austen can desire." And Henry had been promoted from Deputy Receiver for Oxfordshire to be Receiver-General and was planning a trip to Scotland with his nephew, Edward Knight. "Upon the whole his spirits are very much recovered—If I may so express myself, his mind is not a mind for affliction. He is too busy, too active, too sanguine." Love would never blind Jane Austen to facts. This same letter has that delicious description of Miss Lewis, the new wife of an old admirer of Jane's, who was to be "of a silent turn and rather ignorant". It also reported the death of Thomas Leigh, who had succeeded to the Stoneleigh estates, and Jane Austen wrote with sympathy of Mrs. Leigh Perrot "who would now have been mistress of Stoneleigh had there been none of that vile compromise". It was not, in fact, a sentiment that Jane

Leigh Perrot shared. She was happy to take the settlement, and let the estate go.

Jane's last paragraph covers the subject probably nearest to her heart. "You will be glad to hear that every copy of *Sense and Sensibility* is sold and that it has brought me £140 besides the copyright, if that should ever be of any value—I have now therefore written myself into £250—which only makes me long for more." *Pride and Prejudice*, of course, had been sold outright for a hundred and ten pounds to spare Henry trouble. Since the small edition of *Sense and Sensibility* had been published in the winter of 1811 it had taken a year and a half to sell out, but a hundred and ten pounds still seems an intolerably bad bargain for *Pride and Prejudice*. Jane Austen went on to say that, "I have something in hand—which I hope on the credit of P. and P. will sell well, though not half so entertaining." She clearly recognised *Mansfield Park* for what it was, her problem book. Always a stickler at once for good manners and for accuracy, she went on to tell Frank that she had mentioned the *Elephant* and "two or three of your old ships", and ask his permission.

Mansfield Park was finished in June, so that Jane Austen was free to enjoy that summer's daily exchange of visits with the Knights at the Great House. In the autumn she went back to Godmersham with them, by way of London, where she and her three nieces, Fanny, Marianne and Lizzy Knight stayed with Henry at 10, Henrietta Street, while Edward slept at a hotel nearby, and the rest of his huge family made the journey home across country, escorted by his second son George, who was then seventeen. The London party made the most of their three nights in town. The first night they went to the Lyceum for *Don Juan*, "whom we left in hell at half-past eleven". Lizzie and Marianne were delighted, but Jane's delight was "very tranquil", though, "I must say that I have seen nobody on the stage who has been a more interesting character than that compound of cruelty and lust." It hardly sounds like "dear Aunt Jane". The next night they went to *The Clandestine Marriage* and *Midas* at Covent Garden. Lizzie and Marianne were delighted, "but *I* wanted better acting".

In the daytime they shopped for English poplins, and caps like Harriet Byron's in *Sir Charles Grandison*, and "kind, beautiful Edward" gave Jane and Fanny five pounds each. At thirty-seven, and an established author, Jane Austen still found these presents of money very welcome, and would spend this one on twenty yards of poplin for herself and Cassandra. "Do not refuse me. I am very rich." Edward also, like the devoted father he was, helped Jane take his daughters to the dentist, which "cost us many tears". Henry had been unwell and was being a little difficult about plans for a visit to Chawton to fetch Cassandra, and, worse still, he had been indiscreet again. He had met Lady Robert Kerr in Scotland, and she had spoken highly of *Pride and Prejudice*. "Before she knew who wrote it, for, of course, she knows now. He told her with as much satisfaction as if it were my wish." On the other hand Henry had also told Warren Hastings, and received a reaction to which no author could object. "I am quite delighted with what such a man writes about it." And, later in the same letter, "His admiring my Elizabeth so much is particularly welcome to me." And, an odd little phrase, "Mr. Hastings never *hinted* at Eliza in the smallest degree."

Jane Austen had not been to Godmersham for four years, and one inevitably wonders why, but the few letters for the intervening period give no clue, and neither does family tradition. Perhaps she was too much occupied with the pleasures and pains of writing again to find time for one of those interminable Kentish visits in the great house full of nieces and nephews. And of course Edward's family had visited in Hampshire. Certainly, four years had done little to change the pleasant pattern of life at Godmersham, though Jane must have missed both Elizabeth and her old friend, Mrs. Knight.

The children were growing up. Fanny, the eldest, was twenty, and there was a John Plumtre to be considered. Jane Austen thought him "sensible rather than brilliant—There is nobody brilliant nowadays." At thirty-seven, she may have been feeling her age a little as she watched Fanny suffering from "one of the sweet taxes of youth to choose in a hurry and make bad bargains". A letter from Cassandra had reported that the other grown-up niece, James's Anna, was causing trouble. Anna had fallen in love with Ben Lefroy, son of that beloved friend of Jane's who had died in 1804, and Anna's stepmother and grandmother both seemed to be making difficulties. "How can Mrs. J. Austen be so provokingly ill-judging?" wrote Jane. "I should have expected better from her professed if not her real regard for my mother." It is an unusually sharp comment for Jane, or at least for what remains of her letters. But she had been suffering from a pain in her face, made worse by a cold caught on the journey.

The next letter from Godmersham is to Frank, who had answered the one she had written him earlier in the summer. She had to tell him that though she was to be in Kent for two months, there seemed no chance of getting over to Deal to visit his wife Mary and their children. Travelling was still a problem, but at least they were expecting a visit from Charles and his family. She had a sharpish comment on another visitor, the wife of Edward Bridges, who may possibly have proposed to Jane herself in 1808.

She "is a poor honey — the sort of woman who gives me the idea of being determined never to be well — and who likes her spasms and nervousness and the consequence they give her, better than anything else." And then, "This is an ill-natured sentiment to send all over the Baltic!" It is sad to think that four years later, Jane Austen was to describe herself as a "poor honey". For the moment, she seemed almost out of proportion sorry for Edward in his unlucky match. "We have had another of Edward Bridges' Sunday visits. I think that the pleasantest part of his married life must be the dinners, and breakfasts, and luncheons, and billiards that he gets in this way at Godmersham. Poor wretch! he is quite the dregs of the family as to luck."

Frank had given her permission to use the names of his ships, but had warned her that this might betray the secret of her authorship. Her answer is rueful. "The truth is that the secret has spread so far as to be scarcely the shadow of a secret now . . . I believe whenever the third appears, I shall not even attempt to tell lies about it — I shall rather try to make all the money than all the mystery I can of it." She goes on to describe how Henry had given her away to Lady Robert Kerr. And, "A thing once set going in that way — one knows how it spreads! — and he, dear creature, has set it going so much more than once. I know it is all done from affection and partiality — but at the same time, let me here again express to you and Mary my sense of the *superior* kindness which you have shown on the occasion, in doing what I wish — I am trying to harden myself. After all, what a trifle it is in all its bearings, to the really important points of one's existence even in this world!"

It is so rare for Jane Austen to draw this kind of contrast between life here and life everlasting that one can only conclude that she minded Henry's betrayal very much indeed. The same letter has an interesting comment on a preacher she had heard. "He gave us an excellent sermon — a little too eager sometimes in his delivery, but that is to *me* a better extreme than the want of animation, especially when it evidently comes from the heart as in him."

Anna was engaged to Ben Lefroy by now and her Aunt Jane was not over-hopeful about the match. "There is an unfortunate dissimilarity of taste between them in one respect which gives us some apprehensions, he hates company and she is very fond of it — this, with some queerness of temper on his side and much unsteadiness on hers, is untoward." And then, an important postscript: "There is to be a Second Edition of S. and S. Egerton advises it." The second edition of *Sense and Sensibility* came out in November 1813, again at Jane Austen's expense.

The next letter is to Cassandra and has one of Jane Austen's brief, drastic character sketches. "Mrs. Britton called here on Saturday. I never saw her before. She is a large, ungenteel woman, with self-satisfied and would-be elegant manners." With *Mansfield Park* finished and perhaps already at the printer's, Jane was ready for a new start, and this visit was full of raw material for *Emma*. Mrs. Britton reappears with her husband. "I had long wanted to see Dr. Britton, and his wife amuses me very much with her affected refinement and elegance." It sounds as if Mrs. Elton were in the making. And, visiting Canterbury, they called a couple of times on Mrs. and Miss Milles, who were to join Mrs. Stent in composing the Bateses. "I like the mother . . . because she is cheerful and grateful for what she is at the age of ninety and upwards." And as for the daughter, "Miss Milles was queer as usual, and provided us with plenty to laugh at. She undertook in *three words* to give us the history of Mrs. Scudamore's reconciliation, and then talked on about it for half-an-hour, using such odd expressions, and so foolishly minute, that I could hardly keep my countenance."

It was doubtless a safety-valve to be thinking of Highbury in the few quiet times of those crowded days when she actually found herself alone, "very snug, in my own room, lovely morning, excellent fire, fancy me". Edward was always kind, but the rest of the household may have been exhausting. Jane probably shared her sister's anxieties about the nephews and nieces who were being brought up so indulgently. Cassandra obviously felt it necessary to destroy a letter about the nephews, for the next one reads, "As I wrote of my nephews with a little bitterness in my last, I think it particularly incumbent on me to do them justice now, and I have great pleasure in saying that they were both at the sacrament yesterday." Jane Austen goes on with her usual insight, "After having much praised or much blamed anybody, one is generally sensible of something just the reverse soon afterwards. Now, these two boys who are out with the foxhounds will come home and disgust me again by some habit of luxury or some proof of sporting mania." They do sound a little like Tom Bertram, but she has a charming picture of them making rabbit nets in the evening. They "sit as deedily to it, side by side, as any two Uncle Franks could do."

Jane Austen was rereading Mary Brunton's *Self Control* (published in 1810) and not thinking much of it. "My opinion is confirmed of its being an excellently-meant, elegantly-written work, without anything of nature or probability in it. I declare I do not know whether Laura's passage down the American river, is not the most natural, possible, everyday thing she ever does." Jane Austen was to remember this book, when she drew up her spoof *Plan of a Novel* in the last years of her life. There was Southey's *Life of Nelson*, too, but, "I am tired of Lives of Nelson, being that I never read any. I will read this however, if Frank is mentioned in it." Frank had taken a vital despatch to Nelson at Palermo in 1799 and one can only wish we had any record of what he and his sister thought of the curious *ménage à trois* in which Nelson was then living with Sir William Hamilton and his experienced wife, Emma. Perhaps this explains why Jane Austen did not read lives of Nelson. Frank, on the other hand, who served under Nelson in the desperate chase to the West Indies before Trafalgar, had had nothing but praise for him after his death. "I never heard of his equal, nor do I expect again to see such a man," he had written to his fiancée in 1805.

Jane had still not managed to get to Deal. "Here I am in Kent, with one brother in the same county and another brother's wife, and see nothing of them—which seems unnatural—It will not last so for ever I trust—I should like to have Mrs. F. A. and her children here for a week—but not a syllable of that nature is ever breathed." With eleven children of his own to think about, it is perhaps natural enough that Edward took his sisters a little for granted. Cassandra was busy overseeing alterations to Chawton House for him. "He desires me to say that your being at Chawton when he is, will be quite necessary. You cannot think it more indispensable than he does. He is very much obliged to you for your attention to everything —Have you any idea of returning with him to Henrietta Street and finishing your visit then?—tell me your sweet little innocent ideas." There is something at once dry and unmistakable about that last ironic little sentence. Jane and Cassandra were, indeed, a continuing comfort and support to each other.

Jane and Fanny had called on a plain family of Lady Fagg and her five daughters, and were being visited by a Mr. Wigram, "not ill-looking and not agreeable", but at least they had got rid of Mr. Robert Mascall. "I did not like *him* either. He talks too much and is conceited—besides having a vulgarly shaped mouth." One begins to detect something unusually sharp in this batch of letters. "Only think of Mrs. Holder's being dead!—Poor woman, she has done the only thing in the world she could possibly do, to make one cease to abuse her." Lord Brabourne thinks that this was Jane Austen's last visit to Godmersham and it seems possible that she was finding the company of eleven nephews and nieces and their over-indulgent father a little too much. Did she have any time for revising *Mansfield Park*? It seems unlikely, as the letters to

Cassandra were obviously fitted in here and there between other calls on her.

Charles and his family were coming at last, but to a house that already had its complement of visitors, though luckily the billiard table occupied the young men in the evening, leaving Edward, Fanny and Jane, "the library to ourselves in delightful quiet". This quiet was happily interrupted at dinner time next evening by the arrival of Charles and his family, "safe and well, just like their own nice selves . . . dear Charles all affectionate, placid, quiet, cheerful, good humour . . . but poor little Cassy is grown extremely thin and looks poorly." Life on board ship did not suit Cassy and one of the subjects of discussion during this visit was whether she should spend the winter with her grandmother and aunts at Chawton, but Cassy "did not like the idea of it at all", and Charles, a devoted father like all the Austens, did not want to part with her. Jane obviously thought him almost too devoted. "Charles . . . will be as happy as he can with a cross child or some such care pressing on him . . ." And, again, "I think I have just done a good deed — extracted Charles from his wife and children upstairs, and made him get ready to go out shooting, and not keep Mr. Moore waiting any longer." Cassy took too much after her mother's family. "Poor little love — I wish she were not so very Palmery," and her cousins were "too many and too boisterous for her". James's Caroline had felt the same way years before. Clearly, there was something rather overwhelming about the young Knights.

Cassandra was just off to visit Henry in London, no doubt leaving Martha with old Mrs. Austen. "I suppose," said Jane, "my mother will like to have me write to her. I shall try at least." It is a depressing sidelight on her relationship with her mother at this point. Henry had been unwell again, and the next letter, written to Cassandra in Henrietta Street, hopes that she is "seeing improvement in him every day". Charles and his family had left, but their old friend Harriot Moore (née Bridges) was still there with her husband and little boy. "I do believe that he makes her — or she makes herself — very happy. They do not spoil their boy." These were two important points for Jane Austen. She was against the spoiling of children and did not "think it worth while to wait for enjoyment until there is some real opportunity for it".

In Hampshire, Anna's affairs continued to be a problem. Ben Lefroy had been offered a curacy, "which he might have secured against his taking orders", and had refused it. "Upon its being made rather a serious question, [he] says he has not made up his mind as to taking orders so early, and that, if her father makes a point of it, he must give Anna up rather than do what he does not approve. He must be maddish," adds Jane Austen. It seems an extraordinary comment from the creator of Fanny Price and Edmund Bertram. Clearly the rules of *Mansfield Park* were not those of the real world that Jane Austen lived in.

The next letter has a more encouraging report of Anna and her Ben. Jane has had "a very comfortable letter" from her mother about a satisfactory visit from Anna. "This will be an excellent time for Ben to pay his visit—now that we, the formidables, are absent." It is a fascinating, and revealing, comment on Jane and Cassandra and their position in the family. They were "the formidables". In fact, Ben Lefroy did marry Anna in the winter of 1814, and did not take orders until some years later.

Cassandra had sent good "tidings of S. & S.", presumably the second edition. "I have never seen it advertised," said Jane, and, later, "I suppose in the meantime I shall owe dear Henry a great deal of money for printing &c." She had received "more of such sweet flattery" from Miss Sharpe, their friend who had once been governess at Godmersham, and could report proudly that she was "read and admired in Ireland too . . . I do not despair of having my picture in the exhibition at last—all white and red with my head on one side—or perhaps I may marry young Mr. D'Arblay." Since Fanny Burney's son by her French emigrant husband was only born in 1794, this is just Austen-nonsense, like the references, about this time, to Jane's hypothetical marriage to her favourite poet, Crabbe. In fact, she was resigning herself to middle age. "By the bye, as I must leave off being young, I find many douceurs in being a sort of chaperon for I am put on a sofa near the fire and can drink as much wine as I like." It was the young ones now who played the piano, while Aunt Jane could sit on the sofa, and listen, and think her own thoughts.

❧ 13 ❧

HENRY CONTINUED UNWELL. "DEAREST HENRY! WHAT A TURN he has for being ill!" At her own suggestion, Jane visited him that autumn on her way home from Godmersham, travelling up with Edward, who left her in Henrietta Street and took Cassandra down to Chawton with him, doubtless for further discussion of the alterations at the Great House. Henry had his own carriage still, so Jane, like Cassandra, must have been able to visit the Hills at Streatham. When she left, the carriage probably took her down to Great Bookham in Surrey, where she stayed for a while with the Cookes, parents of George and Mary. Jane's godfather, Samuel Cooke, Vicar of Great Bookham, had married Mrs. Austen's first cousin, Cassandra, daughter of Theophilus Leigh, the Master of Balliol. They must have been an interesting household. They were also close to Box Hill. This visit, like the one at Godmersham, must have been germinal to *Emma*.

Unfortunately, there are no letters until the following spring, so we do not know whether Jane Austen actually picnicked on Box Hill, or, for that matter, how she got home from Bookham, but Cassandra's note on the dating of her sister's books records that *Emma* was begun in January 1814, presumably when *Mansfield Park* had had its final polishing and was at the printer's. No doubt the quiet winter months when muddy lanes made visiting difficult were the best for composition. There would be little need for the protection of that invaluable creaking door in the extra cold winter of 1814, when the Thames froze so solid that there were booths and a fair on it, and Napoleon was on the run at last, back across Europe after his defeat by the allied armies at Leipzig the autumn before. "What weather! And what news!" Jane Austen had written in November, while the Duke of Wellington's brother, Lord Wellesley, quoted Pitt to Parliament. Once again, England had saved herself by her exertions, and would, he hoped, save Europe by her example.

By March 1814, when Jane Austen's letters begin again, the long war seemed almost over. Wellington was across the Spanish border, working his way north towards Paris, while the allied armies were closing in from the east. But Jane had matter nearer her heart to think of. She was writing to Cassandra from Henrietta Street after driving up from Chawton with Henry, and they had been reading *Mansfield Park* aloud on the way. The book came out in May, but this was clearly the first time Henry had seen it. Cassandra undoubtedly saw Jane's first drafts, but even Henry seems not to have been consulted until the book was in its final form. Jane Austen may have minded criticism too much to risk exposing herself to it at an earlier stage. Luckily, "His approbation hitherto is even equal to my wishes. He says it is very different from the other two, but does not appear to think it at all inferior . . . He took to Lady Bertram and Mrs. Norris most kindly, and gives great praise to the drawing of the characters. He understands them all, likes Fanny, and, I think, foresees how it will all be." Impossible not to like Henry for this.

The two of them reached London to find that "peace was generally expected", and to have it start snowing again. Jane was reading Lord Byron's *Corsair*, and *The Heroine* by E. S. Barrett, which she found "a delightful burlesque, particularly on the Radcliffe style". This was handsome of her, considering the unlucky fate of her own *Susan* (*Northanger Abbey*). But she could afford to be generous. They had gone on reading and Henry "admires H. Crawford: I mean properly, as a clever, pleasant man". The next letter reports that he "likes my *Mansfield Park* better and better . . . I believe *now* he has changed his mind as to foreseeing the end: he said yesterday at least, that he defied anybody to say whether Henry Crawford would be reformed, or would forget Fanny in a fortnight." And, at last, "Henry has finished *Mansfield Park*, and his approbation has not lessened. He found the last half of the last volume *extremely interesting*."

As always, writing to Cassandra, there was no need to fill in the gaps, but it is impossible not to wish for Henry's view of Mary Crawford, who seems so clearly to trace her ancestry by way of Lady Susan to his own wife Eliza, now dead a year. Of course, it is entirely possible that neither Jane nor Henry recognised this. The Eliza on whom Mary Crawford was ultimately based had been dead much more than a year. She was the frivolous young Eliza of the early letters; the girl who wrote of beaux and balls, of "dear liberty and yet dearer flirtation". Probably Henry, who always loved her, and Jane, who had learned to, had forgotten the early Eliza in the beloved wife and kind sister-in-law, and Jane, if she thought about it at all, merely thought of Mary Crawford as having some affinity with that early, suppressed heroine of hers, Lady Susan. After all, in those happy days before Freud, an author and his or her public did not have to look too closely into the derivation of themes and characters. Shakespeare could write about Hamlet without reference to Oedipus, and Jane Austen, spinster though she was, about love without reference to anything. It was a great advantage to them.

With Henry's approval secured for *Mansfield Park*, Jane Austen could settle to be happy in London. Edward and Fanny Knight were to visit Henry too, and they were all going to Drury Lane to see the famous Kean in *The Merchant of Venice*. "So great is the rage for seeing Kean that only a third and fourth row could be got." They were great playgoers, those Austens, and one can only wish for a record of a family discussion of the use of the play in *Mansfield Park*. Meanwhile, the cold weather continued, snow saved Jane Austen from calls, and Edward and Fanny had a hard drive of it up from Bath, where they had been visiting Edward's ailing mother-in-law, Lady Bridges.

Lucky Edward was in trouble for once. There was some problem about the prosecution of a boy for assault, but Edward's opinion inclined "*against* a second prosecution". Much more serious and more lasting was a legal assault made on him at this time by the blood heir to the Knight estates, a Mr. Baverstock, who claimed the Hampshire property through his mother, arguing that an entail had not been properly set aside. This must have been a cause of very considerable anxiety at Chawton cottage, which would, of course, have been affected, though Jane wrote hopefully at this point, "Edward has a good chance of escaping the lawsuit. His opponent knocks under. The terms of agreement are not quite settled." They were not, indeed. The claim was only settled, at considerable expense to Edward, in 1817, the year of Jane's death.

But for the moment all was gaiety. Edward and Fanny arrived just in time for *The Merchant of Venice*, and next night they all went to *The Devil to Pay* by Charles Coffee, and an Italian Opera. "Excepting Miss Stephens, I daresay *Artaxerxes* will be very tiresome." The snow was so deep that Edward and Fanny stayed an extra night and they saw Miss Stephens again in *The Farmer's Wife*. She proved a disappointment. "All that I am sensible of in Miss Stephens is, a pleasing person and no skill in acting." Edward and Fanny set off for Kent next day, but not before Henry was suspecting "decided attachment" between Fanny and John Plumtre, the young man Jane had earlier described as "sensible rather than brilliant". He had been their constant companion during this visit and had organised the last party to see *The Farmer's Wife*. It was the nieces' turn, now, to be watched and speculated about.

Jane Austen had the usual London errands to do. Her mother wanted her to order their tea at Twining's and pay their bill, but had unfortunately not provided her with the money for it. The public were in mourning for six weeks because of the death of Queen Charlotte's brother, the Duke of Mecklenburg-Strelitz, and Jane had been "ruining myself in black satin ribbon with a proper pearl edge". She never lost her interest in clothes, and sounds rather touchingly like one of her own younger heroines when she worries, at thirty-eight, whether long sleeves will do for the evening.

Cassandra was to join them in town after Edward and Fanny left. "Prepare for a play the very first evening, I rather think Covent Garden to see Young in *Richard*." Martha was at home to look after Mrs. Austen and they had had Charles's daughter Cassandra staying with them. "If Cassandra has filled my bed with fleas, I am sure they must bite herself." Little Cassandra was coming to town with her aunt to rejoin her parents, who were living in Keppel Street. Charles must have been between commands and they were staying with his wife's family. Jane had discovered that Cassandra senior's visit would have to be a short one. As usual the sisters' plans must depend on Henry's rather indefinite ones, and, "By a little convenient listening, I now know that Henry wishes to go to Godmersham for a few days before Easter." This meant a complicated rearrangement of Cassandra's and Jane's own plans, since Cassandra wanted to go to the Leighs at Adlestrop and the two of them also meant to visit the Hills at Streatham. Visits together were a rare indulgence.

In May, *Mansfield Park* came out, being announced in the *Morning Chronicle* for May 23rd and 27th. Disappointingly, it received no reviews, and seems to have made altogether less of an impression than the two previous books. Perhaps it was as a compensation for this lack of critical response that Jane Austen made a collection of the opinions of her family and friends (published in Dr. Chapman's collection of her *Minor Works*). Although there was much praise, the majority view does seem to have placed *Mansfield Park* below *Pride and Prejudice*, but it is pleasant to think of Mrs. James Austen enjoying Mrs. Norris particularly, and Admiral Foote, "surprised that I had the power of drawing the Portsmouth scenes so well".

That May and June were sociable months at Chawton. Edward and his five eldest children were staying at the Great House, complete with Miss Clewes, the current governess, and Fanny's diary reports the usual close relations between the two families. "The cottage dined here", "Papa and I dined at the cottage", "Aunt Jane drank tea here", or, "Aunt Jane and I spent a bustling hour or two shopping in Alton." The word "cottage" was of course something of an understatement for Mrs. Austen's house, but served, for the Knights at least, to distinguish it from the Great House.

The sociable summer was enlivened by the illuminations that celebrated peace, at last, with France, and by a visit from Lady Bridges and her daughter on their way back from their long stay in Bath. In June, Cassandra went up to London to stay with Henry again. Jane was planning another visit to the Cookes at Bookham (perhaps to check a point or two for *Emma*), but would not go until Edward had left the Great House, "that he may feel he has a somebody to give memorandums to, to the last". His sisters were obviously very useful to Edward. It was, in fact, a considerable sacrifice on Jane's part as it meant giving up "all help from his carriage, of course. And, at any rate, it must be such an excess of expense that I have quite made up my mind to it and do not mean to care. I have been thinking of Triggs and the chair, you may be sure, but I know it will end in posting." There were financial advantages about being an actual, published author, even if they were smallish. Jane Austen had her own travelling purse at last.

The Cookes had endeared themselves to Jane by admiring *Mansfield Park* "exceedingly. Mr. Cooke says 'it is the most sensible novel he ever read,' and the manner in which I treat the clergy delights them very much." For a clergyman's family, Edmund Bertram must have been a great improvement on Mr. Collins. Peace was being celebrated with a will. The Tsar Alexander of Russia and his ally the King of Prussia came to visit England with a long train of generals, statesmen and minor princes, and Jane warned Cassandra, "Take care of yourself, and do not be trampled to death in running after the Emperor. The report in Alton yesterday was that they would certainly travel this road either to or from Portsmouth." The English were wild with joy, and the only blot on the festivities was the fact that the unfortunate Prince Regent was hissed wherever he went by the supporters of his wife, Princess Caroline. "I long to know," said Jane Austen cryptically, "what this bow of the Prince's will produce." There is no letter to tell us whether the Chawton household did, in fact, see the European potentates driving by in state on their way to or from London.

Frank was busy with the naval review at Portsmouth, and Jane hoped that Fanny would see the Emperor. And, "Henry at White's! Oh, what a Henry!" White's was one of the most famous clubs of the day, and this must have been a social step up in the world for Henry, perhaps a dangerously expensive one. Apparently Jane and Cassandra were beginning to hope he would marry again, for Jane goes on, "I do not know what to wish as to Miss B., so I will hold my tongue and my wishes."

That summer Anna Austen was occupying herself through what seems to have been a rather indefinitely prolonged engagement by starting a novel of her own, which she sent to her Aunt Jane by instalments for her advice. We must be grateful to her, for it elicited some fascinating comments. "I do not like a lover's speaking in the third person — it is too much like the formal part of Lord Orville, [in Fanny Burney's *Evelina*] and I think is not natural." And then, the established author, the kind and modest aunt goes on, "If *you* think differently however, you need not mind me — I am impatient for more."

More came, and Jane Austen continued encouraging. "*I* read it aloud — and we are all very much amused." She apologised for having been slow in answering a set of questions Anna had sent her. Surprisingly, she did not like Anna's new title, *Which is the Heroine*, so well as the old one, *Enthusiasm*, but then she had only just moved on from the abstract, Johnsonian type of title herself. She was full of practical help. There were no "blunders about Dawlish", but Lyme was too far from it and she had put Starcross instead. She had corrected some minor social errors, and, tactfully, "I *do* think you had better omit Lady Helena's postscript; — to those who are acquainted with *Pride and Prejudice* it will seem an imitation." She also advised Anna not to take her characters to Ireland. "Let the Portmans go to Ireland, but as you know nothing of the manners there, you had better not go with them. You will be in danger of giving false representations. Stick to Bath and the Foresters. There you will be quite at home." And then, Aunt Cassandra "does not like desultory novels, and is rather fearful yours will be too much so" but, "I allow much more latitude than she does — and think nature and spirit cover many sins of a wandering story."

The next letter raises some objections: "more than you will like". There are small points of etiquette and, more serious, "Your descriptions are often more minute than will be liked. You give too many particulars of right hand and left." It is a failing that could never be attributed to Jane Austen herself. Then comes a famous piece of praise: "You are now collecting your people delightfully, getting them exactly into such a spot as is the delight of my life; — three or four families in a country village is the very thing to work on ... You are but *now* coming to the heart and beauty of your book; till the heroine grows up, the fun must be imperfect." It is pleasant to think that Jane Austen thought in terms of "fun" for both author and reader. The young author was perhaps feeling her oats, for her aunt felt it necessary to caution her on a point of style. "Devereux Forester's being ruined by his vanity is extremely good; but I wish you would not let him plunge into a 'vortex of dissipation'. I do not object to the thing," went on practical Aunt Jane, "but I cannot bear the expression — it is such thorough novel slang — and so old, that I daresay Adam met with it in the first novel he opened."

Waverley had just been published anonymously, but Jane Austen was in no doubt as to the author. "Walter Scott has no business to write novels, especially good ones — It is not fair — He had fame and profit enough as a poet, and should not be taking the bread out of other people's mouths — I do not like him, and do not mean to like *Waverley* if I can help it — but fear I must ... I have made up my mind to like no novels really, but Miss Edgeworth's, yours and my own." Unfortunately, Anna's book does not survive, so we cannot fully appreciate her aunt's meticulous criticism. Many years later, after Jane Austen's death she got out the manuscript they had worked over together, and burned it.

Henry moved from Henrietta Street to Hans Place that summer, and Jane actually went up by herself in the public coach to visit him, and wrote a cheerful report of the journey to Cassandra: "It put me in mind of my own coach between Edinburgh and Stirling." Jane could rely on Cassandra to recognise the reference to the young man in *Love and Friendship* who spent all his wife's money, sold everything they had except their coach, and made his living by driving to and fro between Edinburgh and Stirling. Henry had been visiting Godmersham and could tell Jane about the Canterbury Races and Fanny's partners at the grand ball that accompanied them. Mr. Plumtre was still in evidence.

Jane apparently had had doubts about Henry's new house in Hans Place but, "Having got rid of my unreasonable ideas, I find more space and comfort in the rooms that I had supposed, and the garden is quite a love." One tends to forget how London still blended into country. Henry's move may have indicated serious thoughts of re-marriage, for Jane writes, "Henry wants me to see more of his Hanwell favourite, and has written to invite her to spend a day or two here with me ... I am more and more convinced that he will marry again soon, and like the idea of *her* better than anybody else in hand." The "Hanwell favourite" was

Miss Eliza Moore of Hanwell, who reappears later in the letters, but in fact Henry did not remarry until 1820, three years after Jane's death.

Henry was to take Jane home to Chawton, and she was there in September when they received the news of the death of Charles's wife Fanny on the birth of her fourth child. She died at the Nore, where Charles was stationed, and their older daughter, "that puss Cassy", spent a good deal of time from then on with her grandmother and aunts at Chawton. Charles, left with three motherless girls, finally married Fanny's sister Harriet, who had helped to look after them, in 1820, a good year for Austen marriages. There is no letter from Jane to Cassandra about their sister-in-law's death, but, writing to Anna, she seems mainly concerned about its effect on their mother, who "does not seem the worse now for the shock". It meant a temporary end to the public reading aloud of Anna's book, but, "I have read it to your Aunt Cassandra however — in our own room at night, while we undressed — and with a great deal of pleasure." It is one of those small, important reminders of the intensely private life that the two sisters lived together in their tiny back bedroom at Chawton.

While Anna Austen wrote for advice about her novel, Fanny Knight needed it on a more serious subject. Henry had been right in suspecting a romance between her and John Plumtre, and apparently she had talked to her Aunt Jane about her feelings when they were in London together in the summer. Now, in November, she had changed her mind about the suitor her aunt had earlier described as "a very amiable young man, only too diffident to be so agreeable as he might be". Fanny's letter has not survived, but it had surprised her aunt very much. "What strange creatures we are! — It seems as if your being secure of him (as you say yourself) had made you indifferent." Fanny's was a serious situation: "What is to be done? You certainly *have* encouraged him to such a point as to make him feel almost secure of you." Jane went on to plead the young man's cause eloquently. His difficulty seems to have been a lack of manner, particularly when compared with Fanny's own "agreeable, idle brothers". But, said Jane, "Wisdom is better than wit, and in the long run will certainly have the laugh on her side." It sounds as if John Plumtre would have just done for Fanny Price. "As to there being any objection from his *goodness*," said Jane Austen, "from the danger of his becoming even Evangelical, I cannot admit *that*. I am by no means convinced that we ought not all to be Evangelicals."

And then, like the good aunt and intelligent woman that she was, she turned round and argued the other side of the case. "Anything is to be preferred or endured rather than marrying without affection; and if his deficiencies of manner &c &c strike you more than all his good qualities, if you continue to think strongly of them, give him up at once . . . I have no doubt of his suffering a good deal for a time . . . but it is no creed of mine, as you must be well aware, that such sort of disappointments kill anybody." And, in a postscript, the woman of genius reduced the situation to its true proportions: "Your trying to excite your own feelings by a visit to his room amused me excessively — The dirty shaving rag was exquisite! — Such a circumstance ought to be in print. Much too good to be lost." Nor was it. Did Fanny recognise herself in Harriet Smith and her court-plaster?

The two letters Jane Austen wrote to Fanny that autumn about John Plumtre give one a frightening picture of the total lack of privacy in her life. This was a subject, apparently, that must be kept secret even from Cassandra, and when the first letter arrived, "Luckily your Aunt Cassandra dined at the other house, therefore I had not to manoeuvre away from *her* — and as to anybody else, I do not care." In her next letter, Jane warned her niece to "write *something* that may do to be read or told". Motherless Fanny wanted her aunt to make up her mind for her, but Jane Austen had too much sense for that. "You frighten me out of my wits by your reference. Your affection gives me the highest pleasure, but indeed you must not let anything depend on my opinion. Your own feelings and none but your own, should determine such an important point." She urged Fanny not to engage herself. "I should not be afraid of your *marrying him*," she said wisely. "With all his worth, you would soon love him enough for the happiness of both; but I should dread the continuance of this sort of tacit engagement, with such an uncertainty as there is, of *when* it may be completed — Years may pass, before he is independent — You like him well enough to marry, but not well enough to wait . . . nothing can be compared to the misery of being bound *without* love, bound to one, and preferring another." Here speaks the voice of wisdom.

Fanny chose the path of caution. John Plumtre survived his disappointment, married someone else in 1818, and was returned as Member of Parliament for East Kent in the Reform Parliament of 1832. The episode may have shaken Fanny more than she and her aunt expected. She remained single until 1820, when she married a cousin, Sir Edward Knatchbull, as his second wife. By then, there was no Aunt Jane to consult, so we do not know whether he was "the creature you and I should think perfection, where grace and spirit are united to worth, where the manners are equal to the heart and understanding". Probably not. Fanny was twenty-seven by then, and Sir Edward thirty-nine.

Meanwhile, the other grown-up niece, James's Anna, married her Ben Lefroy at last that November in a quiet winter wedding described later by her half-sister, Caroline. Though Chawton was only sixteen miles from Steventon, and Frank was staying at the Great House, the Austen ladies did not go to the wedding, but Jane visited Henry in Hans Place later that month and went to call on the young couple, who were living at Hendon. Her second letter of advice to Fanny was written from Henry's house and mentioned the visit. Anna had bought herself an unexpected purple pelisse and meant to buy a piano, which had shocked an aunt hardened to doing everything in public. "I suspect nothing worse than its being got in secret and not owned to anybody— She is capable of that, you know." This oddly sharp note suggests that something went wrong between Anna and her aunt and friendly critic that autumn. Perhaps it was simply that this was the first marriage to take place in the next generation of Austens, and came as an inevitable shock to the confirmed maiden aunt, but there was probably more to it. Anna was not an easy character, and the circumstances of her engagement had not been easy either.

After the first visit, Anna invited her aunt to come back and stay for a night, but this was declined in a civil bread-and-butter note. "We all came away very much pleased with our visit I assure you." Edward was hopeful that Mr. Baverstock's lawsuit was to be settled, and Jane was sorry not to have a chance to see a letter Anna had had from a cousin. "I like first cousins to be first cousins, and interested about each other. They are but one remove from brother and sister." The relationship of brother and sister, or sister and sister, was, for Jane Austen, perhaps the deepest of all. She had celebrated it, in *Mansfield Park*, in the happy reunion of Fanny and William Price. "Children of the same family, the same blood, with the same first associations and habits, have some means of enjoyment in their power, which no subsequent connections can supply; and it must be by a long and unnatural estrangement, by a divorce which no subsequent connection can justify, if such precious remains of the earliest attachments are ever entirely outlived." They never were among the Austens. The attachments that were outlived seem to have been those between children and parents.

On this visit, Jane was exerting herself to make friends with Henry's "Hanwell favourite", Eliza Moore, and her sister. "At my time of life," she confessed to Fanny, "it is uphill work to be talking to those whom one knows so little." And, of Eliza, "We shall not have two ideas in common. She is young, pretty, chattering, and thinking chiefly (I presume) of dress, company, and admiration."

It was at about this time in Jane Austen's life that Miss Mitford quoted that famous remark of her mother's about the husband-hunting butterfly in a letter and went on to say:

A friend of mine who visits her now, says that she has stiffened into the most perpendicular precise, taciturn piece of "single blessedness" that ever existed, and that, till *Pride and Prejudice* showed what a precious gem was hidden in that unbending case, she was no more regarded in society than a poker or a fire-screen, or any other thin, upright piece of wood or iron that fills the corner in peace and quietness. The case is very different now: she is still a poker — but a poker of whom everyone is afraid. It must be confessed that this silent observation from such an observer is rather formidable . . . A wit, a delineator of character, who does not talk, is terrific indeed!

Two things must be remembered in connection with this portrait of the author as a fierce spinster. One is that the source quoted was a connection of the Mr. Baverstock who was suing Edward for his Hampshire estates, the other, and more important, is that Jane Austen was shy. She never wanted to be lionised, and even after Henry had betrayed the secret of her authorship, she would not be drawn into the kind of social life that would have been open to the author of *Pride and Prejudice*. She refused a chance to meet Madame de Staël, though she had read and enjoyed her books, and it is more than probable that Miss Mitford's acquaintance had made some unfortunate attempt at "drawing out" the new lion and had been snubbed with the quiet ruthlessness of which one can imagine the author of *Mansfield Park* capable.

In the family, it was different. Anna Austen remembered joking so much with her Aunt Jane over their work that Cassandra finally, with streaming eyes, begged them to stop, but she also remembered that when Aunt Jane was grave, she was very grave indeed, graver even than Aunt Cassandra. These are the two sides of the same picture. Like Elizabeth Bennet, Jane Austen allowed herself to be diverted by "follies and nonsense, whims and inconsistencies", and laughed at them whenever she could. Laughter, and its sharper cousin, irony, were Jane Austen's defence against the pressures of society, as Marvin Mudrick has pointed out in *Jane Austen. Irony as Defense and Discovery*. But true laughter and true irony both need a moral basis, and when this was threatened, Jane Austen stopped laughing. Then she was grave, graver even than Aunt Cassandra. Social pretentiousness, like everything else that rang false, might well have turned her into that "poker of whom everyone is afraid".

Lion or no, Miss Jane Austen, the author, was having a rather frustrating time that autumn. The small edition of *Mansfield Park* (probably only fifteen hundred copies) was sold out, she told Fanny, but it was doubtful whether she and Egerton would "hazard a second edition . . . People are more ready to borrow and praise, than to buy — which I cannot wonder at — but though I like praise as well as anybody, I like what Edward calls *pewter* too." She and Henry had a final meeting with Egerton, but it proved unsatisfactory. The second edition of *Mansfield Park* was brought out, at last, in 1816 by the famous publisher Murray, to whom Jane Austen moved after considerable negotiation in the course of the next year. For the moment, she had a right to be discouraged, and it seems to have affected the progress of *Emma*. Writing once more to Anna about her novel she congratulated her on getting on so fast. "I wish other people of my acquaintance could compose as rapidly."

There is a happy tone in this letter which suggests that whatever the trouble had been between Anna and her aunt, it was over. "St. Julian's history was quite a surprise to me," said Jane. "You had not very long known it yourself I suspect — but I have no objection to make to the circumstance — it is very well told — and his having been in love with the aunt, gives Cecilia an additional interest with him. I like the idea — a very proper compliment to an aunt! — I rather imagine indeed that nieces are seldom chosen but in compliment to some aunt or other. I dare say Ben was in love with me once, and would never have thought of *you* if he had not supposed me dead of a scarlet fever." This is Austen-nonsense at its happiest. Jane Austen was accommodating herself to the new position of senior aunt, as well as to the vagaries of her married niece.

❧ 14 ❧

Jane Austen may have been momentarily discouraged, in the autumn of 1814, about her progress with *Emma*, but Cassandra's dates show that it was, in fact, written more quickly than any of her previous books. Begun in January 1814, it was finished in March 1815, and published that December. *Sense and Sensibility* and *Pride and Prejudice*, of course, had been revised and revised again over the years, while *Mansfield Park* had been begun about February 1811, and finished in the summer of 1813. Even then it had not been published until the following May.

With *Emma*, Jane Austen seems to have taken a great step forward in her confidence as a writer. It is clear from her letters that she had been thinking about it as far back as least as the autumn of 1813, and probably earlier. Her usual habit, as David Rhydderch has pointed out in *Jane Austen. Her Life and Art*, was to work on three books at once. "Having milled one work, she begins another during the process of refining a second. The drudgery of correcting one, and ironing the other, was relieved by creating a third." He quotes *Emma* as the great exception to this, but it seems reasonable to assume that she was already thinking about it while she finished *Mansfield Park* in the spring and summer of 1813, and during that autumn. Once one is used to have a set of fictional characters always at the back of one's mind, to be taken up and thought about when the opportunity offers, it is hard to do without them, and Jane Austen would have needed the private half of her double life during the busy summer months at Chawton and the last long autumn visit to Godmersham. As with *Mansfield Park*, she began the actual writing of *Emma* in the quiet of winter, but *Emma*, her most perfect, if not necessarily her most likeable book, reads as if it had been well and truly planned in advance.

162

Unfortunately, there are no letters for 1815 until September, and the only reference to the composition of *Emma* is that one deprecatory one to Anna, "I wish other people of my acquaintance could compose as rapidly." Lacking letters for that eventful spring and summer of 1815, we do not know how the Austen ladies bore the anxiety of the new war that followed Napoleon's escape from Elba. The occupants of the house on the busy Southampton road must have been intensely aware of the build-up of men and material in Flanders. Charles was on active service in the Mediterranean, where Napoleon's brother-in-law Murat had broken faith with the Allies, who had confirmed him in his position as King of Naples. Charles came through the resultant hostilities unscathed, and was able to write to Jane in May 1815 from Palermo that he had met a young man called Fox, who said that "nothing had come out for years to be compared with *Pride and Prejudice, Sense and Sensibility* ... That you may not be too much elated at this morsel of praise, I shall add that he did not appear to like *Mansfield Park* so well as the two first, in which, however, I believe he is singular." The young man in question was Charles James Fox's nephew, and son of Lord Holland, whose wife used to read Jane Austen's novels aloud to her husband when his gout was bad.

Meanwhile, Anna Lefroy and her husband had moved to a house called Wyards, within walking distance of Chawton, and in September Jane wrote to change the arrangements for a visit to her. Charles's motherless eldest daughter Cassy was living at Chawton at the time, and, given a choice between going to the Alton fair or going to Wyards, she had "preferred the former, which we trust will not greatly affront you — if it does, you may hope that some little Anna hereafter may revenge the insult by a similar preference of an Alton Fair to her Cousin Cassy." Anna, in fact, bore her first child, a girl, that October.

Jane was off to London with Henry to conclude the negotiations for a change of publisher. She wrote Cassandra from Hans Place that, "Mr. Murray's letter is come. He is a rogue of course, but a civil one. He offers £450 but wants to have the copyright of *Mansfield Park* and *Sense and Sensibility* included. It will end in my publishing for myself I daresay." Henry's answer to this letter of Murray's has been preserved. The style is characteristic.

Your official opinion of the merits of *Emma* is very valuable and satisfactory ... the quantum of your commendation rather exceeds than falls short of the author's expectation and my own. The terms you offer are so very inferior to what we had expected that I am apprehensive of having made some great error in my arithmetical calculation . . . the sum offered by you for the copyright of *Sense and Sensibility*, *Mansfield Park*, and *Emma* is not equal to the money which my sister has actually cleared by one very moderate edition of *Mansfield Park* — (you yourself expressed astonishment that so small an edition of such a work should have been sent into the world) — and a still smaller one of *Sense and Sensibility*.

Henry had to dictate this letter. He was suffering from what his sister described as "a bilious attack with fever . . . He is calomeling and therefore in a way to be better and I hope may be well tomorrow." But next day Jane changed her tune. "Henry's illness is more serious than I expected." She had sent for Mr. Haden, "the apothecary from the corner of Sloane Street", who "calls it a general inflammation". In accordance with the barbarous medical practice of the time, Haden had taken "twenty ounces of blood from Henry last night, and nearly as much more this morning, and expects to have to bleed him again tomorrow — but he assures me that he found him *quite* as much better today as he expected."
Henry was an excellent patient, she said, and she was still hopeful of getting home soon. Meanwhile, she was busy cancelling engagements. She had put off Edward's boys "till Friday. I have a strong idea of their uncle's being well enough to like seeing them by that time." She proved over-optimistic. Henry grew worse instead of better and Jane's anxious letters brought James and Cassandra hurrying up from Hampshire, and Edward and Fanny from Godmersham. At the end of October, Jane was still nursing Henry and had felt it necessary to write a "preparatory letter" to the Leigh Perrots at Scarlets. She mentioned this to her ten-year-old niece Caroline. James's younger daughter, who was staying at Chawton, had started writing in her turn, and had, inevitably, sent the manuscript to her aunt. Busy nursing her brother, Jane had "not yet felt quite equal to taking up your manuscript", and hoped her "detaining it so long will be no inconvenience". She congratulated Caroline (Anna Lefroy's half-sister) on having become an aunt. "I have always maintained the importance of aunts as much as possible, and I am sure of your doing the same now." She signed herself, "Believe me my dear Sister-Aunt, Yours affectionately J. Austen." It was almost a prophecy. Caroline, the most intelligent of the nieces, lived and died a spinster like her Sister-Aunt.
Terms for *Emma* had been agreed with Murray at last. Murray's friend

and adviser, William Gifford, had been full of praise both for *Pride and Prejudice* and for *Emma*. "I have for the first time looked into *Pride and Prejudice* and it is really a very pretty thing. No dark passages; no secret chambers; no wind-howlings in long galleries; no drops of blood upon a rusty dagger – things that should now be left to ladies' maids and sentimental washerwomen." And, "Of *Emma*, I have nothing but good to say. I was sure of the writer before you mentioned her." Praise from Gifford, the editor of the *Quarterly Review*, was praise indeed. What is surprising is that Murray's reaction was so cautious, but he may well have been influenced by the lack of critical reaction to *Mansfield Park*. And Jane Austen, preoccupied with Henry's illness, was very likely glad to settle the matter by accepting his offer of publication on a commission basis. It was probably just as expensive, and just as understandable a mistake as her outright sale of *Pride and Prejudice*. With only ten per cent of the profits at stake, John Murray the second does not seem to have over-exerted himself in publicising *Emma*. It is significant that Samuel Smiles' *Memoir of John Murray*, with nearly two columns each in its index for Lord Byron and Sir Walter Scott, has just four references for Jane Austen.

On the other hand, Jane Austen, like his other authors, found John Murray an agreeable publisher to deal with. Gifford, pointing out that the manuscript of *Emma*, "though plainly written, has yet some, indeed many little omissions", had offered to revise it. Jane Austen certainly refused this offer, and corrected her own proofs, complaining, as authors will, of the printer's delays, but her letters to Murray himself are increasingly friendly. He lent her books, and gave her good advice; the pity of it is that it did not occur to him to give *Emma* the same kind of pre-publication publicity that he gave *Childe Harold*. But then, the cases were very different. Perhaps if Jane Austen had gone to him with *Pride and Prejudice* it would have been another story.

Meanwhile, a disconcerting thing happened to Jane Austen. Henry continued so ill that Mr. Haden's ministrations had been supplemented by those of one of the Prince Regent's physicians, probably Sir William Knighton, who soon discovered that the sister who was nursing his patient so devotedly was in fact Miss Austen, the author. The Prince Regent, he told her, was a great admirer of her novels and kept a set in every one of his residences. While Jane Austen was recovering from this tribute from the man of whose wife she had written, "Poor woman, I shall support her as long as I can, because she *is* a woman, and because I hate her husband," a further surprise followed. She received a visit from the Prince Regent's librarian, a pompous Mr. Clarke, who invited her to

Carlton House, explaining (as the author of the *Memoir* put it) that he had "the Prince's instructions to show her the library and other apartments, and to pay her every possible attention". He sounds, at least in James Edward Austen-Leigh's report, so like Mr. Collins, that Jane Austen must have felt that one of her characters had come disconcertingly to life.

Worse was to follow. In the course of the visit to Carlton House, which duly took place, Mr. Clarke intimated to Miss Austen that she was at liberty to dedicate her next novel to the Prince Regent. Jane Austen must have been appalled. It is hard to imagine a more unsuitable dedication for *Emma*. Caroline tells us that she had no idea of acting on the permission to dedicate until told by her friends that it was tantamount to a command. She then wrote a masterly little note to Mr. Clarke, asking "whether it is incumbent on me to show my sense of the honour, by inscribing the work now in the press to His Royal Highness; I should be equally concerned," she went on, "to appear either presumptuous or ungrateful."

Edward had taken Cassandra home to Chawton on Henry's beginning to recover, and a letter to her provides a gloss to this. "I hope you have told Martha of my first resolution of letting nobody know that I *might* dedicate, &c for fear of being obliged to do it — and that she is thoroughly convinced of my being influenced now by nothing but the most mercenary motives." Resigning herself to the inevitable, she used the dedication as a spur to Murray's dilatory printers, and received "a fine compliment in return".

She had also received Mr. Clarke's reply by return. His letter settled the question of the dedication and went on to urge her to write a book about "an English clergyman . . . of the present day, fond of and entirely engaged in literature, no man's enemy but his own", in short, himself. He received a more interesting answer than he deserved. Jane Austen wrote to him early in December, when *Emma* was about to be published, the unavoidable dedication having been taken care of in an exchange of letters with Murray. She was suffering from an author's inevitable qualms at such a time. "My greatest anxiety at present is that this fourth work should not disgrace what was good in the others . . . I am very strongly haunted with the idea that to those readers who have preferred *Pride and Prejudice* it will appear inferior in wit, and to those who have preferred *Mansfield Park* very inferior in good sense." She went on, courteously but firmly, to declare herself incapable of writing the book he wanted about a clergyman. "A classical education, or at any rate a very extensive acquaintance with English literature, ancient and modern, appears to me quite indispensable for the person who would do any justice to your clergyman; and I think I may boast myself to be, with all possible vanity, the most

unlearned and uninformed female who ever dared to be an authoress."
Readers who take this claim seriously, do so at their peril.

Mr. Clarke was unsnubbable. Thanking her for the Prince Regent's
presentation copy of *Emma*, he returned to the attack. "Do let us have an
English Clergyman after *your* fancy ... show dear madam what good
would be done if tithes were taken away entirely, and describe him
burying his own mother—as I did ... Carry your clergyman to sea as a
friend of some distinguished naval character about a court ..." And so on.
Jane Austen probably made a note for her *Plan of a Novel*, and returned to
the serious business of nursing Henry back to health. An acute psycholo-
gist before the industry had acquired its technical terms, she recognised
that anxiety about his bank was probably retarding his recovery. "I
wonder that with such business to worry him, he can be getting better, but
he certainly does gain strength." 1815, with the war over at last, and the
inevitable post-war depression setting in, was not a good year for banks.
1816 was to be a worse one.

Mr. Haden was still in devoted attendance, not only on his patient but
on Jane and Fanny. He was on visiting terms now, and Jane wrote
Cassandra that they were looking forward to a quiet evening with him
and Henry's partner, Mr. Tilson. Unfortunately a couple of ladies of their
acquaintance offered themselves for tea. "Here is an end of our extreme
felicity in our dinner guest—I am heartily sorry they are coming! It will
be an evening spoilt to Fanny and me." Jane Austen and Fanny Knight
could recognise quality when they met it, even in an apothecary. Charles
Thomas Haden was to introduce the stethoscope and was a well-known
amateur of music. "I have been listening to dreadful insanity," said Jane
Austen. "It is Mr. Haden's firm belief that a person *not* musical is fit for
every sort of wickedness. I ventured to assert a little on the other side,
but wished the cause in abler hands." For once she had found someone
outside the family to whom she could really talk. "Mr. Haden," she
reported after the dinner party, "brought good manners and clever
conversation ..." She went on to describe "Fanny and Mr. Haden
in two chairs (I *believe* at least they had *two* chairs) talking together
uninterruptedly." And then, a significant note, "Fanny has heard all that
I have said to you about herself and Mr. H."

Cassandra, in Hampshire, seems to have injected a note of caution in her
answer to this letter, and her sister took her up on it. "You seem to be
under a mistake as to Mr. H.—You call him an apothecary; he is no
apothecary, he has never been an apothecary, there is not an apothecary in
this neighbourhood—... he is a Haden, nothing but a Haden, a sort of

wonderful nondescript creature on two legs, something between a man and an angel – but without the least spice of an apothecary." One can only wonder what really happened to that happy trio round the invalid's bed. Lord Brabourne quotes from his mother's diary: "Mr. Haden, a delightful, clever, musical Haden, comes every evening, and is agreeable." And that is the end of Mr. Haden, except that he must have married soon afterwards, for his son, later a prominent doctor and artist, and ultimately Sir Francis Seymour Haden, was born in 1818.

Edward had been staying in Hampshire while his daughter kept her aunt company in Hans Place, but perhaps some warning from Cassandra brought him to town to take Fanny home to Godmersham on December 8th. Henry was much better by now, but old Mrs. Austen was unwell. "I am sorry my mother has been suffering," Jane wrote, "and am afraid this exquisite weather is too good to agree with her! – *I* enjoy it all over me, from top to toe, from right to left, longitudinally, perpendicularly, diagonally." But in fact, she had overtired herself nursing her brother, and, whatever she says, it is hard to imagine him as the easiest of invalids. Altogether, what with Henry's illness, the Prince Regent and Mr. Clarke, and, perhaps most tiring of all, Fanny and Mr. Haden, this must have been an exhausting winter. She actually felt unwell enough in the course of it to consult a doctor, but we do not know who, or what he said.

Jane had been to see Charles's younger, motherless daughters, who were with their Aunt Harriet (later his second wife) in Keppel Street, and sent messages to their sister Cassy, at Chawton. She was doing errands as usual, "encountering the miseries of Grafton House to get a purple frock for Eleanor Bridges". But she still found time to thank Caroline Austen for another instalment of her book. "I wish I could finish stories as fast as you can." And, in a short, straight note, returning some books, she said goodbye to "our precious" Mr. Haden. "As we were out ourselves yesterday evening we were glad to find you had not called – but shall depend upon your giving us some part of this evening – I leave town early on Saturday, and must say 'goodbye' to you." Fanny was gone, and Jane was going. Whatever had happened, was over.

Emma was announced for publication in December 1815, but no reviews of it appeared until the following spring and summer. *Sense and Sensibility* and *Pride and Prejudice* had been reviewed sooner than this, and the delay must have been maddening for an author still smarting under the critics' total silence about *Mansfield Park*. And when they came, the reviews were on the tepid side. The book was described as "harmless amusement" by the *Monthly Review*, while the *British Critic*'s reviewer

Chawton Cottage, where Jane Austen spent the last years of her life
(*Photo British Travel Association*)

Jane Austen's niece Fanny Knight. Portrait by Cassandra Austen. By courtesy of the Jane Austen Society

(*Photo J. Butler-Kearney*)

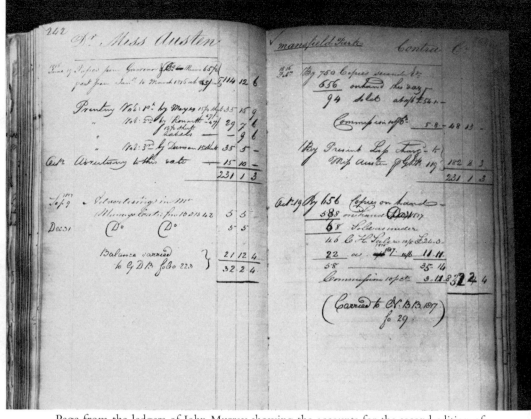

Page from the ledgers of John Murray showing the accounts for the second edition of
Mansfield Park. By courtesy of John Murray

The circulating library in Milsom Street, Bath (*Photo Courtauld Institute of Ar*

Dr. Miss Austen

Emma   Contra.   Cr

Page from the ledgers of John Murray showing the accounts for the first edition of *Emma*.
By courtesy of John Murray

The house in College Street, Winchester, where Jane Austen died. By courtesy of the Jane Austen Society   (*Photo J. Butler-Kearney*)

said that, "It rarely happens that in a production of this nature we have so little to find fault with." *The Gentleman's Magazine* was equally lukewarm. "If *Emma* be not allowed to rank in the very highest class of modern novels, it certainly may claim at least a distinguished degree of eminence in that species of composition. It is amusing, if not instructive; and has no tendency to deteriorate the heart."

But there was comfort in the *Quarterly Review*, which was published by Murray himself. He had written to Sir Walter Scott, "Have you any fancy to dash off an article on *Emma*? It wants incident and romance does it not?" Perhaps Murray thought less highly of *Emma* than Gifford. At least Scott obliged with an unsigned review which appeared in the issue dated October 1815, but only, in fact, published the following March. He began with a general discussion of the value of novels in a passage which may or may not have antedated Jane Austen's own defence of the novel in *Northanger Abbey*. He went on to speak favourably of *Sense and Sensibility* and *Pride and Prejudice*, and then turned to describe *Emma* as "a story which we pursue with more pleasure, if not with deep interest, and which perhaps we might more willingly resume than one of those narratives where the attention is strongly riveted, during the first perusal, by the powerful excitement of curiosity." He congratulated the author on "the force of a narrative conducted with much neatness and point, and a quiet yet comic dialogue, in which the characters of the speakers evolve themselves with dramatic effect." But, alas for Miss Bates, he found that the comic characters became tedious. He was to improve, later, on this rather lukewarm praise. Writing his diary in March of 1826, he said that Jane Austen "had a talent for describing the involvements and feelings and characters of ordinary life which is to me the most wonderful I ever met with." But by then she had been dead nine years.

On April 1st, 1816, Jane Austen returned the copy of the *Quarterly Review* that Murray had lent her, "with many thanks. The authoress of *Emma* has no reason, I think, to complain of her treatment in it, except in the total omission of *Mansfield Park*. I cannot but be sorry that so clever a man as the reviewer of *Emma* should consider it as unworthy of being noticed. You will be pleased to hear that I have received the Prince's thanks for the *handsome* copy I sent him of *Emma*. Whatever he may think of *my* share of the work, yours seems to have been quite right."

In fact, the reception of *Emma* was disappointing, like that of *Mansfield Park*, and the reason is not far to seek. In these two books, Jane Austen had made the mistake so many authors do. After acquiring a public for her light-hearted early works, she changed her tune and wrote two totally adult books. And, by sheer bad luck, the publication of the early novels had been so long delayed that *Mansfield Park* and *Emma* followed as if in natural and immediate succession. No wonder if her readers were surprised. It had been easy to enjoy the surface brilliance and charm, particularly of *Pride and Prejudice*, without taking too much notice of the low, enduring moral note against which the comedy beats out its happy tune. *Sense and Sensibility* and *Pride and Prejudice* can, and often have been treated simply as romantic comedies, and for one reviewer who compares Elizabeth Bennet to Shakespeare's Beatrice there are always half a dozen to accuse Jane Austen of celebrating nothing better than the "husband hunt". *Mansfield Park*, inevitably, confounds them. Fanny Price can be accused of many things, but not of hunting husbands. If she had been on the hunt, she would have married Henry Crawford. The hunting is left to Mary Crawford and the Bertram girls, and very unsuccessful they are at it.

In *Emma*, the whole situation has been turned, ironically, upside-down. Emma hunts husbands—for other people, and nearly destroys her own happiness in the process. The author of the *Memoir* quotes Jane Austen as describing Emma as a "heroine whom no one but myself will much like", and, in fact, certainly in the first half of the book, one rather suspects that even Jane Austen does not much like her. She may be "my Emma" to Mrs. Weston, but she is not to Jane Austen, as Fanny Price was "my Fanny" and Elinor Dashwood "my Elinor". If *Mansfield Park* is Jane Austen's most moral book, *Emma* is her least feminine one, and it is not surprising that it is often preferred by men. In *Beyond Culture*, Lionel Trilling remarks, with a touch of surprise, that Emma has "a moral life as a man has a moral life". Her charm, he says, is based on self-love, and "women in fiction only rarely have the peculiar reality of the moral life that self-love bestows. Most commonly they exist in a moonlike way, shining by the reflected moral light of men." As so often when Jane Austen is the subject, the criticism tells us at least as much about the critic as about the book, but it is none the less perceptive for that. In *The Watsons*, Jane Austen had tried a serious approach to the problem of the husband hunt and had apparently recognised defeat. In *Emma* she turns it into high, ironic comedy. The book might easily have been called *Match-making*, with even Mr. Knightley taking part in the game, when he sends Robert Martin to London after his Harriet. There is not much romance about *Emma*. The romantic, or Cinderella theme has been relegated to a couple of sub-plots, where Harriet Smith and Jane Fairfax work out their destinies as best they may, with a maximum of interference from a heroine with whom her creator refuses to identify herself. Here Lionel Trilling goes wide of the mark. It has been thought, he says, that in the portrait of Emma there is "an air of confession", that in drawing her, Jane Austen was taking account of something offensive that she and others had observed in her own earlier manner and conduct.

It is an extraordinary suggestion. Emma is practically everything that Jane Austen was not. Where Jane Austen was poor, shy, and one of eight, Emma is rich, spoiled, over-confident and to all intents and purposes an only child. Most important of all, where Jane Austen was a realist, Emma is a snob, and a stupid one at that. Where Jane Austen could recognise quality in Mr. Haden, or Elizabeth Bennet bad manners in Lady Catherine, Emma's criteria are purely social. As a result, she is incorrigibly, almost wilfully wrong in her judgments about people, and Jane Austen appears to take pleasure in showing her up over this, as when she wonders whether she will condescend to accept an invitation from the Coles, and is then taken aback when the invitation does not arrive. The real triumph of the book is that Jane Austen has managed to make this unpromising heroine sympathetic, not only to most men, who, as she herself has said, like a woman to be a bit of a fool, but to many women. This is largely because Emma is prepared to learn by experience, when once it has hit her hard enough. Like Marianne Dashwood before her, she ends by reversing all her own first principles, and it is a pleasure to watch her.

As rich and subtle as *Mansfield Park*, *Emma* has a lightness of tone that is notably absent from the story of Fanny Price. This is Jane Austen's purest and driest comedy. Where *Mansfield Park* dealt in adultery, elopement and corruption, the most wicked thing that happens in *Emma* is its heroine's own rudeness to Miss Bates at the famous picnic on Box Hill. It is a measure of the quality of the book that this one flippant, cruel remark carries a more convincing moral load than any of Maria or Julia Bertram's misbehaviour. It is the crucial point of the book, the moment when Emma turns her clear sight into herself for the first time. Jane Austen's books are always, to some extent, concerned with the problem of learning by painful experience, but in *Emma* this is the dominant theme, and the extraordinary richness of the book is due to the fact that so many of the characters are capable of doing so. Even Mr. Knightley, like Darcy before him, must learn to be teased by his wife. Emma learns to know herself, and the Emma she learns to know is delightful.

It is a curious thing that while *Pride and Prejudice* is constantly and unsuccessfully being dramatised, *Emma*, which is practically a drama as it stands, is seldom touched. Do producers fight shy of it because of the accusation of snobbery that is so frequently and unjustly levelled at it? Or does it strike them as lacking the vital element of melodrama? Perhaps when we see Ivy Compton-Burnett's novels, which claim their descent so directly from it, as a television series, we may see *Emma* put on again. The dialogue is some of the best Jane Austen wrote, which means it is some of the best in the English language, with even the breathless Miss Bates contributing vitally to the progress of the narrative. Altogether it is a brilliant book, technically an immense advance over *Pride and Prejudice*, and if one goes obstinately on preferring *Pride and Prejudice*, it is probably because the latter still has the glow of youth upon it. And yet, in one of those impossible desert island situations, I think, for one's single book, one would be wise to choose *Mansfield Park* or *Emma* rather even than *Pride and Prejudice*. "Wisdom is better than wit," as Jane Austen told Fanny, "and in the long run will certainly have the laugh on her side." People who begin by loving *Pride and Prejudice*, may end by rereading the later novels more often.

$$\begin{array}{c} \maltese \; 15 \; \maltese \end{array}$$

WHILE JANE AUSTEN WAS FINISHING *EMMA*, THAT EVENTFUL spring of 1815, she must also, as usual, have been busy planning her next book. Cassandra's note tells us that *Persuasion* was begun that summer, but it must have been laid aside in the autumn when Henry became ill. No doubt, Jane Austen made a new start on it when she got home at last in December; though once again she must have been interrupted by a visit she and Cassandra paid, at the turn of the year, to their old friends Mrs. Heathcote and her sister Miss Bigg, who were now settled at Winchester. Mrs. Heathcote's clergyman husband had died in 1802, and she and her sister had set up house in the Close at Winchester some time in 1814.

Jane and Cassandra went on from there to pay a short visit to the James Austens at Steventon, and it may well be from this time that some of Caroline Austen's memories of her aunt can be dated. Was it on this visit that she was told the ravishing stories she remembered about fairies who all had characters of their own? And did she keep "creeping up" to her aunt, until her mother warned her off? It seems likely. Before Jane Austen became, even to her quiet extent, what she called "a wild beast", it is doubtful if it would have occurred to Mrs. James Austen that her child's attentions could be any less welcome than the little Middletons' were to the Miss Steeles.

In fact, Jane Austen obviously welcomed eleven-year-old Caroline's affection. "She seemed to love you, and you loved her naturally in return," said Caroline. Several letters to her survive from this period, and one of them is worth quoting whole. "I wish I could finish stories as fast as you can—I am much obliged to you for the sight of Olivia, and think you have done for her very well; but the good for nothing father, who was the real author of all her faults and sufferings, should not escape unpunished. I hope *he* hung himself, or took the surname of *Bone* or underwent some direful penance or other." The secret of Jane Austen's success with children was simple: she treated them as equals. Another letter to Caroline, dated in March, 1816, carries on a lively discussion of *Olympe et Théophile* by Madame de Genlis. "You are quite my own niece in your feelings towards Madame de Genlis ... It really is too bad! — Not allowing them to be happy together, when they *are* married."

If Jane Austen had hoped to have silenced Mr. Clarke with her last letter, she had been mistaken. The egregious clergyman wrote to her again that March. He had just been appointed chaplain and secretary to Prince Leopold of Saxe-Coburg, who had arrived in England to marry the Prince Regent's heir, Princess Charlotte. Mr. Clarke thought that Jane Austen might like to dedicate her next book to Prince Leopold, and went on to say that, "Any historical romance, illustrative of the august house of Coburg, would just now be very interesting."

He received the answer he deserved. After the usual courtesies, Jane Austen went roundly to work with him.

> I am fully sensible, [she said] that an historical romance, founded on the House of Saxe-Coburg, might be much more to the purpose of profit or popularity than such pictures of domestic life in country villages as I deal in. But I could no more write a romance than an epic poem. I could not sit seriously down and write a serious romance under any other motive than to save my life; and if it were indispensable for me to keep it up and never relax into laughing at myself or other people, I am sure I should be hung before I had finished the first chapter. No, I must keep to my own style and go on in my own way; and though I may never succeed again in that, I am convinced that I should totally fail in any other.

Mansfield Park and *Emma* may not have been received with the acclaim they deserved, but Jane Austen had too much sense to let this influence her into a new start so drastic as the one Mr. Clarke suggested. On the other hand, *Persuasion* does, to an extent, hark back to the style of the earlier novels. In it, as in her two first published books, the love story is the dominant theme, with the moral issues relegated to the background. But whether this is due to a change in herself, or to her awareness of a falling off of enthusiasm in her audience, there is no way of knowing.

Some time in 1816 Henry bought back the long-lost *Susan* from Crosby for the ten pounds he had paid for it, and then had the pleasure of telling the dilatory publisher that the book he had neglected was by the author of *Pride and Prejudice* and *Sense and Sensibility*. It is significant that he chose to mention those two, rather than the more recently published *Mansfield Park* and *Emma*. This transaction probably took place in the early months of 1816, for in March disaster struck Henry. Jane had obviously been anxious about his affairs in the autumn when she was in Hans Place nursing him. It had been a bad time for him to be ill. Waterloo had brought both peace and financial crisis to the exhausted country. Hardest hit, as always, were the small men, whether in society or in business. A dramatic fall in the price of corn ruined small farmers and country banks alike, and in March the Alton bank with which Henry's London one had connections failed and dragged Austen, Maunde and Tilson down with it. Henry's bankruptcy was a family disaster. Edward Knight and James Leigh Perrot, who had stood sureties for twenty thousand and ten thousand pounds respectively when Henry became Receiver-General of Taxes for Oxfordshire, lost their money. Edward took it like the Austen and the gentleman he was, but James Leigh Perrot undoubtedly took it hard. Even Jane lost thirteen pounds, part of the profits from the first edition of *Mansfield Park*, which had been banked in Henrietta Street. Writing to thank Murray for the loan of the *Quarterly Review* with Scott's anonymous piece in it, she makes her only reference to Henry's disaster. "In consequence of the late event in Henrietta Street, I must request that if you should at any time have anything to communicate by letter, you will be so good as to write by the post, directing to me (Miss J. Austen), Chawton, near Alton: and that for anything of a larger bulk, you will add to the same direction, by Collier's Southampton coach." It was a far cry from the pseudonymous Mrs. Ashton Dennis.

In April, Miss Elizabeth Leigh, Thomas Leigh's sister and Cassandra's godmother, died. "We all feel that we have lost a most valued old friend," wrote Jane to Caroline, but added philosophically, "The death of a person at her advanced age, so fit to die and by her own feelings so *ready* to die, is not to be regretted." Despite the inevitable mourning, family visiting went on as usual. Henry had been down at Godmersham, doubtless being comforted in his bankruptcy by the brother whose twenty thousand pounds he had lost. And at the beginning of May, Edward, Fanny, and a little later, her brother Edward Knight junior were all coming to Chawton. Jane wanted to arrange a visit from James's Caroline to her cousin Cassy, who was with them as usual, but "we *must* wash before the Godmersham party come", so the visit would have to be a short one. Those were the days of the great spring wash.

175

It had been a long, hard winter. Henry's illness and bankruptcy had told on Jane, and so must anxiety about their "own particular brother" Charles, whose ship H.M.S. *Phoenix* was wrecked in a gale off Smyrna that February. No blame attached to him, but the episode must have been at once a setback to his career and a source of long worry to his family. At all events, it was at this time, according to the authors of the *Life*, that Jane's health began to fail, although she had already made at least one visit to a London physician when she was with Henry that winter. The first signs of trouble were probably digestive (she was later to speak of "bile" as the source of her complaint) and her ill health was probably the reason for a three-week visit she and Cassandra paid to Cheltenham in May. Cheltenham, like Bath, was known for its medicinal waters. Henry had been going there, no doubt for an occasional "cure", since as early as 1808. And unlike Bath, Cheltenham had no old unhappy associations, and, perhaps more important, no risk of meeting irate Leigh Perrots.

On the way back from Cheltenham the sisters visited their old friends the Fowles at Kintbury, who noticed a change in Jane. She was no longer the vigorous woman who loved to walk, and who could enjoy good weather "all over me, from top to toe, from right to left, longitudinally, perpendicularly, diagonally". More disturbing still, the Fowles noticed that Jane went about paying visits to her favourite haunts, as if for the last time. But this may well have been wisdom after the event.

Cassandra and Jane visited Steventon on the way home, which was never restful, and even at Chawton life must have been busier than usual. Frank and his wife Mary came to stay, with their two daughters, Cassy and Mary Jane, and when they returned to London they took Cassy, Cassandra senior and Martha with them, so that Jane was left alone to look after her mother and little Mary Jane, who was just nine. James's wife, the other Mary, had been ill, and old Mrs. Austen was doubtless "not quite well", as usual. And to make matters worse, that was a terrible summer. Writing to James's son Edward, Jane Austen described meeting a neighbour. "I talked of its being bad weather for the hay—and he returned me the comfort of its being much worse for the wheat." She could still manage the old light note for the young. Edward was just home from Winchester and she teased him a little about this, and about his school-mates whom they had watched passing their window. "We saw a countless number of postchaises full of boys pass by yesterday morning— full of future heroes, legislators, fools, and villains." Probably because James's Mary was still unwell, Edward and his father came to stay at Chawton a few days later, and Jane wrote to Edward's sister Caroline that his visit "has been a great pleasure to us. He has not lost one good quality or good look and is only altered in being improved by being some months older than when we saw him last. He is getting very near our own age, for *we* do not grow older of course."

Which probably meant that at forty she was feeling her age, and the encroaching symptoms of the disease that would kill her. In an article for the *British Medical Journal* of July 1964, Doctor (now Sir) Zachary Cope, analysed Jane Austen's own description of her symptoms and proved, conclusively in my view, that she died of an illness that had not then been identified, Addison's disease of the adrenal bodies. He attributes the beginning of the illness to the shock of Henry's bankruptcy, but no doubt the long anxiety of the months that led up to it played its part too, as well as worry over Charles. It is equally sad to think that Jane's favourite brother's disaster was the beginning of her own, and to remember that these days her illness could probably be kept under control by hormone injections.

In the spring and summer of 1816, it seems likely that Jane was beginning to feel rather less well than usual, suffering perhaps from fits of fatigue and faintness, and digestive upsets. She doubtless dosed herself in the same practical spirit with which she had dosed her mother for so long, and went on coping with life as it came. She had both *Persuasion* and *Susan* to work on, and must have returned to her old habit of polishing one book while she wrote another. An anonymous novel called *Susan* had come out while Jane Austen's book lay dormant with Crosby, so now her heroine was being turned into Catherine Morland while she finished *Persuasion*.

Revising *Susan* for the third time, Jane Austen seems to have worked with a light hand. A close revision would undoubtedly have removed that old family joke about Mr. Morland, "a very respectable man, though his name was Richard". Tired, ailing and busy, Jane Austen probably went through her old book quite fast, changing Susan to Catherine throughout, sighing and smiling over the dated references to Mrs. Radcliffe and the *Mysteries of Udolpho*, and adding a note for the reader explaining what had happened to the book and why parts of it had been made "comparatively obsolete" by the passage of thirteen years. Jane Austen must by this time have been enough of a professional to recognise the dangers of too heavy a revision of this light-hearted early work, so close in spirit to the *Juvenilia*.

The most significant bit of revision, in my view, is that of the famous defence of the novel, in Chapter Five:

Alas! If the heroine of one novel be not patronised by the heroine of another, from whom can she expect protection and regard? I cannot approve of it. Let us leave it to the reviewers to abuse such effusions of fancy at their leisure, and over every new novel to talk in threadbare strains of the trash with which the press now groans. Let us not desert one another; we are an injured body. Although our productions have afforded more extensive and unaffected pleasure than those of any other literary corporation in the world, no species of composition has been so much decried. From pride, ignorance, or fashion, our foes are almost as many as our readers.

This is no unpublished novelist speaking. This is the voice of the author of *Mansfield Park* and of *Emma*, and it tells us a painful deal of how she felt about the reception of her masterpieces. *Emma* had come out in December 1815, and the second edition of *Mansfield Park* in February 1816, so it must have been towards the end of the year, or the beginning of 1817, that she learned that her profit on *Emma* had been almost wiped out by the loss on the second edition of *Mansfield Park*. She actually received the balance of £38 18s. due to her in February 1817. There are no references to what must have been a bitter disappointment in her surviving letters or in the family's records, but her own financial blow must have been doubly painful in the light of Henry's bankruptcy. The two shocks together may well have combined to contribute to the insidious onset of her last illness. It may not only have been Keats who felt that his "name was writ in water".

But Jane Austen's active, hopeful spirit found comfort where it could. As she had done for the neglected *Mansfield Park*, she made a collection of the opinions of her family and friends on *Emma*. It must have been wonderfully cheering to think that, "Mr. Jeffrey [of the *Edinburgh Review*] was kept up by it three nights", while her brother Charles liked it better "even than my favourite *Pride and Prejudice*". Frank, too, had an encouraging comment. He "liked it extremely, observing that though there might be more wit in *Pride and Prejudice* — and a higher morality in *Mansfield Park* — yet altogether, on account of its peculiar air of nature throughout, he preferred it to either." The naval brothers always turned up trumps. And Mr. Haden reappeared briefly to be "quite delighted with it", and admire the character of Emma.

The four men were in a minority, however. The general view was probably expressed by the Leigh Perrots who "saw many beauties in it, but could not think it equal to *Pride and Prejudice* — Darcy and Elizabeth had spoilt them for anything else." There was an interesting division of opinion between Anna Lefroy and her husband. He "did not like the heroine so well as any of the others", while she "preferred Emma to all the heroines". And then there was Mr. Sherer, the Vicar of Godmersham, who was displeased with Jane Austen's pictures of clergymen. It is fascinating how self-revealing people's comments on Jane Austen's books tend to be. But it must have been discouraging for her to have the general voice declare *Emma* inferior to *Pride and Prejudice*. It is hard on an author to have published her most obviously attractive book so early in her career. As for *Sense and Sensibility*: nobody mentioned it.

In the end, Jane Austen changed her mind about *Northanger Abbey*, writing to Fanny next spring that, "Miss Catherine is put upon the shelf for the present, and I do not know that she will ever come out—but I have a something ready for publication, which may perhaps appear about a twelvemonth hence. It is short, about the length of *Catherine*." In fact, *Persuasion*, though at the time she and Cassandra were discussing the merits of *The Elliots* for its title. It is entirely understandable that at this point Jane Austen should prefer the mellow, autumnal *Persuasion* to the light-hearted *Northanger Abbey*, and it is simply one of life's ironies that Henry should have brought the two of them out together, in one set of four volumes, the year after her death.

While she was finishing *Persuasion*, Aunt Jane's double life continued. She wrote to Caroline Austen on July 15th, 1816, thanking her for yet another literary work. "I have been very much entertained by your story . . . it made me laugh heartily, and I am particularly glad to find you so much alive upon any topic of such absurdity, as the usual description of a heroine's father." Three days later, she wrote "finis" to *Persuasion*, but, says James Edward Austen-Leigh in his *Memoir*:

Her performance did not satisfy her. She thought it tame and flat, and was desirous of producing something better. This weighed upon her mind, the more so probably on account of the weak state of her health; so that one night she retired to rest in very low spirits. But such depression was little in accordance with her nature, and was soon shaken off. The next morning she awoke to more cheerful views and brighter inspirations: the sense of power revived; and imagination resumed its course. She cancelled the condemned chapter, and wrote two others, entirely different, in its stead.

By some miracle, the original chapter was preserved, so that this is the one instance where we have both Jane Austen's first and second thoughts.

It makes one wish, more than anything else could, that she had not been so sweeping in her destruction. What, one can only wonder, did she find wrong with the first version? It contains one of her most direct and charming proposal scenes. Where the final version has Wentworth propose by letter, the cancelled passage does it in a short, swift conversation in which Anne denies the rumour that she is engaged to Mr. Elliot. This ends with "a silent, but a very powerful dialogue—on his side, supplication, on hers acceptance—Still, a little nearer—and a hand taken and pressed—and 'Anne, my own dear Anne'—bursting forth in the fullness of exquisite feeling—and all suspense and indecision were over."

It is sad to have lost this, even in the interests of Jane Austen's moving and significant comparison of the feelings of men and women, as discussed by Anne Elliot and Captain Harville and overheard by Wentworth. Perhaps, if she had had time and strength, she might have contrived to combine what was best in both versions. As it stands, her final version is clearly still in need of revision. At the end of Chapter Eleven, Anne makes a long speech in defence of her own line of conduct ending, "A strong sense of duty is no bad part of a woman's portion", and Captain Wentworth's answer, in which he refuses to forgive Lady Russell "yet", is an almost complete non-sequitur.

Because *Persuasion* is at once the most feeling and, in tone, the saddest of Jane Austen's books, critics tend to treat it as autobiographical. This, they say, is the story of that lost love of hers, given a happy ending. If it is, she has certainly taken good care to disguise it. Anne Elliot, like Fanny Price, is totally unlike her creator. She is quiet, shy, reserved—and persuadable. There is little wit or liveliness about her, and, perhaps most significant of all, she tires easily. When she goes for a walk with the Musgrove sisters, she has to thank Captain Wentworth's surprising solicitude for a lift home in his sister's carriage. And, in the cancelled chapters, she celebrates her happiness by a sleepless night and pays "for the overplus of bliss, by headache and fatigue".

This is not the Jane Austen we have learned to know, any more than *Persuasion* is her story, and it seems to me an insult to such an artist even to entertain the suggestion that for her last finished novel she should have turned to autobiography. The young Jane, who had the courage to change her mind overnight, and reject the advances of Harris Bigg Wither, would never have let herself be persuaded out of her own happiness. It is as absurd as to imagine Elizabeth Bennet yielding to the bullying of Lady Catherine de Bourgh.

If Jane did put something of herself into *Persuasion*, it seems to me most likely that it was in the character of Lady Russell. She had spent a good deal of thought and care, not long before, on her niece Fanny's love affair with John Plumtre, and had obviously been deeply aware of the responsibility of an adviser in such a situation. She, in fact, had refused to act the part of Lady Russell. "You frighten me out of my wits by your reference." But this exchange may well have started her thinking about such a position, and the kind of woman who might plunge in with advice where angels feared to tread. Lady Russell and Lady Catherine de Bourgh may not be sisters, but they might easily be cousins.

In his *George Meredith and English Comedy*, V. S. Pritchett has a challenging aside in which he describes Jane Austen as a war novelist, pointing out that the facts of the long war are basic to all her books. She knew all about the shortage of men, the high cost of living, and, most particularly, about the vital part played by the Navy. Starting *Persuasion* in 1815, with Waterloo won, she seems, consciously or otherwise, to have designed it as her tribute to the brutes and heroes who had made survival possible for the British Isles. From the first moment when Anne Elliot speaks up for the Navy, "who have done so much for us", and then goes on to reveal surprising knowledge of naval affairs in her summary of Admiral Croft's career, the alert reader will recognise that in this book the moral theme is rather different from that of Jane Austen's earlier work.

It is, at first sight, a weakness of the book that Anne Elliot has nothing to learn. When the story opens, she has long recognised the mistake she made when she yielded to persuasion and sent Captain Wentworth away. Throughout the book, she behaves perfectly, as she always has; so much so as almost to justify her creator's comment in a letter to Fanny, "You may *perhaps* like the heroine, as she is almost too good for me." Fanny had always liked the "pictures of perfection" that made her aunt "sick and wicked". Indeed, in my opinion, one of the advantages of Jane Austen's first, as opposed to her final, version of the conclusion is that it omits Anne's self-justificatory speech: "I must believe that I was right, much as I suffered from it." As this did not save the book from being attacked, by critics in training for the Victorian era, for advocating rash marriages, one can only regret that Jane Austen cancelled Anne's original answer to Wentworth's jealousy over Mr. Elliot: "When I yeilded [on the first occasion, eight years before] I thought it was to duty — But no duty could be called in aid here — In marrying a man indifferent to me, all risk would have been incurred, and all duty violated." To the end, Jane Austen would go on condemning the marriage of convenience, however convenient it might seem.

But the fact that Anne and Wentworth have both, actually, recognised their mistake long before the story opens does weaken the book. Here is no conflict, only anxiety lest Wentworth may have entangled himself too far with absurd Louisa Musgrove. Here, too, significant perhaps of the author's impaired health, is a failure of the comic spirit. There are no comic characters to be compared with those in *Emma*, and indeed Jane Austen has been accused of one of her greatest failures in her handling of Mrs. Musgrove's "large, fat sighings" over the fate of her scapegrace son.

For me, this particular accusation is cancelled out by another; the suggestion that Jane Austen ignores the fate of the ordinary seaman who was, in fact, the reluctant backbone of the British Navy. One might have thought that the Portsmouth scenes in *Mansfield Park* were answer enough to this, but it is surely an instance of Jane Austen's artistry that she should have taken care, in *Persuasion*, where every other naval character is on the side of the angels (even if Captain Benwick havers a bit about which angel) to introduce poor Dick Musgrove, who had been "sent to sea, because he was stupid and unmanageable on shore", and whose family had had "the good fortune to lose him before he reached his twentieth year". It sounds a heartless enough passage, and has been often attacked, but if you consider *Persuasion* as a book on the navy, it serves, quite obviously, a useful function. It is out of this material, Jane Austen is telling us, that the Captain Wentworths and Admiral Crofts fashioned the weapon that would defeat Napoleon. And, just in case the reader, involved in the moving reconciliation, at last, between Wentworth and Anne, should have forgotten the moral theme of the book, Jane Austen concludes with it. Anne "gloried in being a sailor's wife, but she must pay the tax of quick alarm for belonging to that profession which is, if possible, more distinguished in its domestic virtues than in its national importance."

When Jane Austen told Fanny, in the spring of 1817, that she had "a something ready for publication, which may perhaps appear about a twelvemonth hence," she probably meant that *Persuasion* was nearly, but not entirely finished to her satisfaction. A last revision before publication would, no doubt, have taken care of the major awkwardness of the book, the behaviour of Mrs. Smith. Anne loved her, and we are clearly expected to, but how can we, when she behaves with the self-centred hypocrisy Jane Austen hated almost as much as anything. Thinking that Anne has decided to marry William Elliot, she says nothing about his true character, but hopes, instead, that Anne will persuade him to sort out her own tangled affairs for her. It is more than she deserves that Wentworth ultimately does so. Clearly, Jane Austen was aware, at some level, of this weakness in Mrs. Smith's character, for she gives her the kind of frozen metaphor she had criticised in her niece Anna's work. There is not much to choose between Anna's "vortex of dissipation" and Mrs. Smith's "Oh! he is black at heart, hollow and black!"

One must, however, recognise that *Persuasion* shows a small, important change in Jane Austen's style. There is more landscape and more emotion, and indeed, the two tend to go together. There is the famous description of Lyme and Charmouth, and of the Lyme party who "soon found themselves on the sea shore, and lingering only, as all must linger and gaze on a first return to the sea, who ever deserve to look on it at all". And, even in the straight narrative, figurative language is creeping in. "Prettier musings of high-wrought love and eternal constancy, could never have passed along the streets of Bath, than Anne was sporting with from Camden-place to Westgate-buildings. It was almost enough to spread purification and perfume all the way."

Persuasion is not, inevitably, as highly wrought a book as *Emma*, but it is easier to enjoy, and it is immensely interesting in that it shows Jane Austen trying a new balance between the surface romantic plot and the underlying moral theme. If, in some ways, *Persuasion* harks back to the early successes, where the romantic story was the dominant motif, it also looks forward, most significantly, to *Sanditon*, where, one suspects, the moral theme was to be the dominant. Was *Persuasion*, with its autumnal, melancholy note, Jane Austen's farewell to romance? If she had been able to finish *Sanditon*, would it not have been an entirely new departure?

With *Persuasion* finished, Jane Austen may have felt that her state of health demanded a holiday. The only other work that was probably written in 1816 is the comic *Plan of a Novel*, in which the established author put together and made mock of all the various suggestions kind friends had made for her future works. Mr. Clarke, the Prince Regent's librarian, contributed largely to it, but so to quite an extent did Jane Austen's own family. Fanny Knight apparently had insisted that a heroine must be of "faultless character ... accomplished ... all perfection" and, despite such adventures as being carried away by the anti-hero and often reduced to work for her bread and worn down to a skeleton and now and then starved to death, she must "throughout the whole work, be in the most elegant society and living in high style". "The name of the work *not*," concluded Jane Austen, "to be *Emma*—but of the same sort as S. & S. and P. & P."

It is quite possible that, aside from her unsatisfactory state of health, Jane Austen was simply too busy, in the late summer and autumn of 1816, to consider starting a new book. Henry's affairs were to the fore as usual. He had recovered, resilient as always, from bankruptcy, and decided to become a clergyman. It may be owing to the influence of his favourite sister, who had written Fanny that perhaps they ought all to be Evangelicals, that he, in fact, was known in later life for the pronounced Evangelical tone of his preaching.

Meanwhile, James's Mary was still unwell, and Cassandra had taken her and her daughter Caroline to try the waters at Cheltenham, while her son Edward stayed at Chawton. "Edward is a great pleasure to me," Jane wrote to Cassandra, and, "Henry . . . wishes to come to us as soon as we can receive him – is decided for Orders." Charles, too, wanted to come to stay bringing his sister-in-law and his little girls. Both naval brothers were on shore now, and Frank and his family were living at Alton, where Frank's wife was pregnant again, and, "seldom either looks or appears quite well – Little embryo is troublesome I suppose." Jane and Edward had dined with them and walked the two miles home from Alton by moonlight, which does not sound as if she was very unwell, but she goes on to say, "Thank you, my back has given me scarcely any pain for many days – I have an idea [she anticipates modern psychologists] that agitation does it as much harm as fatigue, and that I was ill at the time of your going, from the very circumstance of your going."

In fact, Jane was missing Cassandra badly. "When you have once left Cheltenham, I shall grudge every half day wasted on the road." Martha Lloyd was at Chawton, but just the same Jane needed Cassandra practically as well as emotionally. Their nephew Edward had just left, and she admitted that she was not sorry for it. "I wanted a few days quiet, and exemption from the thought and contrivances which any sort of company gives – I often wonder how *you* can find time for what you do, in addition to the cares of the house – and how good Mrs. West[1] could have written such books and collected so many hard words with her family cares, is still more a matter of astonishment! Composition seems to me impossible, with a head full of joints of mutton and doses of rhubarb."

Jane Austen may have found mutton and rhubarb unconducive to authorship, but she was thinking about her next book just the same, and had evidently discussed it with Cassandra. In this same letter she has an interesting passage about their old friend Miss Sharpe, from whom she had had a letter. "Quite one of her letters – she has been again obliged to exert herself – more than ever – in a more distressing, more harassed state – and has met with another excellent old physician and his wife,

[1] Author of *Alicia de Lacy, an Historical Romance,* 1814, and other novels.

with every virtue under heaven, who takes to her and cures her from pure love and benevolence—Dr. and Mrs. Storer are *their* Mrs. and Miss Palmer—for they are at Bridlington." The Palmers were to become Parkers, and Bridlington Sanditon, but both reference and style suggest the unfinished work that was to be begun, as usual, in January, and named *Sanditon* by Henry after its author's death.

❧ 16 ❧

DID CASSANDRA SEE AN ALARMING CHANGE IN HER SISTER WHEN she got back from Cheltenham that autumn? Sir Zachary Cope has described Addison's disease as proceeding slowly (and in those days inexorably), without any great pain, and with intermissions of apparently improved health. It is quite possible that neither Jane Austen herself, nor the people who were constantly with her, had yet recognised any serious cause for alarm, but Cassandra, coming back after an absence of some length, would not be so easily deceived. The fact that there are no more letters from Jane to her suggests that from now on ailing or pregnant sisters-in-law would have to take care of themselves. Cassandra would stay with Jane.

The family as a whole do not seem to have been unduly anxious, and it would have been in character for Jane Austen to make as little fuss about herself as possible. Family visiting went on as usual. Writing cheerfully to James's son Edward in December, Jane admitted, in passing, that she was not strong enough to walk to Wyards, though she insisted, "I am otherwise very well." Both Henry and Charles were staying with them. Charles was now much better in "health, spirits and appearance". The shipwreck had doubtless told on him too. Henry "writes very superior sermons. You and I must try to get hold of one or two, and put them into our novels — it would be a fine help to a volume." Edward was writing now, and Jane had already told Cassandra that his novel was "extremely clever; written with great ease and spirit . . . and in a style, I think, to be popular". Jane had heard from Edward's mother that he had mislaid two and a half chapters. "It is well that *I* have not been at Steventon lately," she wrote him, "and therefore cannot be suspected of purloining them —

two strong twigs and a half towards a nest of my own, would have been something—I do not think however that any theft of that sort would be really very useful to me. What should I do with your strong, manly, spirited sketches, full of variety and glow?—How could I possibly join them on to the little bit (two inches wide) of ivory on which I work with so fine a brush, as produces little effect after much labour."

This must, though she conceals it admirably in the rest of the letter, have been one of the times of low spirits described in the *Memoir*, and doubtless due to her illness. Her description of her method of work has been quoted over and over again by her critics, and I suppose it is no more ironic that this serious bit of self depreciation should be taken *au pied de la lettre* than that her comic ones were. If Jane Austen was a miniaturist, then the whole world was her background. Her little bit (two inches wide) of ivory is her microcosm, which predicates the rest of the universe. And I am sure that, except in moments of ill health and discouragement, she knew this. She was not, it is true, to know that critics to come would discuss in all earnestness whether she owed the greater debt to Plato or Aristotle, to Dr. Johnson or Lord Shaftesbury. If she could have known, she would probably have dissolved into one of her fits of delighted laughter. But, "the most unlearned and uninformed female who ever dared to be an authoress" was artist enough to recognise her own quality, so long as she had the strength to function as artist and critic.

There must have been a remission of her illness about this time, perhaps when the house became quieter after the departure of Charles and Henry. By January 1817, she had awakened once again "to more cheerful views and brighter inspirations". The sense of power must have revived; and imagination resumed its course. She started a new book that was to be totally unlike the others. She had probably been discussing her plans for it with Cassandra for some time, but no doubt the associations of this book, unfinished because of her sister's death, were too painful for Cassandra to give any clue as to what she had planned for it. All we have is eleven short chapters, but they are enough to show that *Persuasion* had ended the first stage of Jane Austen's literary career. It was the last of her romantic comedies, and had already begun to show a sea-change. Now the keen, cold intelligence that had created Sir Walter Elliot and his odious daughter Elizabeth would turn more entirely to social satire. In her art, as in her life, Jane Austen had always spoken with two voices, but so far it had been possible for romantically-minded readers to ignore the bass note of irony, concentrating on the gay treble of the heroine's adventures. This would, from the evidence of the eleven existing chapters, have been impossible with *Sanditon*. If completed, it would probably have provided the same kind of shock to devoted readers that an addict of Shakespeare's romantic comedies might feel on turning from *As you Like It* to *All's Well that Ends Well*.

Thanking the Countess of Morley for a letter of congratulation on *Emma*, Jane Austen had written, in December 1815, that it encouraged her to "believe that I have not yet—as every writer of fancy does sooner or later—overwritten myself". She was writing *Persuasion* at the time, and had perhaps already decided that it was to be her last romantic comedy. Now, at forty-one, she must have decided it was time to break entirely new ground. In the new book she bravely started in January 1817 everything was to be different. The opening, with a carriage accident in the first sentence, is as unlike as possible to her usual leisured run-in, while Mr. Parker, one of the characters to be satirised, holds the field for the whole of the first chapter. The heroine (or one of them) is not introduced until the end of the second chapter, by which time the tone of dry comedy is well established. Charlotte Heywood was presumably to share the honours as heroine with Clara Brereton, who is not introduced until Chapter Six, when Charlotte (already established as the intelligent observer who sees most of the game) instantly recognises her as "a complete heroine".

There was to be a hero to match. Sir Edward Denham, like Catherine Morland before him, has over-indulged himself in romantic fiction, and feels in honour (or dishonour) bound to seduce Clara Brereton, who is in the classic position of penniless dependant. Jane Austen lets us see him considering the possibilities of "the neighbourhood of Tombuctoo" as the scene of his beloved's seduction, and deciding, regretfully, that economy indicates that he must "prefer the quietest sort of ruin and disgrace for the object of his affections, to the more renowned". Jane Austen was trying her hand here, for almost the first time, at extensive inner study of her male figures, and a title for the book, which she had discussed with Cassandra, is surely significant in this context. She had considered calling it *The Brothers*, in honour of the three Parkers: Mr. Parker, of the carriage accident and the absurd passion for sea-air; his gluttonous brother Arthur, who has such a neat hand with a slice of toast; and Sidney, the third, presumably Charlotte's hero, who only makes his appearance in the last chapter Jane Austen wrote.

Speculation is idle, but attractive. Was the plot to contain two ruins, or near ruins, those of Clara Brereton, and of Sanditon itself, the seaside resort into which Mr. Parker had put all his money? Sanditon, certainly, was to play an infinitely more important part in the story that the setting ever had before in Jane Austen's novels. If one scene tends to leap to the mind as crucial for most of the other books—Box Hill for *Emma*, Lyme Regis for *Persuasion*, Sotherton for *Mansfield Park*—in *Sanditon* the place dominates the book. It is lovingly described, in the quick, allusive style Jane Austen had allowed herself at times before, as in Mrs. Elton's famous monologue among the strawberries at Donwell. But if speculation about plot is idle, discussion of style in this much altered first draft is almost absurd. If she had lived, she would undoubtedly have changed so much . . .

Among other things, I imagine she would have given a fairly drastic pruning to the whole episode of Mr. Parker's valetudinarian and busy sisters, but how characteristic of Jane Austen to have written, in pencil, in discomfort, during her last illness, about so absurd a pair of hypochondriacs. She had laughed all her life. Now, gallantly, was she laughing at death? On March 17th, she put down her pen on a characteristic note of humour, and never picked it up again. But enough of *Sanditon* (or *The Brothers*) remains to suggest that its completion might have sadly disconcerted the faithful band of readers who had always loved *Pride and Prejudice* best. With the one desolating exception of Jane, the Austens were a long-lived family. If she had lived, might she not have developed into a formidable, Victorian Ivy Compton-Burnett?

From January 17th to March 17th, Jane Austen went on indomitably working away at *Sanditon* in pencil if necessary; reclining, when her discomfort grew too great, on a mock sofa made of three chairs, because, as she quietly explained to a niece, if she had used the one real sofa her mother might not have liked to. Jane maintained, of course, that her three chairs were just as comfortable, and nobody thought to buy a second sofa. But this was very likely as much Jane Austen's fault as anyone's. She would go on laughing to the end, and she would think of everyone else but herself. Writing to Caroline in January 1817, she was preoccupied as always with language. "Your Anne is dreadful. But nothing offends me so much as the absurdity of not being able to pronounce the word shift. I could forgive her any follies in English, rather than the mock modesty of that French word." Uncle Charles, meanwhile, "has a sad turn for being unwell", but, "*I* feel myself getting stronger than I was half a year ago and can so perfectly well walk to Alton, *or* back again, without the slightest fatigue that I hope to be able to do both when summer comes." She had been visiting the Frank Austens at Alton, "and though the childern are sometimes very noisy and not under such order as they ought and easily might, I cannot help liking them and even loving them, which I

189

hope may be not wholly inexcusable in their and your affectionate aunt." Life at the Frank Austens' sounds rather like life at the Musgroves'.

Though Caroline was only sixteen miles away at Steventon, it was not easy for her and her aunt to meet, which is sad, as by now Jane Austen seems to have recognised a true kinswoman in the eleven-year-old daughter of her least favourite sister-in-law. "The pianoforte often talks of you," she says in a postscript to this last letter, "in various keys, tunes, and expressions I allow — but be it lesson or country dance, sonata or waltz, *you* are really its constant theme. I wish you could come and see us, as easily as Edward can." For Edward, the sixteen miles between Steventon and Chawton were a morning's ride; for his little sister, they were an impossible barrier, or, if she went, it must be with the father and mother who brought out the best, one suspects, neither in her nor in her aunt.

That January, Jane Austen wrote a long letter to her old friend Alethea Bigg, who was staying with her sister and brother-in-law, the Hills, in Streatham. It is a sad letter, just because Jane wrote so confidently about her health: "*I* have certainly gained strength through the winter and am not far from being well; and I think I understand my own case now so much better than I did, as to be able by care to keep off any serious return of illness. I am more and more convinced that *bile* is at the bottom of all I have suffered, which makes it easy to know how to treat myself." In fact, the weakness and the digestive upsets were continuing, and as she had cosseted her brothers through very similar afflictions at various times in their lives, it was both reasonable and characteristic to take her own symptoms lightly.

The other family news was good. James's Edward remained a favourite, and James, who seems to have been unwell too, was better. His daughter Anna Lefroy, who had borne two children in two years, was looking better than since her marriage. And Henry was now curate of Bentley, near Alton, and was expected at Chawton "very soon, perhaps in time to assist Mr. Papillon on Sunday. I shall be very glad when the first hearing is over. It will be a nervous hour for our pew, though we hear that he acquits himself with as much ease and collectedness, as if he had be n used to it all his life." Henry was, at last, settled for life. He remarried in 1820, and continued as perpetual curate of Bentley until his death in 1850.

Mr. Hill's nephew, the poet (and poet laureate) Southey had written a *Poet's Pilgrimage to Waterloo*, and Jane told Alethea that the Austens had been reading it with "much approbation. Parts of it suit me better than much that he has written before." A friend of Alethea's was in France, and Jane hoped her letters from there were satisfactory. "They would not be satisfactory to *me*, I confess, unless they breathed a strong spirit of regret for not being in England." Jane Austen had always been a passionate Englishwoman. The autumn before, commenting on one of the Lefroys' return from France, she had written to Cassandra, "He is come back from France, thinking of the French as one could wish, disappointed in everything."

A charming postscript to her letter to Alethea Bigg shows Jane Austen the housewife still, and still in charge of the wine. The wet summer had meant a shortage of honey for the home-made mead they drank at Chawton. Now, "The real object of this letter is to ask you for a receipt, but I thought it genteel not to let it appear early. We remember some excellent orange wine at Manydown, made from Seville oranges ... and should be very much obliged to you for the receipt, if you can command it within a few weeks." Some housewives make marmalade with their Seville oranges after Christmas, but the Austens meant to make wine that year. The French wine that one drank in affluent Kent must have been more prohibitively expensive than ever, at this point, in Hampshire, where one economised.

It is possible that by now, Fanny Knight, at Godmersham, had been made a party to some of her Aunt Cassandra's anxiety about their beloved Jane. It was not a subject Cassandra would have been likely to discuss either with her brothers or with their mother, who had established, years before, the fact that she must be protected from family anxiety of any kind. But Fanny, the dear niece, "almost another sister", and twenty-four that January, would have been a natural confidante. After Jane Austen's death, Cassandra was to write to Fanny thanking her for the letters with which she had cheered her aunt's deathbed. "Never shall I forget the proofs of love you gave her during her illness in writing those kind, amusing letters at a time when I know your feelings would have dictated so different a style. Take the only reward I can give you in my assurance that your benevolent purpose *was* answered; you *did* contribute to her enjoyment."

Fanny had done better than that. She had provided a distraction. Remembering the exchange about Mr. Plumtre years before, and that light-hearted agreeable flirtation with Mr. Haden, she now produced a Mr. Wildman of Chilham Castle, near Godmersham, for her aunt's consideration. Perhaps she did not do it entirely seriously. Her letters do not survive, but they certainly served their purpose. "You are the delight of my life," wrote her aunt. "Such letters, such entertaining letters as you

191

have lately sent! — Such a description of your queer little heart! ... Who can keep pace with the fluctuations of your fancy, the capriccios of your taste, the contradictions of your feelings?" Jane Austen was not too ill to enjoy playing with words for her favourite niece. "It is very, very gratifying to me to know you so intimately," she went on. "You can hardly think what a pleasure it is to me, to have such thorough pictures of your heart — Oh! what a loss it will be when you are married. You are too agreeable in your single state, too agreeable as a niece. I shall hate you when your delicious play of mind is all settled down into conjugal and maternal affections." And then, with a characteristic turn of argument, "And yet I do wish you to marry very much, because I know you will never be happy till you are."

Fanny had apparently been brooding a little, or pretending to, about John Plumtre, the rejected suitor, who showed signs of marrying someone else. "My dearest Fanny, I cannot bear you should be unhappy about him." And, earlier, "Why should you be living in dread of his marrying someone else? — (Yet how natural!) — You did not choose to have him yourself; why not allow him to take comfort where he can?" And, a subtle reminder, "You cannot forget how you felt under the idea of its having been possible that he might have dined in Hans Place." Had Fanny been nervous of a possible encounter between staid John Plumtre and entertaining Mr. Haden?

Jane Austen was at her most realistic both about spinsterhood and about marriage in this batch of letters. "Single women have a dreadful propensity for being poor — which is one very strong argument in favour of matrimony." But she had long since faced the fact that marriage, too, held its hazards. Mrs. Deedes, one of the vast Bridges tribe in Kent, had just had another child, and Jane had a characteristic comment. "Good Mrs. Deedes! — I hope she will get the better of this Marianne, and then I would recommend to her and Mr. D. the simple regimen of separate rooms." And, again, of her niece Anna, "Poor animal, she will be worn out before she is thirty — I am very sorry for her." It was an argument for Fanny's delay in choosing a husband. "By not beginning the business of mothering quite so early in life, you will be young in constitution, spirits, figure and countenance, while Mrs. William Hammond is growing old by confinements and nursing."

Meanwhile, Fanny, the incorrigible creature, had been making her suitor, Mr. Wildman, read one of her aunt's books, without telling him who had written it. "Have mercy on him," said the author. "Tell him the truth and make him an apology." Fanny had quoted poor Mr.

Wildman's adverse opinion to her aunt, who "had great amusement in reading it, and I *hope* I am not affronted". But, "He and I should not in the least agree of course, in our ideas of novels and heroines – pictures of perfection as you know make me sick and wicked." There were no pictures of perfection in *Sanditon*. Jane Austen went on to confess that she had told Henry about *Persuasion*. "Do not be surprised at finding Uncle Henry acquainted with my having another ready for publication. I could not say No when he asked me, but he knows nothing more of it – You will not like it, so you need not be impatient. You may *perhaps* like the heroine, as she is almost too good for me." It seems to settle the question of whether Jane Austen saw herself in Anne Elliot.

Mrs. Frank Austen was to be confined again, and Charles was seriously worried about his second daughter, Harriet, who was suffering from headaches that might indicate water on the brain. And there was anxious news, too, from Scarlets, where Mrs. Austen's brother James Leigh Perrot was seriously ill. Ailing herself, Jane Austen wrote of this without hypocrisy. "I shall be very glad when the event at Scarlets is over, the expectation of it keeps us in a worry, your grandmamma especially; she sits brooding over evils which cannot be remedied and conduct impossible to be understood." Austens and Leigh Perrots had drifted far apart over the years, but the impossible conduct was not yet at an end.

Fanny's brothers were growing up. William and Henry had both been visiting at Chawton and their aunt was delighted with them. But, "You will have a great break-up at Godmersham in the spring, you *must* feel all their going. It is very right however." Fanny, at twenty-four, had been mother and older sister both since she was sixteen and would inevitably feel the change caused by her younger brothers' leaving home. But Jane Austen did not want her to plunge into marriage on this account. "Sweet Fanny, believe no such thing of yourself – Spread no such malicious slander upon your understanding . . . Do not speak ill of your sense, merely for the gratification of your fancy – Yours is sense, which deserves more honourable treatment – You are *not* in love with him. You never have been really in love with him."

And then, one of those practical postscripts. "Uncle Henry and Miss Lloyd dine at Mr. Digweed's today, which leaves us the power of asking Uncle and Aunt Frank to come and meet their nephews here." It is hard to imagine how that modest house at Chawton could have accommodated four grown women, Uncle Henry and the two Knight nephews. Even with Cassandra in charge of the housekeeping, it can scarcely have been the ideal atmosphere for an invalid, however fond she was of all the people who crowded the house. It is possible that on this, as on other occasions, the Great House was used as an overflow, or annexe, but the burden of housekeeping would still have fallen on the Cottage. Caroline Austen said, "It was altogether a comfortable and ladylike establishment, though I believe the means that supported it were but small." One must hope that when sons and nephews arrived, they brought, tactfully, the kind of contribution Anna Austen Lefroy made when she sent her grandmother a turkey that winter.

Jane Austen was by now acknowledged to be ill. Her disease manifested itself now here, now there. In February she reported herself "almost entirely cured of my rheumatism ... Aunt Cassandra nursed me so beautifully!" On March 13th she had "got tolerably well again, quite equal to walking about and enjoying the air; and by sitting down and resting a good while between my walks, I get exercise enough." She was planning, when spring came, to start riding the donkey which they kept to pull Mrs. Austen (or her ailing daughter) in a donkey cart. "It will be more independent," said Jane Austen characteristically, "and less troublesome than the use of the carriage, and I shall be able to go about with Aunt Cassandra in her walks to Alton and Wyards."

Her next letter to Fanny, dated March 23rd, is less encouraging. "I certainly have not been well for many weeks, and about a week ago I was very poorly, I have had a good deal of fever at times and indifferent nights, but am considerably better now, and recovering my looks a little, which have been bad enough, black and white and every wrong colour. I must not depend upon being ever very blooming again. Sickness is a dangerous indulgence at my time of life." For Jane Austen, whose "eloquent blood spoke through her modest cheek", this disfigurement of her clear complexion must have been something of a last straw. And, for Sir Zachary Cope, it is the clinching argument as to her complaint. The mottled black and white effect is significant of Addison's disease. The illness had obviously made great, silent strides forward during that too-busy, too anxious winter, and Jane Austen was right in thinking sickness "a dangerous indulgence" at her time of life. But, whatever her secret feelings, she was not going to admit to them. "Air and exercise is what I want," she told Fanny briskly, and, "Aunt Cass is such an excellent nurse, so assiduous and unwearied!" Jane Austen was now established as an invalid, and Cassandra as her nurse.

But she did not lose interest in the outside world. Henry might hate London now, but Jane still followed the gossip. "If I were the Duchess of Richmond, I should be very miserable about my son's choice. What can be expected from a Paget, born and brought up in the centre of conjugal infidelity and divorces?" Jane Austen knew all about Henry William Paget, Lord Uxbridge and later Marquess of Anglesey, whose liaison with the Duke of Wellington's sister-in-law had made it difficult for the two men to serve together in the army. By the time of Waterloo, two divorces and two marriages had turned Mrs. Wellesley into Lady Uxbridge. At Waterloo, her husband commanded Wellington's cavalry brilliantly, and, if she heard of it, which she probably did, Jane Austen would have enjoyed a laconic exchange between them. "By God," said Uxbridge, looking down, "I've lost my leg." "Have you, by God?" said Wellington, and rode on.

By now, Caroline Austen as well as Fanny must have been writing letters intended to cheer up an invalid, for Jane Austen wrote to her on March 26th, "Pray make no apologies for writing to me often." She had "taken one ride on the donkey and like it very much," but admitted, "A great deal of wind does not suit me, as I have still a tendency to rheumatism. In short I am a poor honey at present. I will be better when you can come and see us." She doubtless meant to be, but it is sadly significant that she had abandoned *Sanditon* ten days before.

There was one pleasant piece of news for Caroline. Jane Austen had received nearly twenty pounds for the second edition of *Sense and Sensibility*. This was the last literary payment she was to receive during her lifetime. A note she wrote during the last months of her life lists the "Profits of my novels, over and above the £600 in the Navy Fives", as follows:

Residue from 1st Edition of *Mansfield Park* remaining in Henrietta Street, March 1816	£13 7s.
Received from Egerton on 2nd Edition of *Sense and Sensibility*, March 1816	£12 15s.
February 21st, 1817. First profits of *Emma*	£38 18s.
March 7th, 1817. From Egerton. 2nd Edition of *Sense and Sensibility*	£19 13s.

Presumably the £13 7s. was lost in Henry's bankruptcy, so this makes Jane Austen's total earnings during her lifetime £671 16s.

Doctor Chapman accounts for the £600 in the Navy Fives as follows: *Pride and Prejudice*: £110, *Sense and Sensibility*: £140, *Mansfield Park*: £320, together with a first payment of about thirty pounds on the second edition of *Sense and Sensibility*, which was published late in 1813. Apparently Egerton made up his books and paid his authors annually in

March, so Jane Austen finally got her thirty pounds odd for the second edition of *Sense and Sensibility* in March 1815. It was like the author of *Persuasion* to put her money into the Navy five per cents, and one can only hope that she got her thirty pounds a year regularly. It would have been a welcome addition to the income of the "comfortable and ladylike establishment". The Austen ladies' income must have shrunk considerably since the time of old Mr. Austen's death, when Henry had written optimistically about how well off his mother and sisters would be on their four hundred and sixty pounds a year. It will be remembered that this was to be made up of contributions of a hundred pounds from Edward and fifty each from James, Frank and Henry to supplement Mrs. Austen's own small income, and Cassandra's, from the thousand pounds left her by her fiancé. Henry's fifty obviously stopped on his bankruptcy in 1816, and Frank, too, seems to have stopped paying in 1816. When Jane Leigh Perrot finally wrote her sister-in-law with an offer of financial help in 1820 she got a grateful and detailed reply. James had continued to pay his annual fifty pounds up to his death the year before, and had also allowed his mother the forty pounds a year interest on the South Sea Stock belonging to her mentally deficient brother Thomas. Mrs. Austen's own income was only a hundred and sixteen pounds a year plus six pounds rent from a little land at Steventon. Charles, the youngest son, had never contributed anything, and Frank may have been involved to some extent in Henry's bankruptcy, for his contributions also ceased in 1816, and, though he later offered to resume them, his mother would not let him. He had responsibilities enough of his own: by 1820 his wife was bearing their ninth child. Edward, however, had given his mother two hundred pounds a year as well as "my house rent, supplies me plentifully with wood and makes me many kind presents". But Edward had eleven children to start in the world, and at the time of his sister's death, still had the lawsuit about the Hampshire estates hanging over him.

❋ 17 ❋

IT MUST HAVE BEEN A SAD WINTER AT CHAWTON. BUT THERE was worse to come. On March 28th, Mrs. Austen's rich brother James Leigh Perrot died and left a will that did not even mention her. Everything went to his wife for her lifetime, much of it absolutely, but with a large sum tied up in trust to revert to James Austen and his heirs when she died, together with legacies of a thousand pounds each to such of James's brothers and sisters as should survive their aunt. It is impossible not to feel malice in this will, though the charitable have argued that James Leigh Perrot wished, most of all, to show his confidence in the wife who had been wrongly tried, so long ago, in 1800. Other defenders have pointed out that James Leigh Perrot had lost ten thousand pounds on Henry's being declared bankrupt in 1816. But this hardly holds water, since his will was made in March 1811.

It is very likely, granted Mrs. Austen's habitual ill health, that her brother assumed that he would survive her. Perhaps she was suffering from one of her ailments when he drew up his will in 1811. If so, it was as unlucky as the circumstances that kept her from her sister-in-law's side at her trial, years before. As Jane Austen's letters show, relations between Austens and Leigh Perrots had never been easy, and unfortunately there is a two-year gap in her correspondence before the date when James Leigh Perrot made his will. Had he and his difficult wife, for some reason, taken the move to Chawton in ill part? Or had he simply assumed that Edward was in a position to do everything that was necessary for his mother?

At all events, just when medical expenses must have been mounting, and spirits low, the ladylike establishment at Chawton got nothing. It was a blow, and admitted as such. Jane Austen, who had written, so long ago, about the legacies that never seemed to come their way, could not manage to make a joke of this. She confessed, in a letter to Charles:

> A few days ago my complaint appeared removed, but I am ashamed to say that the shock of my uncle's will brought on a relapse, and I was so ill on Friday and thought myself so likely to be worse that I could not but press for Cassandra's returning with Frank after the funeral last night, which she of course did, and either her return, or my having seen Mr. Curtis, or my disorder's choosing to go away, have made me better this morning. I live upstairs however for the present and am coddled. I am the only one of the legatees who has been so silly, but a weak body must excuse weak nerves. My mother has borne the forgetfulness of *her* extremely well—her expectations for herself were never beyond the extreme of moderation, and she thinks with you that my uncle always looked forward to surviving her.

Jane Austen, who had such high standards of behaviour herself, must have minded the unkindness of the will as much as the financial disappointment. Once again the world was at work enriching James—at least in prospect—at the expense of the rest of his family. Jane went on to say that her mother "heartily wishes that her younger children had more, and all her children something immediately". In fact, James did not survive to inherit. He died in 1819, the last year of his life having been embittered by a curiously mean action of Jane Leigh Perrot's, who had withdrawn the annuity of a hundred pounds her husband had given James in 1808. Perhaps her offer of help to her sister-in-law, after James's death, was some kind of a sop to her conscience. If so, it was a belated one.

James Leigh Perrot's will probably marked one more downward stage in his niece's last illness. A disease that is brought on by mental distress will be advanced by it. But she wrote bravely and kindly to Charles, and was even able to speak well of the aunt she had never liked, who "felt the value of Cassandra's company so fully, and was so very kind to her, and is poor woman so miserable at present . . . that we feel more regard for her than we ever did before". Charles was having a hard time. 1817 was a bad year for naval officers, and he, too, must have had hopes from his uncle's will. The news of it seems to have made his sister-in-law (who had looked after his daughters since his wife's death) ill too, and then there was little Harriet, with her headaches. "As for your poor little Harriet," wrote her Aunt Jane, "I dare not be sanguine for her." And, one of those significant postscripts of hers: "I have forgotten to take a proper-edged sheet of paper." It was perhaps difficult to remember mourning paper for an uncle who had behaved so unkindly as James Leigh Perrot.

The Austens were not the only ones to be left out of James Leigh Perrot's will. There was no mention either of his nephew Edward Cooper, the only surviving child of Jane Leigh, sister to James Leigh Perrot and Cassandra Austen senior. As executor of his uncle's will, James Austen had had the unpleasant duty of breaking this news to his cousin, and the result was an affronted letter to poor Jane. Beginning properly with regrets for her ill health and "the solicitude and agitation of mind" that her mother must have felt, he went on to his own grievance. "There was probably no reason why I should have expected any distinguished notice in his will: but I certainly never seriously anticipated the probability of being altogether excluded from it. And I must express to you that the circumstance of being thus disowned by him at last does hurt me a good deal." Being a clergyman, he indulged himself in describing the prayers he had said for his uncle during his last illness, and in looking forward to a meeting "in another world, where mis-apprehension, mis-judgment, and mis-representation will have no place". Did Jane Austen feel haunted by Mr. Collins?

We do not know whether she answered her cousin's letter, but at the end of April she sat down and wrote her own will, simple and straight-forward like one side of its author. "To my dearest sister Cassandra Elizabeth everything of which I may die possessed or which may be here-after due to me subject to the payment of my funeral expenses and to a legacy of £50 to my brother Henry and £50 to Madame Bigion." This latter was the faithful maid of Henry's wife Eliza, who had cared for him after her death and had probably lost her savings in his bankruptcy. Dated April 27th, Jane Austen's will named Cassandra as sole executrix, but the signature was not witnessed, and Charles's brother and sister-in-law had to swear to its validity after Jane Austen's death. Once again, no doubt, the two sisters had been conspiring together, as they had so often done before, to spare their mother pain. The will must be made, for Jane was too clear-headed to leave muddle, or the kind of misery her uncle had created, behind her, but it must be kept secret. This may be the explanation of the surprising — in that age — appointment of Cassandra as executrix, but it may well be that after long and varied experience of her brothers Jane Austen felt Cassandra the most competent to act. It is a text for feminists. Henry, however, acted with Cassandra as literary executor. After all, he had handled all Jane Austen's books, though with varying success.

Jane Austen's Will

I Jane Austen of the Parish of Chawton do by this my last Will & Testament give and bequeath to my dearest Sister Cassandra Elizth everything of which I may die possessed, or which may be hereafter due to me, subject to the payment of my Funeral Expences, & to a Legacy of £50. to my Brother Henry, & £50. to Mde Bigeon — which I request may be paid as soon as convenient. And I appoint my said dear Sister the Executrix of this my last Will & Testament.

Jane Austen

April 27. 1817

[Reproduced by permission of the Public Record Office, London]

This will must have been written in an interval of a serious bout of illness that struck Jane Austen that April. She had rallied briefly from the shock of her uncle's will and then succumbed to a new attack, worse than any she had suffered before. Writing to her old friend Miss Sharpe on May 22nd she described herself as better, but admitted to having been "very ill indeed". She had kept her bed "since the 13th of April, with only removals to a sofa", but, "*Now*, I am getting well again ... and *really* am equal to being out of bed, but that the posture is thought good for me." Their local apothecary from Alton had not been able to control her complaint, but Mr. Lyford[1] from Winchester had done so at last, and she now intended to go to Winchester and put herself under his care, rather than going to London, which had also been considered.

The Austens had admitted at last that their Jane was very ill indeed. "How to do justice to the kindness of all my family during this illness, is quite beyond me! — Every dear brother so affectionate and so anxious! — and as for my sister! — Words must fail me in any attempt to describe what a nurse she has been to me. Thank God! she does not seem the worse for it *yet*, and as there was never any sitting-up necessary, I am willing to hope she has no after-fatigues to suffer from." And then, characteristically, "I have so many alleviations and comforts to bless the Almighty for! — My head was always clear, and I have scarcely any pain; my chief sufferings were from feverish nights, weakness and languor."

With a touch of her old humour she described herself as "really a very genteel, portable sort of an invalid". James was to lend his carriage to take her the sixteen miles to Winchester. "Now, that's a sort of thing which Mrs. J. Austen does in the kindest manner! — But still she is in the main *not* a liberal-minded woman, and as to this reversionary property's amending that part of her character, expect it not my dear Anne — too late, too late in the day." Even the shadow of death would not stop Jane Austen facing facts. She had studied character too long and too closely to be ready for easy, optimistic solutions. And that she was aware of death, hovering, but temporarily withdrawn, is clear from the end of this letter: "I have not mentioned my dear mother; she suffered much for me when I was at the worst, but is tolerably well. — Miss Lloyd too has been all kindness. In short, if I live to be an old woman, I must expect to wish I had died now; blessed in the tenderness of such a family, and before I had survived either them or their affection. — You would have held the memory of your friend Jane too in tender regret I am sure." There is valediction in every line.

[1] Probably a connection of the other Mr. Lyford, who had attended Mrs. Austen earlier.

It was at about this time that Caroline Austen had her last sight of her aunt. She was visiting her half-sister Anna Lefroy at Wyards, while her parents were at Scarlets helping Jane Leigh Perrot arrange her late husband's affairs. Calling at Chawton, Caroline and Anna were taken upstairs to where their aunt "in her dressing-gown . . . was sitting quite like an invalid in an arm-chair, but she got up and kindly greeted us, and then, pointing to seats which had been arranged for us by the fire, she said: 'There is a chair for the married lady, and a little stool for you, Caroline.' " "I was struck," Caroline reported, "by the alteration in herself. She was very pale, her voice was weak and low, and there was about her a general appearance of debility and suffering; but I have been told that she never had much acute pain. She was not equal to the exertion of talking to us, and our visit to the sick room was a very short one, Aunt Cassandra soon taking us away. I do not suppose we stayed a quarter of an hour; and I never saw Aunt Jane again."

The circumstances of this visit suggest one of the many good reasons that must have decided the move to Winchester. There was Mr. Lyford, of course, that "man of more than provincial reputation", as he is described in the *Memoir*. Jane Austen, who thought him "*very good*", obviously had confidence in him, and the move to Winchester was much easier than one to London, with its sad memories of Henry's bankruptcy. And, clearly, a move had to be made. Chawton Cottage may have seemed "very snug" when the Austen ladies moved in, but it was no place to nurse a serious illness. One look at the tiny bedroom traditionally assigned to Cassandra and Jane makes one wonder how they could have fitted in a chair and a little stool by the fire, as well as the bare minimum furnishings of a bedroom. Perhaps Martha Lloyd, who had presumably been given the larger front room next to Mrs. Austen's, had vacated it on Jane's illness, and it is also possible that the house was to some extent remodelled during the nineteenth century, but the fact remained that all the bedrooms at Chawton were too close together to give even a minimum of privacy. And at seventy-seven Mrs. Austen had a right to be protected from the anguish of her younger daughter's death, and Jane a right to be spared the pain of trying to protect her. One can only imagine the silent suffering of the "feverish nights" to which she confessed, when any undue movement must inevitably rouse her dear sister and nurse, and, in all probability, the other occupants of the cramped first floor at Chawton. It may well have been with feelings of relief that the two sisters left the invaluable Martha to look after their mother, and set off on their last journey together.

It rained all the way to Winchester that 24th of May, and Jane, in the carriage with Cassandra, was anxious about her brother Henry and her nephew William Knight, who rode beside them. Did she peer out, through the spring rain, at the new green of rolling downs and leafing hedgerows and remember that other hedge, where Anne Elliot had heard more than she bargained for, or how she herself had written, long ago, to ask Cassandra what the hedges were like in Northamptonshire? Whatever she thought, she probably felt that it was her last sight of spring.

Their old friend Mrs. Heathcote had found them excellent lodgings in College Street, with "a neat little drawing room with a bow-window overlooking Dr. Gabell's garden". The house still stands, with its green view towards the Palace wall. Mrs. Heathcote was nearby in the Close, but her sister Alethea Bigg was "frisked off like half England, into Switzerland". There were nephews, one Knight and one Heathcote, at Winchester College to keep them in touch with life, which Jane Austen would not let go easily. On May 27th she was writing to another nephew, James Edward Austen, who was now at Exeter College, Oxford, to say that she was "gaining strength very fast ... Mr. Lyford says he will cure me, and if he fails I shall draw up a memorial and lay it before the Dean and Chapter, and have no doubt of redress from that pious, learned, and disinterested body." Did she believe Mr. Lyford? It seems doubtful. The end of this letter strikes an unusual note of gloomy introspection. "If ever you are ill, may you be as tenderly nursed as I have been, may the same blessed alleviations of anxious, sympathising friends be yours, and may you possess—as I dare say you will—the greatest blessing of all, in the consciousness of not being unworthy of their love. *I could not feel this.*"

Jane Austen may sometimes have written a sharp thing, but I am sure she never consciously wrote a false one. She must have meant it when she told her nephew that she felt unworthy of her family's love. Was this simply the depression attendant on her illness, or was she spiritually casting up her accounts? Owing to Cassandra's ruthless destruction of so many of her letters we do not know all the sharp things that Jane Austen said or wrote in her lifetime, but her standards were high: she would have remembered. And, particularly, writing to James Edward, son of James and Mary, she must have remembered the impatience towards them that shows even in the expurgated letters that remain. Facing death, she may well also have regretted that long failure of communication between herself and her mother.

One more letter survives from this time, undated, and to an unknown recipient. Quoted by Henry in his *Biographical Notice* of his sister, it has been heavily cut. After speaking of Cassandra, her "tender, watchful, indefatigable nurse", Jane Austen must have gone on to describe the bitter blow of James Leigh Perrot's will. This passage has been cut, but the characteristic conclusion preserved: "But I am getting too near complaint. It has been the appointment of God, however secondary causes may have operated . . . You will find Captain —— a very respectable, well-meaning man, without much manner, his wife and sister all good humour and obligingness, and I hope (since the fashion allows it) with rather longer petticoats than last year." It was like Jane Austen to go on trying "To move wild laughter in the throat of death".[1]

But though she would go gallantly on pretending to the last, her family could no longer be deceived. Cassandra, it is true, went on writing hopefully to their mother at Chawton, and Mrs. Austen passed on the deceptively good news to her grand-daughter, Anna Lefroy. "Mr. Lyford says he thinks better of her than he has ever done, though he must still consider her in a precarious state." Mrs. Austen would not be warned. "I had a very comfortable account of your Aunt Jane this morning; she now sits up a little." She was writing to Caroline, and added a significant note: "Your Mamma is there . . . which I am very glad of. Cassandra did not quite like the nurse they had got, so wished Mrs. J. A. to come in her stead, as she promised she would whenever she was wanted."

It was an irony Jane Austen was equipped to appreciate that of all the women she had known, and the few that she had really loved, it should be her sister-in-law, James's Mary ("*not* a liberal-minded woman") who promised Cassandra to come when she was needed, and came. Martha was busy looking after old Mrs. Austen; Frank's Mary was occupied with her ninth child; and Fanny, the beloved niece, was only twenty-four. She stayed in Kent and noted in her diary, "another hopeless account from Winchester". But she went on writing "those kind, amusing letters" to her aunt, and one actually arrived, and was opened and looked at, on the last morning of Jane Austen's life.

At Steventon, there were no illusions now. Mary Austen had been summoned to Winchester early in June, and at that time her husband wrote to their son James Edward in Oxford, "I grieve to write what you will grieve to read; but I must tell you that we can no longer flatter ourselves with the least hope of having your dear valuable Aunt Jane restored to us . . . She is well aware of her situation . . . with such a pulse it was impossible for any person to last long, and indeed no one can wish it—an easy departure from this to a better world is all that we can pray for."

[1] Shakespeare's *Love's Labour's Lost*.

Jane was incorrigible. She went on thinking about living, and the living. It must be at about this time that she sent her message to Caroline Austen about reading more and writing less. No doubt this was conveyed by Caroline's mother, now installed as second nurse, sharing the nights with Cassandra and the maid, in the comfortable lodgings in College Street. Edward, Henry and James were all close at hand now, and Frank not far off at Alton. Did Jane Austen remember the old, sociable family days at Steventon? The day before her death, according to Henry, she wrote a set of mildly comic verses about Winchester and St. Swithin. But then, verse had never been her strong point. What she was doing, and doing brilliantly, was keeping the family tone light to the last.

"She retained her faculties, her memory, her fancy, her temper, and her affections, warm, clear, and unimpaired, to the last." It is Henry speaking, only five months after her death. "Neither her love of God, nor of her fellow creatures flagged for a moment. She made a point of receiving the sacrament before excessive bodily weakness might have rendered her perception unequal to her wishes. She wrote whilst she could hold a pen, and with a pencil when a pen was become too laborious."

She had two clergymen brothers, now, to administer the sacrament. That duty done, her manners remained perfect to the end. "Her last voluntary speech," says Henry, "conveyed thanks to her medical attendant." James Edward Austen-Leigh, writing his *Memoir*, years later, recalled an even more significant remark. On her deathbed, Jane Austen turned to her sister-in-law, James's tiresome wife, Mrs. Norris *in petto*, who had come to help nurse her. "You have always been a kind sister to me, Mary." That last duty done, she was, to all intents and purposes, alone with Cassandra, as, in a way, she had always been. She slept a great deal through the last few days of her life, but even Cassandra did not realise how near the end was, that night of July 17th. Writing to Fanny, after it was all over, Cassandra said she "had no suspicion how rapidly my loss was approaching—I *have* lost a treasure, such a sister, such a friend as never can have been surpassed—she was the sun of my life, the gilder of every pleasure, the soother of every sorrow." The end, at last, came quickly, as her brother had hoped for her, and she had hoped for others. "She felt herself to be dying about half an hour before she became tranquil and apparently unconscious. During that half hour was her struggle, poor soul." When asked if she wanted anything, she replied, "Nothing but death," and died, as she would have wished, in her sister's arms, very early on the morning of July 18th.

She was buried in Winchester Cathedral on the 24th, early in the morning, so as not to interrupt the regular services, with three of her brothers, Edward, Henry and Frank in attendance, and James Edward there representing his father, who was unwell. Years later, writing his *Memoir* of his aunt, James Edward remembered the occasion. "Her brothers went back sorrowing to their several homes. They were very fond and very proud of her. They were attached to her by her talents, her virtues, and her engaging manners; and each loved afterwards to fancy a resemblance in some niece or daughter of his own to the dear sister Jane, whose perfect equal they yet never expected to see."

"*Not* to have found Aunt Jane at Chawton," wrote Caroline Austen, long afterwards, "*would* have been a blank indeed," and a nephew who visited the house in later years confessed to being always disappointed. He expected particular happiness in that house, and found it there no longer. The laughter had died from Chawton Cottage; but only half of Jane Austen's double life was over. The laughter lives on: in Elizabeth and Emma; in Mr. Collins and Miss Bates; at Sotherton and Box Hill and Sanditon. Jane Austen did not deal much in death in her novels. It was life, and the living of it, that she cared about. And the testament she left, more important than any memorial, whether at Winchester or Westminster, lies in the six novels, where:

> Sudden in a shaft of sunlight
> Even while the dust moves
> There rises the hidden laughter.[1]

---

[1] From *Burnt Norton* by T. S. Eliot.

Appendix I

JANE AUSTEN'S LITERARY EARNINGS

Jane Austen's own statement, quoted in the Life.

Profits of my novels over and above the £600 in the Navy Fives.

Residue from the 1st Edit. of *Mansfield Park* remaining in Henrietta St., March 1816.	£13 7s.
Received from Egerton, on 2nd Edit. of *Sense and Sensibility,* March 1816.	£12 15s.
February 21st, 1817. First Profits of *Emma.*	£38 18s.
March 7th, 1817. From Egerton. 2nd Edit. of *Sense and Sensibility.*	£19 13s.

The £600 in the Navy Fives constituted earnings from the earlier books:

First edition of *Sense and Sensibility.*	£140
Pride and Prejudice sold outright.	£110
Therefore, before Jane Austen wrote her note, *Mansfield Park* and the 2nd Edition of *Sense and Sensibility* must have made:	£350

Figures from John Murray's Ledgers.

All books published on a commission of 10%: then all profits to author.
Emma. 2,000 copies printed in 1815.

Author's (or representative's) account:	1816	£221	6	4
	1817	72	1	9

Author's (or representative's) account: 1817   £15 7 4
                                               1818   3 1 9
     1819   12 5 9
     1821   48 10 0

Author's (or representative's) account:	1817	£15	7	4
	1818	3	1	9
	1819	12	5	9
	1821	48	10	0

Balance of copies sold at sale.

Mansfield Park. 2nd Edition. 1,750 copies printed February 1816.

Author's (or representative's) account:	1816	*Loss of* £182	8	3
	1817	Credit 21	12	4
	1819	,, 22	4	6
	1820	,, 19	1	0
	1821	,, 56	0	6

Balance of copies sold at sale.

Northanger Abbey and Persuasion. 1,750 copies printed December 1817.

Author's (or representative's) account:	1818	£533	14	11
	1819	23	0	2
	1820	39	2	6

N.B. *Sense and Sensibility* cost 15/- for three volumes.
     Pride and Prejudice cost 18/- for three volumes.
     Mansfield Park cost 18/- for three volumes.
     Emma cost 21/- for three volumes.
     Northanger Abbey and Persuasion, with Henry Austen's *Biographical Notice,* cost 24/- for four volumes.

Appendix II

Cassandra's note on the dating of Jane Austen's novels. Reproduced in the Oxford Edition of the *Minor Works*.

First Impressions begun in October 1796. Finished in August 1797. Published afterwards, with alterations and contractions under the title of *Pride and Prejudice*.

Sense and Sensibility begun November 1797. I am sure that something of this same story and characters had been written earlier and called *Elinor and Marianne*.

Mansfield Park begun sometime about February 1811—Finished soon after June 1813.

Emma begun January 21st, 1814, finished March 29th, 1815.

Persuasion begun August 8th, 1815, finished August 6th, 1816.

Northanger Abbey was written about the years '98 and'99.

C.E.A.

N.B. The precise dates given for *Emma* and *Persuasion* suggest that the manuscripts at least of these books must have survived until Cassandra wrote her note.

Appendix III

Northanger Abbey

No one would take Catherine Morland for a heroine. She is neither beautiful, nor brilliant, nor penniless, nor hopelessly in love. In short, she is the antithesis of the Gothic heroines of Jane Austen's day. Growing up in the Wiltshire village where her father is clergyman, she gets her first chance at romance when childless neighbours, the Allens, invite her to go to Bath with them. But at first Bath disappoints her high expectations. Mr. Allen is sensible, but silent; Mrs. Allen thinks of nothing but clothes and gossip. And they have no friends.

Even Catherine's first ball is a bitter disappointment of crowded rooms and no partner. Her second is better. The master of ceremonies introduces a young clergyman called Henry Tilney who dances with her and teases her agreeably. And next day Mrs. Allen meets an old friend, Mrs. Thorpe, who is in Bath with her daughters. Catherine and the oldest one, Isabella, instantly become dearest friends, exchanging details of the latest "horrid" romances they have read, and happily discussing Henry Tilney and Catherine's elder brother, James, who is at Oxford with Isabella's brother, John.

Catherine's only sorrow is that Mr. Tilney has disappeared; she is too innocent to understand Isabella's heavy hints about her own brother James. Soon James Morland and John Thorpe arrive. James is a young clergyman, sensible in everything but being in love with Isabella. Thorpe is a vapid young man, who decides at once to be in love with Catherine, whom he mistakenly thinks an heiress. He engages to dance with her at that night's ball, but is late in claiming her hand. Henry Tilney reappears with his sister Eleanor and asks Catherine to dance, but she has to refuse him and spend a miserable evening with John Thorpe.

Isabella and James are happy together, but Catherine is increasingly disillusioned with John Thorpe. Worst of all, he threatens her ripening friendship with the Tilneys by lying about her engagements. The first time he does this, he succeeds, but the second time she runs after the Tilneys to explain. Their father, General Tilney, treats her with extraordinary kindness and soon invites her to go back to Northanger Abbey with them. Catherine is in ecstasy. The Abbey is sure to be just like the ones she has read about, with a ghost, at least, or a skeleton somewhere. Meanwhile James and Isabella get engaged, but Isabella is disappointed with the financial provision Mr. Morland senior is prepared to make for them. The Thorpes have been deluding themselves about the Morland finances. Catherine is surprised that, in James's absence, Isabella should dance and flirt so happily with Henry's elder brother, handsome Captain Tilney. She consults Henry about this, but he laughs at her affectionately as usual, only becoming serious when he sees that she is really concerned, and reassuring her as best he may.

At first, Northanger Abbey is a disappointment. It is so modern, so comfortable, that there seems little chance of ghost or skeleton. But alone in her room at night, with the wind rising outside, Catherine gives way to the romantic fears that Henry has jokingly raised on the journey there. She has just found a mysterious document in a chest, when her candle blows out, and she retires to bed in terror. Next morning the document turns out to be a laundry list. She feels a fool, but is too happy to be angry with herself for long. Only the General is curiously oppressive. Effusively polite to Catherine, he has a quelling effect on his children. Catherine is soon convinced that he either murdered his wife, or, more likely, has shut her up in some remote part of the house. Henry finds her investigating the late Mrs. Tilney's room and gently disabuses her. Once again she feels a fool, but forgives herself, since Henry has. Even the news that James and Isabella have broken off their engagement cannot cloud her happiness for long. And a palpably insincere letter from Isabella, who has lost both James and Captain Tilney, and wants James back, opens her eyes at last. She feels very grown up. Henry has gone back to his parsonage a few miles away, and one happy day, when General Tilney and the girls visit him there, the General's behaviour makes it clear that he looks on Catherine as its future mistress.

But it is a relief when he goes to London for a week, even though Henry can spend only a part of his time with the two girls. He is away when the General returns home, unexpectedly, late at night, and gives furious orders that Catherine is to leave next morning. Eleanor, his reluctant messenger, does everything she can to console Catherine, and at least sees to it that she has enough money for her expenses. The angry General will not even send a servant with her. She must set out on her long day's journey alone. But she is too unhappy to be frightened. What can she have done to anger the General so? And what will Henry think when he gets the pitiful little farewell message she leaves for him?

She reaches home safely, and her family's warm greetings are some consolation. But she cannot help pining for Henry, and her mother is soon anxious about her. A few days later, Henry himself appears, defying his father to propose to her. The General was misled by John Thorpe into thinking Catherine an heiress and therefore ordered his son to court her. Then he met Thorpe again in London, was told that she was penniless, and ordered Henry never to see her again.

The Morlands refuse to sanction the engagement until the General gives his consent. Luckily, the young man who left the laundry list in the spare room at Northanger Abbey becomes a viscount and is able to marry Eleanor, whom he has always loved. The General is mollified by this, and by the discovery that Catherine is not penniless after all, and consents to Henry's marriage. They are all ready "to begin perfect happiness".

Sense and Sensibility

Sensible Elinor and over-sensitive Marianne Dashwood are the daughters of a widow, whose husband has just died, leaving her in straitened circumstances, and charging his son by a previous marriage to look after them. But John Dashwood is weak and his wife Fanny selfish. Mrs. Dashwood and her three daughters are soon delighted to accept the offer of a cottage on the Devonshire estate of Sir John Middleton, a connection of hers.

Marianne indulges her grief at leaving their old home. Elinor, who has more cause, since she loves Fanny's brother, Edward Ferrars, is silent. At Barton Cottage they at once find themselves involved in the social life of the big house. Sir John's idea of bliss is to get a few young people together for a dance; his wife thinks of nothing but society and her spoiled children. Her gossiping, vulgar mother, Mrs. Jennings, is staying at Barton Park, and is soon teasing the Dashwood girls about beaux, and Marianne about another guest, Colonel Brandon, an older man, whom Marianne dismisses as beyond marriage. He wears a flannel waistcoat.

To Elinor's silent grief, Edward does not visit them, but Marianne has a romantic encounter with a handsome young man called Willoughby, who is staying with a relative in the district. Marianne and Willoughby make no secret of their delight in each other's company and are naturally the target of much gossip. Colonel Brandon receives an urgent summons to London, and Willoughby too leaves suddenly, and with no promise of returning. Marianne is in despair, but a distraction is provided by a visit, at last, from Edward Ferrars, who surprises them by revealing that he has already been in the district a fortnight, staying with his old tutor. And at first he is so reserved and so strange that his visit gives Elinor little pleasure. Entirely dependent on his capricious mother, he tells them that he wishes now that he had insisted on entering one of the professions. He only stays a week, and Marianne is shocked that Elinor takes his going with such apparent calm.

Mrs. Jennings' other daughter, silly Charlotte Palmer, and her rude husband, have joined the party at Barton Park, and when they go, Sir John invites two Miss Steeles, connections of his wife's, to stay. Both are vulgar, but Miss Steele is thirty and plain, Miss Lucy young and pretty. They soon endear themselves to Lady Middleton by their sycophantic attentions to her spoiled children, and Lucy makes a great point of telling Elinor (in deepest confidence) all about her secret engagement to—Edward Ferrars. At first, Elinor cannot believe it, but it is all too evidently true. The Misses Steele's uncle is the tutor Edward has been visiting. It is soon obvious to Elinor that Lucy is holding a reluctant lover to a rash engagement. She suffers, endures Lucy's confidences, and says nothing.

Mrs. Jennings invites Elinor and Marianne to go to London with her, and to Elinor's amazement Marianne insists on accepting. Her longing to see Willoughby outweighs her scorn of kind, vulgar old Mrs. Jennings. But Willoughby proves elusive. More and more distressed, Marianne writes to him in vain, finally accosts him at a party and is brutally snubbed. One more letter elicits a ruthless answer, announcing his engagement to someone else. The news is soon official, and Marianne's real anguish is increased by the well-meant condolences of Mrs. Jennings and her circle. Colonel Brandon visits Elinor to tell her that Marianne has had a lucky escape. His sudden summons to town from Barton Park was because Willoughby had seduced his ward, whose sad story he tells. Perhaps if Marianne knows this, it will help her to forget Willoughby . . .

The Middletons come to town, bringing the Misses Steele with them, and Elinor is again forced to endure Lucy's confidences. Worse still, John and Fanny Dashwood, and Edward himself, soon arrive. Fanny and her tyrannical mother, old Mrs. Ferrars, suspect Edward of loving Elinor, and disapprove. Being rich himself, at least in expectation, he must marry money. They make a point of being kind to Lucy, and slighting Elinor. Misled by this, Lucy's sister blurts out the whole story of the secret engagement. The result is a series of scenes, and Edward's disinheritance in favour of his conceited younger brother, Robert. Despite this, Lucy still refuses to free Edward, protesting her great love.

The news of this engagement, and Elinor's long knowledge of it, shocks Marianne, who feels guilty about the way she has been indulging her own grief over Willoughby, while Elinor has suffered in silence. It is a relief to both when the Palmers invite Mrs. Jennings to bring them to their house, which is on the way home to Barton. Before they leave, Colonel Brandon asks Elinor to act as his intermediary in offering a small living on his estate to Edward, who intends to become a clergyman now that he has been disinherited. It is a painful office to Elinor, but she discharges it, and is rewarded by Lucy's effusive happiness.

At the Palmers' country house, Marianne neglects her health and becomes gravely ill. Fearing infection, the Palmers leave, but Mrs. Jennings stays, and finally Colonel Brandon (also a guest) offers to fetch Mrs. Dashwood. The night they are expected, Marianne passes through a crisis and begins to recover. Elinor hears a carriage, hurries downstairs to give her mother the good news, and is confronted by—Willoughby. He has abandoned his new wife to come and enquire after Marianne, and to tell Elinor that he always has and always will love her, but has allowed material considerations to outweigh this, and made himself unhappy for ever. To her amazement, Elinor finds herself sorry for him, and promises to give Marianne his message when she is strong enought to bear it.

He leaves, and Mrs. Dashwood and Brandon arrive to be greeted with the news of Marianne's recovery. When she is a little stronger Elinor tells her about Willoughby's visit. Back, at last, at Barton, Marianne is all plans for reform, But Elinor is suffering silently for lack of news of Edward. One day their servant comes back from Exeter with the news that, "Mr. Ferrars is married." He has met the young couple and Lucy has particularly charged him with messages for them.

Elinor is bearing this with her usual fortitude, when Edward himself appears, and after some initial misunderstanding, explains that Lucy has in fact married his younger brother, Robert. Amazement and delight are equally mixed. At last the way is clear for Edward and Elinor. Mrs. Ferrars ungraciously agrees, and gives them enough to marry on, but Robert and clever Lucy are soon established as her favourite children.

Edward and Elinor marry and settle in the parsonage on Colonel Brandon's estate, and presently Marianne submits to the "extraordinary fate" of marrying the man she once thought too old for marriage, and better still, of loving him.

Pride and Prejudice

When a young, unmarried man rents the nearby big house, Netherfield Park, there is great excitement in the Bennet family. Mrs. Bennet is a silly woman, with two sensible daughters, Jane and Elizabeth, and three who take after herself, Lydia, Kitty and Mary. Mr. Bennet gets his pleasure out of teasing his wife, as now, when he pretends he will not call on the eligible newcomer. Mr. Bingley and his guests make their first public appearance at a local ball. Bingley is a pleasant-looking young man, but he is outshone by his rich and handsome friend, Mr. Darcy. Darcy, however, alienates public opinion by dancing only with Bingley's two sisters, one married, one single. Bingley dances happily with Jane Bennet, and Elizabeth overhears him urging Darcy to ask her to dance. Lively Elizabeth makes a joke of his answer. She is "not handsome enough to tempt *me*".

Bingley's two sisters make friends with Jane Bennet, and Elizabeth watches Bingley's attentions to her sister with pleasure. She is unaware that Darcy is becoming attracted to herself, and gives him a lively set-down when he asks her to dance at a party given by their friends the Lucases. Jane is invited to dine at Netherfield, is made to ride there by her mother, and catches cold. Anxious about her, Elizabeth walks there and arrives, flushed, and with muddy petticoats, thus arousing Miss Bingley's scorn, and Darcy's admiration. Jane is really ill, and both sisters stay on at Netherfield. Jane is in love with Bingley by now, but is too well-bred to let it show. Elizabeth continues to spar with Darcy.

Returning home, the two girls learn that their cousin, Mr. Collins, is to visit them. He is the heir to the estate, which is entailed. This is a sore point with Mrs. Bennet, who cannot understand the law of succession to heirs male. As she and her husband have saved nothing, this is a serious business for their daughters, who have only small dowries. Mr. Collins has written a silly letter, and turns out to be a comically silly, pompous man, but he arrives prepared to make the best amends in his power by marrying one of the Bennet girls. His eye first lights on Jane, but Mrs. Bennet, who is delighted with his plan, explains that Jane has another interest. He transfers his "affections" to Elizabeth.

Meanwhile a regiment has been quartered in the nearby town of

Meryton and the younger Bennet girls are uniform mad. A charming young man called Wickham has just joined the regiment and meets the young Bennets at the house of their aunt, Mrs. Philips. Elizabeth has already witnessed an odd encounter between Wickham and Mr. Darcy. Now, he tells her how Darcy, whose father was his patron, has refused to fulfil his obligations to him. Much attracted to Wickham, Elizabeth is confirmed in her dislike of Darcy. Mr. Collins, too, turns out to be acquainted with Darcy. His rectory is on the estate of Darcy's aunt, Lady Catherine de Bourgh. His sycophantic praise of Lady Catherine adds to Elizabeth's dislike of her nephew.

Mr. Bingley gives a ball at Netherfield, and to Elizabeth's surprise and disappointment, Wickham does not come. It is a painful evening. All her family save Jane contrive to make public fools of themselves in one way or another, and sparring with Darcy is no consolation for Wickham's absence. Worst of all, she sees Darcy close by when her mother is boasting about the match she expects between Jane and Bingley. Next morning, Mr. Collins proposes to Elizabeth and refuses to take no for an answer. Mrs. Bennet sides with him; Mr. Bennet with Elizabeth. In the end, he goes off in a huff, is comforted by Elizabeth's friend Charlotte Lucas, and amazes everyone by proposing to her a few days later. Elizabeth, who loves Charlotte, is shocked when she accepts him, but Charlotte, who is plain, twenty-seven and realistic, says this is her last chance, and she must take it.

A note from Miss Bingley announces that their whole party is leaving Netherfield at once and returning to London. Elizabeth suspects that Bingley's sisters are trying to separate him from Jane, but is confident that they will not succeed. She has forgotten Charlotte's warning that Jane might conceal her feelings too well for her own good. Jane is quietly unhappy, and proportionately pleased when her favourite aunt and uncle, the Gardiners, come to stay, and invite her to go back to London with them. But there, disappointment awaits her. Miss Bingley calls, formally, once. There is no word from her brother. Worse still, Miss Bingley refers to his engagement to Darcy's sister as a certain thing.

Meanwhile Mrs. Gardiner has warned Elizabeth against falling in love with the penniless, charming Wickham, and Wickham himself has proved fickle, falling publicly in love with a plain girl who has just inherited ten thousand pounds. One way and another, Elizabeth is actually glad to go and visit Charlotte, who has married Mr. Collins and settled down at Hunsford Parsonage, on Lady Catherine's estate. Mr. Collins is as silly as ever, but Charlotte manages him admirably. Lady

Catherine is a domineering snob, and astounded when Elizabeth stands up to her.

Mr. Darcy and his cousin Colonel Fitzwilliam come to stay with Lady Catherine, and Charlotte is amazed at the frequency of Darcy's visits to the Parsonage. Even Elizabeth is surprised when she keeps meeting him on her walks. One day, she meets Fitzwilliam, who is loud in his praises of Darcy, and tells her how he saved his friend Bingley from a disastrous marriage. This upsets her so much that she pleads headache and stays at home when the Collinses go to the big house that evening. She is amazed to be visited by Darcy, who plunges into a proposal that begins, inauspiciously: "In vain have I struggled."

Elizabeth rejects him, furiously, and tasks him with his bad behaviour both to Wickham and to Jane. Next day, when she is out walking, he gives her a letter. At first it makes her angrier then ever, but gradually it carries conviction. Jane's calm good manners had convinced him that she did not love Bingley, and Elizabeth must admit that her family are not a desirable connection. As for Wickham, Darcy's story is very different from his, and finally convincing. Among other misdeeds, Wickham actually tried to seduce Darcy's sister, Georgiana. The letter ends, "God bless you." Elizabeth cannot help a small change in her feelings towards Darcy. It is no longer possible absolutely to hate him.

Jane and Elizabeth return home together, and are delighted to hear that the regiment is to leave Meryton for Brighton. When Lydia is invited to accompany a flighty young officer's wife, Elizabeth urges her father to refuse his permission, but he will not exert himself to do so, and Lydia goes off in high spirits. Elizabeth goes on a sightseeing tour in Derbyshire with the Gardiners, and is taken aback when they propose visiting Darcy's house, Pemberley. But a few discreet enquiries assure her that Darcy is not in residence. They go, and she cannot help thinking that she might have been mistress of this splendid house. The Gardiners, who have heard only of Darcy's pride and Wickham's sufferings (for Darcy's letter to Elizabeth was strictly confidential), are astonished at the housekeeper's praise of her master as she shows them round. In the gardens, they are suddenly joined by Darcy himself, who has just arrived. Both he and Elizabeth are too confused to say anything very sensible, and he leaves without being introduced to the Gardiners, but rejoins them later and amazes them by making Mr. Gardiner free of his fishing, and inviting the ladies to meet his sister. What has happened to proud Mr. Darcy?

Bingley and his sisters are staying with the Darcys, so the general meeting is fraught with tension, but Elizabeth is proof against Miss

Bingley's spiteful darts, and she likes tall, shy Georgiana Darcy. A letter from Jane ends this happy episode. Lydia has eloped from Brighton – with Wickham. Hurrying to find her uncle and enlist his help, Elizabeth encounters Darcy and pours out the whole wretched story. He sympathises, promises silence; they talk incoherently, and part. Elizabeth knows that Lydia's disgrace (for why should Wickham marry her?) must ruin her sisters.

The Gardiners are all sympathy, and they return at once to Meryton. Mr. Bennet is already in London, trying to find the vanished couple, and Gardiner goes after him. At first, things look worse and worse. They learn that Wickham left Brighton because he was heavily in debt. What hopes are there of a marriage, considering Lydia's small dowry? Besides, the couple cannot be traced ... Then, after Mr. Bennet has returned home, a letter from Mr. Gardiner brings better news. Lydia and Wickham have been found in London lodgings. Wickham has agreed to marry Lydia, and she is already safe with her aunt and uncle.

Mr. Bennet wonders how much money his brother-in-law has paid out to achieve this "happy" result. Mrs. Bennet is in ecstasy: a daughter married at last. Wickham is transferring to a north country regiment, and after some discussion it is agreed that, for appearance' sake, the young couple shall come home for a few days after their marriage. They arrive, hardened, impenitent, even boastful. A chance remark of Lydia's to Elizabeth reveals that Darcy was at her wedding. Puzzled, Elizabeth writes to Mrs. Gardiner to ask the meaning of this. A long answer registers surprise at the question. Archly, Mrs. Gardiner says she expected Elizabeth to know all about it. She has been assuming that Darcy's interest in Lydia's fate stems from an engagement with Elizabeth, and still imagines that this will soon take place. She reveals that it was Darcy who discovered the couple, and Darcy who made all the arrangements and put up the money to bribe Wickham into marriage.

Next comes the news that the Bingleys are back at Netherfield, and soon Bingley and Darcy come to call. Since only Elizabeth knows the true state of the case, Mrs. Bennet is appalled that disagreeable Mr. Darcy should spoil Jane's first meeting with her lost lover. An uncomfortable meeting follows, but soon Jane and Bingley are as happy as ever, and this time he proposes. Mrs. Bennet's triumph is complete. Lydia's match is nothing to Jane's.

Lady Catherine de Bourgh arrives, unannounced, insists on seeing Elizabeth alone, and demands that she promise never to marry Darcy. Though she has no hope, Elizabeth refuses to give any such undertaking, and Lady Catherine leaves in a rage. Next day, Mr. Bennet receives a letter from Mr. Collins warning him not to sanction a match between Elizabeth and Darcy. Bennet, who knows nothing of the change in Elizabeth's feelings, finds this very funny, and expects her to share his amusement.

Darcy is away. Will he come back? If he does, Elizabeth feels she must thank him for what he has done for Lydia. He arrives, encouraged by Lady Catherine's angry report of her meeting with Elizabeth. Elizabeth seizes a chance to thank him, and gets a proposal in return. Her happiness is only clouded by her family's predictable reaction. Even Jane is amazed at first, and it serves her right when Elizabeth tells her she thinks she first started falling in love with Darcy on seeing his beautiful grounds at Pemberley. Mr. Bennet takes some convincing, but Mrs. Bennet is soon in a seventh heaven. "Jane's is nothing to it." Mr. Bennet writes advising Mr. Collins to back Darcy, who has more to give, and Elizabeth soon recovers her old liveliness. "Did you admire me for my impertinence?" she asks Darcy. He is not likely to return to his old, proud ways.

Mansfield Park

Many years ago, Sir Thomas Bertram married one of three sisters. Lady Bertram is an amiable nonentity. Childless Mrs. Norris lives on Sir Thomas's estates and is very busy about the education of his children. The third sister, Mrs. Price, married beneath her, and is now the mother of a large, impoverished family at Portsmouth. When the story opens, Mrs. Norris has persuaded Sir Thomas that they should adopt the eldest Price girl, Fanny, between them. Fanny arrives and Sir Thomas soon sees that mean Mrs. Norris intends him to have all the expense of her education.

Miserably shy and frightened at first, Fanny is comforted by her cousin Edmund, but submits to plenty of good-natured bullying from his older brother Tom and his sisters Maria and Julia. Growing up, Tom gets into debt and his father takes him with him to Antigua, where he has business about his estates, but sends him back alone when he finds how long this will take. In Sir Thomas's absence, Mrs. Norris encourages an engagement between Maria and a stupid, rich Mr. Rushworth. Then the young Bertrams make friends with a brother and sister named Henry and Mary Crawford, who have come to stay with their half-sister, Mrs. Grant, the vicar's wife. This charming, lively couple of Londoners make a great change in life at Mansfield Park, and Mary Crawford is half inclined to fall in love with Tom Bertram — and his expectations. But Tom goes away, and she is surprised to find how well Edmund takes his place. Fanny, who always loved Edmund, watches, and suffers.

They all go to spend the day with Mr. Rushworth and his mother at Sotherton Court, where Henry Crawford is to give advice about possible "improvements" to the grounds. It is a hot, unlucky day. Maria and Julia are both a little in love with Crawford by now, and Rushworth is jealous. Fanny, who has been included in the party by Edmund's arrangement, watches it all — particularly Edmund's attentions to Mary Crawford. Only Mrs. Norris is happy: she has begged all kinds of domestic trifles from the housekeeper. The day holds an unpleasant surprise for Mary Crawford, who learns that Edmund is intended for the Church. She had really begun to consider marrying him, but a mere clergyman is impossible. She will tease him out of it. Fanny watches, as usual, and suffers. She tries to warn Edmund of possible danger in Henry Crawford's attentions to Maria, but he laughs it off.

Tom returns to Mansfield Park, bringing a stupid Mr. Yates who is stage mad. Soon they all catch the infection, except Edmund and Fanny, who are appalled when the others plan to put on a rather vulgar play called *Lovers' Vows*. Sir Thomas is at sea on the dangerous voyage home, and besides the play is full of undesirable possibilities for flirtation. Mr. Crawford chooses Maria to play opposite him, whereupon Julia walks out in a huff. Mary Crawford hopes to act with Edmund. Distressed when she learns he does not mean to take part, she sets to with a will to persuade him. In the end, reluctantly, he gives in, but Fanny will not, and Edmund has to defend her against the others, and particularly Mrs. Norris.

The estate carpenter turns Sir Thomas's study into a theatre; rehearsals begin; Edmund and Mary both call on Fanny in her cold little upstairs room to ask her to rehearse their embarrassing love scene, are delighted with the coincidence, and rehearse it together. Mrs. Norris is happily busy promoting the activities of the young people, while Fanny does her best to help Rushworth learn his part, and watches, with anxiety, his increasing jealousy of Maria and Crawford.

They are busy rehearsing, when Julia appears, aghast, to announce that Sir Thomas has arrived. The members of the family hurry to welcome him, and Fanny, creeping timidly in after the others, is surprised at the warmth with which stiff Sir Thomas greets her. But the moment of discovery cannot be long delayed. Visiting his study, Sir Thomas finds it a theatre, with Yates ranting out a speech. If he is angry, he hides it: nothing shall spoil his homecoming. But the theatre is soon a study once more, and Yates leaves in disgust. Crawford, too, goes, without proposing to Maria, as she had expected.

Sir Thomas approves of the Crawfords, but soon recognises Rushworth for the fool he is, and asks Maria if she wishes him to free her from her engagement. Furious at Crawford's defection, Maria assures her father that she is perfectly happy about her prospective marriage. It soon takes place, and the new Mr. and Mrs. Rushworth leave for Brighton, taking Julia with them. Now Crawford has gone, jealousy between the sisters is at an end.

Fanny is now the nearest thing to a daughter at Mansfield Park. Rather against her will, she finds herself involved in a friendship with Mary Crawford, who will talk to her about Edmund. Lady Bertram is surprised when Edmund and Fanny are invited to dine at the parsonage together, but Sir Thomas says Fanny must go, and sees to it that she has the carriage, rather than walking, as her Aunt Norris expects. Arriving, she and Edmund find that Crawford has returned.

Sir Thomas has noticed a great improvement in Fanny's looks, and so does Henry Crawford. He tells his sister that he means to entertain himself by making Fanny fall in love with him—just a little. Mary is delighted that he will stay, and merely warns him not to lead poor little Fanny too far. It occurs to neither of them that she may be proof against his charms.

Meanwhile, Fanny's favourite brother William comes to stay at Mansfield Park. William has been started in the Navy by Sir Thomas, has done well, and is home on leave. It is the first time he and Fanny have met since her adoption, though they have corresponded steadily ever since Edmund helped little Fanny rule the lines for her first letter.

The whole Mansfield party dine at the vicarage, and Sir Thomas begins to suspect that Crawford is in love with Fanny. It is a less happy evening for Mary, since Edmund's proposed benefice of Thornton Lacey, not far away, is a subject of discussion. Sir Thomas's return, which made Maria's marriage possible, is also the signal for Edmund to take orders. But everything else is forgotten when Sir Thomas decides to give a ball for Fanny and William. Fanny's chief problem is how to wear the amber cross William brought her. Mary Crawford offers her a choice of several gold chains, and, when she chooses one, reveals that it was a present to herself from her brother. Fanny tries to refuse it, but is over-ruled. Then Edmund, too, presents her with a chain ... After much debate, Fanny ends by wearing both. And she cannot help feeling happy when Edmund confides his conviction that he can never marry Mary: she has been spoiled by her education: she has told him she will never dance with him after he has taken orders.

At the ball, Crawford's attentions to Fanny confirm Sir Thomas's suspicions. William has to leave for London next day, and Crawford goes with him. Edmund, too, leaves for a final course of study before his ordination. They are a quiet group at Mansfield Park. Lady Bertram congratulates herself that they will always have Fanny, but Sir Thomas is not so sure.

Henry Crawford tells Mary that he has actually fallen in love with Fanny, and Mary is amazed and delighted at Fanny's luck. It turns out that Henry's visit to London was to introduce William to his own uncle, the Admiral, and the Admiral has now secured his much-desired promotion to lieutenant. Henry visits Fanny to tell her this, and then goes straight on to propose. Her delight turns to horrified surprise. She has watched him flirting too often to believe him serious. But next day he makes his proposals to Sir Thomas in form. Since Fanny cannot bring herself to tell Sir Thomas about Crawford's behaviour with her cousins, he is amazed and angry when she persists in refusing him, but hopes that time will bring her to her senses. Edmund, who has grieved Mary Crawford by staying away longer than he had planned, returns, and grieves Fanny by his arguments on Crawford's behalf. Mary Crawford also teases her; taking it for granted that she will soon succumb. It is a relief to Fanny when the Crawfords leave for London.

Sir Thomas, who wants Fanny to recognise what a chance she is missing, arranges for her to go home for the first time since her adoption. William is to visit Mansfield Park again and take Fanny back with him. She is delighted, and full of dreams of home at last. The reality is a shock. Her father drinks and swears; her mother is an incompetent slattern; her brothers and sisters are unmanageable, and the house filthy. Worst of all, William is greeted with his sailing orders and leaves at once. Fanny settles down to make the best of things, and soon finds a friend and pupil in her neglected younger sister Susan. But she pines for news of Mansfield Park, which she now looks on as her real home. Edmund has gone to London. Has he proposed to Mary Crawford? A gossipy letter from Mary herself sets her heart at rest for the moment, and mentions a flirtation between Yates and Julia. The Rushworths and Julia are now settled in London.

Mr. Crawford visits Portsmouth and pleases Fanny by his tactful attentions, and talk of Mansfield Park. By now, she is acutely homesick. Two months have passed; there is no talk of her return; her health is suffering from the confinement of the little house at Portsmouth. But worst of all is her anxiety about Edmund. And a letter from him, when it comes at last, brings little comfort. It is full of Mary. He has not proposed yet; he is still worried by her frivolity; but Fanny is sure he will forget his scruples, propose, and be miserable.

A letter from Lady Bertram announces that Tom is seriously ill, and Fanny longs to be at home to help nurse him, but still there is no word about her return. Mary Crawford writes that if Tom will only die, Edmund will be able to sink the clergyman in the "sir". Another letter follows surprisingly fast: Fanny must take no notice of a wicked rumour that is going round. But the rumour is true. Maria Rushworth has run away with Henry Crawford. To make bad worse, Julia elopes with Yates. In this crisis, Fanny is wanted at last at Mansfield Park, and Edmund comes to fetch her, and her sister Susan, whom Sir Thomas has thought of inviting. Edmund is ill and wretched, though the news of Tom is better. But he knows he has lost Mary. It is some time before he can bring himself to tell Fanny about their last interview; when Mary ended everything by her frivolous attitude towards her brother's adultery.

Tom recovers, and Julia marries Mr. Yates. As for Lady Bertram, when Fanny arrives, she actually gets up from her sofa, hurries forward, embraces her, and says, "Dear Fanny! now I shall be comfortable." Crawford soon abandons Maria, and Sir Thomas establishes her in seclusion with Mrs. Norris for her companion. The way is clear for Edmund and Fanny, and, "Exactly at the time when it was quite natural that it should be so, and not a week earlier, Edmund did cease to care about Miss Crawford, and became as anxious to marry Fanny, as Fanny herself could desire." Sir Thomas may have failed with three of his own children, but he has succeeded in bringing up his daughter-in-law. Tom reforms, Fanny is the daughter he wanted, and Susan will take her place with Lady Bertram.

Emma

Handsome, clever, rich, and nearly twenty-one, Emma Woodhouse has had few sorrows in her life. Her mother died when she was a small child, but was replaced by a loving governess, Miss Taylor. Her older sister, Isabella, married a Mr. John Knightley some years ago, and Emma has been left the mistress of her father's house, Hartfield; to all intents and purposes an only child, with all the hazards that implies. When the story opens, Miss Taylor has just married a neighbour, Mr. Weston, and Emma and her father are spending their first evening alone together. Missing her friend (for Miss Taylor was more friend than governess), Emma exerts herself to cheer up her valetudinarian father, and is delighted when another neighbour calls. This is Mr. Knightley, older brother of her sister's husband, a man in his middle thirties, and one of the few people who can see faults in Emma. He is also a good friend, and helps her through this difficult evening, but is shocked when she speaks of having "made" the match between Miss Taylor and Mr. Weston. But Emma will not be curbed, and talks in her lively way of making an equally good match for the clergyman, Mr. Elton.

She soon finds a possible wife for Elton in Harriet Smith, an older pupil at the local boarding school. Harriet is somebody's illegitimate daughter, knows nothing of her parentage, and has been left at the school, where her fees are anonymously paid. She is pretty, silly, eighteen and soon devoted to Emma. She is also devoted to a young farmer called Martin, brother of two of her school friends. But Emma decides that Harriet's unknown father is a gentleman, and she is worthy of better things ... for instance, of Mr. Elton. She soon convinces Harriet that Elton likes her, and Harriet obligingly falls in love with him. Young Martin proposes, in a surprisingly good letter, and Emma has some difficulty in persuading Harriet to refuse him. Learning of this, Knightley, who is Martin's landlord, and helped write his letter, is furious.

Emma does her best to precipitate a proposal from Elton, but he is strangely slow, and she is distracted by a Christmas visit from her sister, Isabella Knightley, her husband and children. This is a chance for Emma to make up her quarrel with the other Mr. Knightley, and she is glad to do so. But the visit is not pure pleasure. Mr. John Knightley, a London lawyer, is sometimes impatient with his father-in-law's fads and fancies. Emma and the other Mr. Knightley work together to keep things going smoothly ...

They are all invited to dine with the Westons, but at the last moment Harriet is unwell and cannot go. The evening is spoiled for Emma by Elton's attentions to herself, but worse is to follow. By accident they drive back home in a carriage together; he seizes her hand and proposes. In a painful scene, she affronts him by her assumption that his attentions have been to Harriet Smith. He goes angrily off to Bath, and Emma has the painful duty of breaking the truth to Harriet, who takes it beautifully and makes her feel worse than ever. She will make no more matches.

But she cannot help being interested in the idea of Frank Churchill, Mr. Weston's son by a previous marriage, who changed his name when he was adopted by his dead mother's rich family. He has never visited his father, but everyone expects that he will come now, to pay his respects to his new stepmother. He does not come, and Mr. Weston excuses him on the grounds of the tyranny of his aunt (and adoptive mother) Mrs. Churchill. Knightley will have none of this. Anyone can do their duty.

Walking out together, Emma and Harriet pay a call on Mrs. and Miss Bates. Mrs. Bates is the impoverished widow of a clergyman. Aged and infirm, she lives in lodgings with her devoted, garrulous daughter. Their main interest in life is Mrs. Bates's orphaned grand-daughter, Jane Fairfax, who has grown up in the family of Colonel Campbell, her dead father's friend. Now Miss Campbell has married a Mr. Dixon, and Emma learns that Jane is coming to stay with her grandmother, while the Campbells visit their daughter in Ireland. Jane is twenty-one, and penniless. She must earn her living as a governess.

She is also beautiful and accomplished, and Emma finds it hard to like her. She means to do better on this visit, but how can she, when Jane does everything so well, and is so intolerably cold and reserved? Jane has actually met Frank Churchill when at Weymouth with the Campbells, but Emma cannot get her to gossip about him. A painful distraction is the news of Elton's engagement, about which Harriet must be comforted. And Harriet is fluttered by a meeting with Miss Martin and her brother, who have been wonderfully kind to her. Emma takes her to call on the Martins, but limits her visit to the minimum quarter of an hour of token politeness, thus hurting their feelings.

Everything is forgotten in the arrival of Frank Churchill at last. Emma is aware that the Westons have ideas about her and him, and rather wonders if she shares them, specially when he turns out to be an extremely handsome, charming young man. His manners are perfect. He even makes a point of calling on Jane Fairfax, since, he explains, they are slightly acquainted. Soon he and Emma are discussing Jane. He finds her in poor looks, he says, and is interested to hear Emma's opinion of her piano-playing.

Next day, Frank shocks everyone by going off to London to have his hair cut. Mr. Knightley is confirmed in his view that he is a puppy. Emma has a preoccupation of her own. Some rather underbred people called Cole are giving a dinner party—and have not invited her. She has always thought that, if invited, she will refuse, but not to be invited is something else again. The invitation comes at last, and she accepts. Mr. Knightley brings Miss Bates and Jane Fairfax in his carriage, and Mrs. Weston suggests to Emma that he and Jane may marry. Emma is horrified. Knightley must not marry: think of his poor little nephews.

Jane Fairfax has received an anonymous gift of a piano. Most people assume that it is from Colonel Campbell, but Emma tells Frank that she suspects a more interesting giver. She suspects that Mr. Dixon (Miss Campbell's new husband) is secretly in love with Jane, and that is the real reason why she has been sent home. Later, she feels guilty about telling Frank this.

Next day, Emma, Harriet, the Westons and Frank Churchill all go to hear the new piano, and Frank shocks Emma by teasing Jane about its anonymous giver. They have had a little dancing at the Coles' party, and now the Westons think of giving a ball at the local inn, and Frank's visit is prolonged for the purpose. Then a letter summons him home. Mrs. Churchill is ill and the ball must be postponed. He calls to say goodbye to Emma; starts to say something; stops. He must, she thinks, be more in love with her than she had realised. She rather tries to love him in return, but it will not do. But he would be just the thing for Harriet. Poor Harriet certainly needs comforting, for Mr. Elton brings home his showy, vulgar bride. Even Emma suffers a little as the new bride takes precedence of her, and, worse still, patronises her. Sensing Emma's dislike, Mrs. Elton transfers her patronage to Jane Fairfax, and is soon looking out for desirable situations for her. Discussing this surprising friendship with Mrs. Weston and Mr. Knightley, Emma is led on to hint at the possibility of an engagement between Knightley and Jane. He denies it, rather red in the face, but Mrs. Weston is not convinced.

Frank Churchill is coming back, and Emma is somehow sure now that she does not love him. The ball takes place at last, but it holds as much pain as pleasure. Emma has to take second place to Mrs. Elton, while Mr. Elton snubs Harriet ruthlessly by refusing to dance with her. Emma is delighted when Knightley saves the situation by asking Harriet to dance. Later, she herself dances with him. After all, she says, they are not really brother and sister, and, no indeed, says he.

Next day, Frank Churchill rescues Harriet from a band of gipsies, and Emma is soon seriously planning a match between them. Harriet must be feeling better, for she destroys the piece of sticking plaster that Mr. Elton once handled, and some other precious, nonsensical souvenirs. She tells Emma she will never marry, and Emma urges her not to worry if the man she loves is a little above her socially. Emma is thinking of Frank Churchill. Harriet is delighted and grateful.

Summer comes, with calls and parties. Frank continues his attentions to Emma, and Mr. Knightley begins to suspect him of double-dealing. Is there not some secret between him and Jane Fairfax? He suggests this to

Emma, but she laughs at the idea. He gives a party at his home, Donwell Abbey, where he runs a modern farm, with the assistance of a manager, William Larkins. They all eat strawberries; Mrs. Elton badgers Jane Fairfax about a position she has found for her, and Jane walks off home alone. Soon afterwards, Frank Churchill arrives late, and in a very bad temper.

Next day, the same party go on a picnic to Box Hill. At first, everyone seems dull, Frank Churchill particularly so; then he cheers up and begins to flirt outrageously with Emma. Intoxicated by this, Emma is rude to harmless Miss Bates. Later, Knightley takes her to task for this, and she is miserable. Next day she calls to apologise, and is aware of bustle before she is shown in. Miss Bates explains that Jane is unwell. She has accepted the post Mrs. Elton found for her and is feeling the reaction. She is to leave in a fortnight. Frank, too, has gone. Mrs. Churchill is ill again.

Returning home, Emma finds Knightley visiting her father, and is pleased with his approval of what she has been doing. Next day, they are all amazed by the news of Mrs. Churchill's death. Emma's hopes rise for Harriet. Now Frank will be free to marry. Jane Fairfax is still ill, and Emma tries to be friendly, offering arrowroot and rides in her carriage, but is refused. Two weeks later she learns why. Mrs. Weston sends for her and breaks it to her that Frank and Jane have been secretly engaged all the time. The Westons have just learned this and are angry and anxious lest Emma has been misled by Frank's apparent attentions to herself. She reassures Mrs. Weston, and they are soon busy unravelling the strange story of the winter's deceptions. In the end, the strain of the secret engagement had told on Jane. She and Frank had quarrelled on the day of the party at Donwell; she had broken off the engagement and agreed to go as a governess. Now, with Mrs. Churchill's death, Frank is free to marry her, and all is well.

Once again, Emma has the painful duty of breaking the news to Harriet. But this time she is in for a surprise. Harriet is amazed at her concern. It is not Frank she loves, but Mr. Knightley, who rescued her, not from gipsies, but from Elton's rudeness. Emma is appalled. At last she understands that Knightley must marry no one but herself. He has been away in London, and when he returns he and Emma have a difficult discussion of the surprising engagement. Emma is finally forced to assure him that she was not betrayed into love by Frank's deceptive attentions. Something Knightley says makes her think he is going to tell her of his love for Harriet. She begs him to stop. At last, after some misunderstanding, the truth comes out. It is Emma he loves.

For the last time, Emma must break something to Harriet. But this is serious. She arranges for Harriet to visit her sister in London, then breaks the news of her engagement to Knightley by letter. But how can they marry without fatally upsetting Mr. Woodhouse? They agree that Knightley will have to come and live at Hartfield so long as his father-in-law is alive. But even so, when they break the news, he takes it badly. Mrs. Weston (who has just had a baby) helps to talk him round, and Mr. Weston spreads the news (officially a secret) all over the neighbourhood.

Knightley breaks it to Emma that Harriet has been seeing young Martin in London, by his arrangement, and has actually accepted him. He is afraid she will be angry, but she is delighted. She is happy enough, now, to face Frank Churchill and tease and be teased about the past. Jane finds it less funny. Harriet returns, happy in her engagement, and her father comes forward on the occasion and turns out to be a prosperous tradesman. So much for Emma's dreams. And she cannot persuade her father to agree to her marriage. Luckily, there is an outbreak of petty robbery in the district, and Mr. Woodhouse is so frightened that he sees the advantages of a resident son-in-law. Mrs. Elton thinks nothing of the wedding: "Very little white satin, very few lace veils; a most pitiful business!"

Persuasion

Sir Walter Elliot of Kellynch Hall cares only about his title, his appearance, and his eldest daughter, Elizabeth. A widower, with three daughters, he and Elizabeth once hoped that she would marry the heir to the title, Mr. Elliot, but Elliot actually repelled their advances. At twenty-nine, Elizabeth, as proud as her father, is still handsome, and still single. The youngest daughter, Mary, has married a respectable young neighbour, Charles Musgrove, but the middle one, Anne, is also single, at twenty-seven, and, worse still in her father's view, has lost her looks. Neglected by her father and sister, Anne turns to her dead mother's friend, Lady Russell, for company.

When the story opens, Sir Walter has run into debt through his habitual extravagance, and Lady Russell, Anne, and his man of business, Mr. Shepherd have combined to persuade him to let Kellynch Hall and take a cheaper house in Bath. It is 1814, and Mr. Shepherd suggests that Admiral Croft, on shore because of the peace with France, might make a good tenant. Croft and his wife are childless, and his wife's brother used to live in the district. Anne, who has proved surprisingly knowledgeable about the Navy, supplies the name: it was a Mr. Wentworth. Nobody else seems to remember that eight years ago she was briefly engaged to another brother, Captain Wentworth, but allowed herself to be persuaded by her father and Lady Russell into breaking off the engagement. Captain Wentworth then had no money; only the prospect of advancement in his hazardous profession. Watching, from afar, as he rises to success, Anne has increasingly regretted their bitter parting. She should not have let herself be convinced that it was in his interest to break off the engagement. Her only comfort now is that neither her own sister, Mary Musgrove, nor Wentworth's sister, Mrs. Croft, knows anything about the bygone affair. It is all over, and must be forgotten.

Lady Russell is delighted about the move to Bath, hoping it will break up an unfortunate friendship between Elizabeth and Mr. Shepherd's widowed daughter, sycophantic Mrs. Clay. But in the end Elizabeth invites Mrs. Clay to go to Bath with her, while Anne is left behind to stay with Lady Russell and with her sister Mary Musgrove, who is ailing as usual. Anne is glad to be of use, but she too is anxious about Mrs. Clay, and actually makes an effort to warn Elizabeth about what she suspects are her designs on their father. Elizabeth will not be warned. Mrs. Clay is plain and elderly; it is an absurd suspicion. Mrs. Clay goes to Bath, and Anne spends a week with Lady Russell before going to Mary's house at Uppercross, not far away.

Mary is sorry for herself as usual, but cheers up when they go to call on her husband's parents and sisters at the Great House. Anne soon finds herself, as always, the confidante of both sides in a rather difficult relationship. The Musgroves find Mary proud and tiresome, and make no secret of their wish that Anne had accepted Charles Musgrove, who proposed to her first. Now, Anne is treated as a confirmed spinster. When the young people have impromptu dances at the Great House, she plays the piano for them.

The Crofts move into Kellynch Hall and come to call on Mary. Anne takes to them at once, but is disconcerted by the news that Captain Wentworth is coming to stay with them. Old Mrs. Musgrove, too, takes this hard. It brings back memories of her dead son, a young scapegrace who was sent into the Navy, served under Captain Wentworth, and wrote of his kindness. One of Mary's little boys has had a bad fall, and Anne has to take charge, since Mary cannot manage an invalid.

Charles and Mary meet Wentworth at the Great House, and Charles brings him to call on the way to a day's sport. It is a painful meeting for Anne, but soon over, and her feelings unnoticed. Later, Mary tells her that Wentworth has found her wretchedly altered. It is true. Wentworth has never forgiven Anne, and now intends to marry—anyone but her.

Henrietta and Louisa Musgrove are gay and attractive; he soon forms part of their circle. Anne listens to his talk of his career; thinks of what might have been; and is silent. *He* has not changed, except towards her. She watches his patience with old Mrs. Musgrove's "large fat sighings" over her lost son, and listens to his discussion with the Crofts about life in the Navy. Wentworth does not approve of women on board ship, whereas Mrs. Croft has been happiest when sailing with her husband. This evening, like many others, ends with dancing—and with Anne playing for it. She hears Wentworth enquire about this, and learn that she has quite given up dancing. He is coldly polite to her. It is worse than anything.

Wentworth's attentions to the Musgrove girls continue, and their cousin, Charles Hayter, who loves Henrietta, becomes jealous, and keeps away. Wentworth and Hayter meet at the Musgroves' cottage, where Anne has been having an awkward tête-à-tête with Wentworth. She is looking after the sick little boy, and when Mary's other child climbs on her back, it is Wentworth, not the children's kinsman, who comes to her rescue.

A few days later the young people all go for a walk together, and Louisa encourages Henrietta to call on the Hayters. She wants Wentworth to herself. After some discussion, Henrietta and Charles go to call, while the others idle about, waiting for them. Anne, tired, sits down beside a hedge and presently hears Louisa and Wentworth coming down the track along its centre. Louisa is telling Wentworth about Henrietta and Charles Hayter, and Wentworth is admiring the firm support she has, apparently, given her sister. There is nothing like firmness in a woman, he says. Still involuntarily eavesdropping, Anne then hears Louisa tell him how much they all wish she, Anne, had married their brother instead of Mary.

Charles Hayter comes back with Henrietta and Charles Musgrove, and they all start to walk back together. Anne is really tired now, but when they meet Admiral and Mrs. Croft in their carriage, she does not put herself forward on the general offer of a lift. Wentworth speaks to his sister, and Anne finds herself in the carriage, liking the odd, kind Crofts better than ever.

The young people make up a party to drive over to Lyme Regis and spend the night. Wentworth has friends there, Captain Harville and his family, and Captain Benwick, who was engaged to Harville's dead sister. Anne cannot help but suffer as she watches the friendly relations between the three naval officers. But the sea air puts colour into her cheeks and life into her step. She is aware of being admired by a handsome stranger they meet, and also aware of Wentworth noticing this. Later, after the stranger has left, they learn that he was in fact Anne's cousin, Mr. Elliot, Sir Walter's heir. That evening, Captain Benwick tells Anne all about his lost love, and she does her best to brace and cheer him, thinking he indulges his grief too much.

Next day they all go for a last walk on the sea wall (or cobb) and Louisa insists that Wentworth jump her down from the upper level. She falls and loses consciousness. Everyone panics except Anne. The Harvilles join them and insist that Louisa be taken to their house. After some debate, it is decided that Charles and Anne shall stay to help nurse Louisa, while the others go back and break the news to her parents. Wentworth appeals to Anne: "You will stay, I am sure; you will stay and nurse her." But in the end tiresome Mary insists on staying instead.

The Musgroves hurry to Lyme to be near their daughter, and Wentworth goes back too. Anne is sure that he loves Louisa and will propose as soon as she is better. Perhaps luckily, it is time for her to return to Lady Russell's and then accompany her to Bath. It is not easy to talk calmly about Wentworth with Lady Russell, who knows of the past, but Anne does her best. She and Lady Russell call on the Crofts, but Wentworth is still in attendance on Louisa at Lyme. Charles and Mary call in on their way back from there, and report that Louisa is recovering. Charles teases Anne about Captain Benwick's partiality for her, but Mary does not think he is good enough for an Elliot. Lady Russell and Anne rather expect him to call, but he does not come.

In Bath, Anne finds her father and sister absorbed as always with their own affairs, with their very good house and their elegant acquaintance. Among these is Sir Walter's heir, Mr. Elliot, who has made his apologies and been received once more as a member of the family. Elizabeth is hopeful again, and Anne is afraid that Mrs. Clay has hopes of her own. Mr. Elliot calls and is pleased and surprised to discover that the unknown lady he admired at Lyme is his cousin. Lady Russell is soon entertaining hopes about him and Anne, and Anne does enjoy his company, though with reservations. Is he quite what he seems? While Sir Walter and Elizabeth cultivate some titled connections, the Carterets, Anne is renewing her friendship with an old school friend, a widowed Mrs. Smith, who is now living, ailing and poor, in Bath. It turns out that the nurse who attends her also works for friends of Mr. Elliot's, and Mrs. Smith is full of gossip about them.

Anne is anxious about the friends she has left behind, and at last the

Crofts arrive in Bath, bringing a letter from Mary. It contains surprising news. Captain Benwick and Louisa Musgrove are engaged. It is astonishing, and Anne cannot help wondering how Captain Wentworth feels about it. Nor can she quite help rejoicing that he is free again. Soon he joins the Crofts in Bath. He and Anne meet in the street: a strange, embarrassed, self-conscious meeting. And what will Lady Russell do when she meets him? They pass him in the street. Lady Russell stares, then explains; she was looking for some unusual curtains. She has not noticed Wentworth.

The Elliots go to a concert with the Carterets. Anne sees Wentworth and makes a point of speaking to him. Politeness demands it. They have an interesting if awkward discussion of the match between Louisa and Captain Benwick, but are interrupted by the arrival of the Carterets. But Wentworth's behaviour has almost convinced Anne that he loves her . . . She hopes he will join her later, but instead Mr. Elliot does so, and mystifies her by telling her that he has long since been used to hearing her praises. Elliot is still monopolising her attention when Wentworth comes up again to bid her a hurried farewell. Can he actually be jealous?

Next morning, Anne visits Mrs. Smith, who drops hints about a romantic attachment on Anne's part. Anne's blushes cease when she realises her friend is speaking of Mr. Elliot. The gossiping nurse has told Mrs. Smith of Elliot's interest in Anne, and she now asks her to speak to him on her behalf. Mr. Elliot, it appears, was a close friend of her husband's, and is executor of his will. When Anne makes it clear that there is no question of an engagement between herself and Elliot, Mrs. Smith changes her story. She breaks out against Elliot, who led her husband into extravagance and than refused to help him. He has actually refused to act as executor, so that she has been unable to claim a small inheritance. Mrs. Smith also explains Elliot's new politeness to Sir Walter. He has decided that a title is worth having, has heard rumours of Mrs. Clay's designs, and has come to Bath in the hope of frustrating them.

Returning home, Anne is relieved to hear that Elliot has left Bath for a few days. It gives her time to decide whether and how to unmask him. They receive a surprise visit from Charles and Mary, who have come to Bath with the Musgroves. The Harvilles have come too, and Anne, calling at their hotel, finds a large, confused party which is soon joined by Charles, Harville and Wentworth. But Anne is distracted by Mary, who calls her to the window to see Elliot talking to Mrs. Clay outside in the street. This is odd, as Elliot is supposed to be in London. When Anne asks Mrs. Clay about this, later, she admits the meeting and describes her own surprise at learning that Elliot has had to put off his journey.

Anne is to spend the next day with the Musgroves, and arrives to find Harville and Wentworth already there. It is happiness. It is misery. Wentworth is writing a letter for Harville, who draws Anne aside to confide to her his distress over Benwick's engagement. He might have mourned longer for Harville's dead sister. But women are like that. Anne speaks up for women. "All the privilege I claim for my own sex (it is not a very enviable one, you need not covet it) is that of loving longest, when existence or when hope is gone."

Harville and Wentworth leave, but Wentworth hurries back, on a pretext, and presses a letter into Anne's hands with a glowing look. He has heard what she said to Benwick. "You pierce my soul," he writes. Does she indeed love him still? one word will decide whether he join her that evening, or never. Anne is in agony. He has gone. Suppose she gets no chance to speak. She looks so ill that it is noticed, and Charles is deputed to see her home. Captain Wentworth catches them up on the way, and Charles is delighted to relinquish his charge. Soon, all is clear and happy between them. And this time, Sir Walter and Lady Russell approve. Mr. Elliot, disappointed, leaves Bath—and takes Mrs. Clay with him. She may even manage to make him marry her. Wentworth recovers Mrs. Smith's lost inheritance, and, as for Anne, only the dread of a future war can dim her sunshine.

Bibliography

For Jane Austen's *Novels*, *Letters* and *Minor Works*, the Oxford Edition. Edited by R. W. Chapman.

Family Records

Biographical Notice by Henry Austen. Published in John Murray's edition of *Northanger Abbey and Persuasion*, 1818.

A Memoir of Jane Austen. By James Edward Austen-Leigh. Richard Bentley, 1870. Second Edition, 1871, included *Lady Susan* and other fragments.

Jane Austen: Her Homes and Her Friends. By Constance Hill. John Lane, 1902.

Letters of Jane Austen. Edited with an introduction by Edward, Lord Brabourne. Richard Bentley, 1884.

Jane Austen's Sailor Brothers. By J. H. and E. C. Hubback. John Lane, 1906.

Jane Austen: Her Life and Letters. By W. and R. A. Austen-Leigh. Smith, Elder, 1913.

Personal Aspects of Jane Austen. By M. A. Austen-Leigh. John Murray, 1920.

Austen Papers. 1704–1856. Edited by R. A. Austen-Leigh. Privately printed by Spottiswoode, Ballantyne & Co, Ltd., 1942.

Cornhill. No. 973, 1947–8. Letter from Lady Knatchbull to her sister.

My Aunt Jane Austen, A Memoir. By Caroline Mary Craven Austen. Spottiswoode, Ballantyne & Co. Ltd., 1952.

Theodore Besterman, *The Publishing Firm of Cadell & Davies*. Oxford University Press, 1938.

Frank W. Bradbrook, *Jane Austen & her Predecessors*. Cambridge University Press, 1966.

Arthur Bryant, *The Age of Elegance*. Collins, 1950.

Lord David Cecil, *Jane Austen*. Cambridge University Press, 1935.

R. W. Chapman, *Jane Austen, Facts & Problems*. Clarendon Press, ᴛ948.

R. W. Chapman. Essays in *The London Mercury*, 1930–31, and in *Transactions of the Royal Society of Literature, VIII*.

Sir Zachary Cope. In *British Medical Journal*, July, 1964.

W. A. Craik, *Jane Austen, the Six Novels*. Methuen, 1965.

Reginald Farrer. In the *Quarterly Review*, No. 452, July, 1917.

E. M. Forster, *Aspects of the Novel*. Arnold, 1927.

E. M. Forster, *Abinger Harvest*. Arnold, 1936.

H. W. Garrod. In *Transactions of the Royal Society of Literature, VIII*.

D. W. Harding. In *Scrutiny, VIII*, March, 1970.

Elizabeth Jenkins, *Jane Austen*. Gollancz, 1958.

Margaret Kennedy, *Jane Austen*. Barker, 1950.

Mary Lascelles, *Jane Austen and Her Art*. Clarendon Press, 1939.

Marghanita Laski, *Jane Austen and Her World*. Thames & Hudson, 1969.

Q. D. Leavis. In *Scrutiny*, June, 1941, September, 1941, January, 1942, Spring, 1944.

Robert Liddell, *The Novels of Jane Austen*. Longman, 1963.

Percy Lubbock, *The Craft of Fiction*. Cape, 1921.

Kenneth L. Moler, *Jane Austen's Art of Allusion*. University of Nebraska Press, 1968.

Marvin Mudrick, *Jane Austen. Irony as Defense & Discovery*. University of California Press, 1968.

F. A. Mumby, *Publishing and Bookselling*. Cape, 1930.

Walter Raleigh, *The English Novel*. Murray, 1894.

David Rhydderch, *Jane Austen. Her Life & Art*. Cape, 1932.

Sir Walter Scott. Anonymous article in *The Quarterly Review XLV*, October, 1815.

Samuel Smiles, *Memoir and Correspondence of the Late John Murray*. John Murray, 1891.

B. C. Southam. In *Notes & Queries. CCVI*, 1961.

B. C. Southam, *Jane Austen's Literary Manuscripts*. Oxford University Press, 1964.

B. C. Southam, *Jane Austen. The Critical Heritage.* Routledge & Kegan Paul, 1968.

B. C. Southam, *Critical Essays on Jane Austen.* Routledge & Kegan Paul, 1968.

C. L. Thomson, *Jane Austen. A Survey.* Horace Marshall, 1929.

J. M. S. Tompkins, *The Popular Novel in England.* 1770–1800. Methuen 1909.

G. M. Trevelyan, *History of England.* Longman, 1926.

Rachel Trickett, *Address* to the Jane Austen Society, 1970.

Lionel Trilling, *Beyond Culture.* Secker & Warburg, 1966.

Lionel Trilling, *The Opposing Self.* Secker & Warburg, 1955.

R. J. White, *The Age of George III.* Heinemann, 1968.

Andrew Wright, *Jane Austen's Novels. A Study in Structure.* 1953, revised 1962.

Index

Index

*(The novel synopses and the bibliography are not indexed. Abbreviations: A. Austen;
J. A. Jane Austen)*

appearance, 25–26, 39, 46, 91, 98, 114–15, 160, 194, 201; domestic arts, 21–22, 32–33, 57, 96, 113, 116, 191; health, 20, 66–68, 96, 129, 144, 168, 176–8, 183–4, 186–187, 190–1, 194–5, 198, 200–5; music, 13, 21, 49, 79, 109, 113, 115–16, 133, 149, 167, 190

as aunt, 13, 35, 42, 90, 98, 104–6, 146, 149, 155, 159, 161, 164, 173–4, 176, 190–1; as daughter, 13, 57, 60, 83, 86, 88, 111, 148, 157; as dramatist, 37, 171–2; as poet, 37, 87, 112, 128, 204; as reader, 36–38, 47, 61–62, 67, 102, 109–10, 133–4, 146–7, 151; as sister, 13, 21, 43, 49, 77, 83, 147, 157, 159, 205

views on: children, 19–20, 89, 97–98, 101–2, 148, 173; death, 42, 54, 68, 89, 110, 111, 175, 189, 201, 206; literary style, 69, 127–8, 132–3, 155–6, 161–2, 174, 180, 187; marriage, 33, 58, 82–83, 85, 88, 181, 192; religion and morals, 14, 30–31, 42–43, 88, 110, 115–16, 137–9, 146, 157, 166, 184, 205; women's status, 33, 38, 58, 82–83, 136, 140, 160, 192

Austen, John (distant connection), 99

Austen, Mary Jane (dtr. of Frank and Mary A.), 99, 109, 176

Austen, Maunde and Tilson, 100, 109, 167, 175

Austen Papers, 1704–1856, ed. R. A. Austen-Leigh, 12, 23, 44, 235

Austen, Philadelphia, *see* Mrs. Tysoe Saul Hancock

Austen-Leigh, James Edward (son of James and Mary A.; author of *A Memoir of Jane Austen*), 11–13, 18–19, 22, 26, 33, 43–44, 46, 72, 85, 91, 101–2, 113–14, 125–6, 166,

170, 176, 179, 184, 186–7, 190, 203–6, 235

Austen-Leigh, Mary Augusta, *see Personal Aspects of Jane Austen*

Austen-Leigh, R. A., *see Jane Austen: Her Life and Letters* and *Austen Papers*

Austen-Leigh, W., *see Jane Austen: Her Life and Letters*

Authors' Society, *see* Society of Authors

Badcock, Mr. and Mrs., 78, 79

Baltic, 142, 145

Barrett, E. S. (*The Heroine*), 151

Basingstoke, 34, 36, 49, 55, 57, 59, 61, 73

Bath, 18, 32–33, 39, 50–52, 68, 70, 74–76, 78–80, 82–83, 85, 87–92, 96, 109, 152, 154–5, 176

Baverstock, Mr., 152, 159–60, 196

Bendish, Miss, 90

Benn, Miss, 135, 140

Bentley, Richard, (publisher), 125

Bentley (near Alton), 190

Bessborough, Lady, 130

Bigg, Alethea, 36, 61, 65, 76, 82, 103, 105, 107, 173, 190–1, 203

Bigg, Catherine, *see* Mrs. Herbert Hill

Bigg, Elizabeth, *see* Mrs. Heathcote

Bigg Wither, Mr., (Manydown), 36 His three daughter were called Bigg.

Bigg Wither, Harris, (son of the above), 36, 75, 82–83, 103, 180

Bigion, Mme., 199

Billington, Mrs., 92

Biographical Notice, by Henry Austen, 11, 26, 204

Blackall, Rev. Samuel, 58, 60, 81

Blackall, Mrs. (*née* Lewis), 58, 142

Blake, William, 121

Bolton, Lord, and son, 66

243

Bonaparte, *see* Napoleon
Bond, John, 59–60, 73, 75, 77
Bookham (Great Bookham, Surrey),
    19, 69, 150, 154
Brabourne, Edward, Lord, *see Letters
    of Jane Austen*
Bridges, Sir Brook, 26, 108
Bridges, Lady, 90, 103, 152, 154
Bridges, Edward and Mrs., 103, 144–5
Bridges, Eleanor, 168
Bridges, Elizabeth, *see* Mrs. Edward
    Austen Knight
Bridges, Harriot, *see* Mrs. Moore
Bridges, Louisa, 101
Bridlington (Sanditon), 185
Brighton, 66, 69, 75
British Critic, 130, 133, 168–9
British Medical Journal, 177
Britton, Dr. and Mrs., 146
Brontë, Charlotte, 51, 64, 104
Brophy, Brigid, 20
The Brothers, see Sanditon
Brown, Capability, 29
Browning, Robert, 120
Brunton, Mary (*Self Control*), 146–7
Brydges, Sir Egerton (*Arthur Fitzal-
    bini*), 26, 60, 84
Buchanan (*Christian Researches in Asia;
    Apology for Promoting Christianity
    in India*), 133
Bullock, William (Liverpool Museum),
    118
Bunyan, John (*Pilgrim's Progress*),
    138
Burdett, Sir Francis and Lady, 141
Burdett, Miss, 141
Burney, Fanny (Mme. d'Arbley;
    Evelina, Cecilia, Camilla), 31, 47,
    50–51, 62, 67–68, 98, 104, 121–2
    142, 149, 155
Burns, Robert, 120
Byron, Lord, 77, 122–3, 125, 134–5,
    151, 165

Byron, Lady (*née* Annabella Mil-
    banke), 134–5

Cadell (publishers), 50, 72, 123
Cage, Mrs., 65
Calland, Mr., 65
Campbell, Thomas, 120
Caroline, Princess of Wales, 140, 154,
    165
Catherine, by J.A., 18, 38, 130, 179;
    179; Edward Stanley, 130; Miss
    Wynne, 18
Cavendish, Lady Harriet, 32
Cawley, Mrs. (*née* Cooper), 21
Chamberlayne, Mrs., 79, 80
Chapman, Dr. R. W., 14, 15, 37, 140,
    153, 195
Charlotte, Princess, 140, 174
Charlotte, Queen, 153
Charmouth, Dorset, 183
Chaucer, Geoffrey, 13
Chawton Cottage, Hants., 97, 106–7,
    109, 111–13, 115–16, 128–9, 132–
    133, 135, 141–2, 144, 148, 150–4,
    157, 159, 162, 164, 166, 168, 173,
    175–6, 184, 190–4, 197, 202–6
Chawton House, 100, 106, 113, 116,
    129, 132, 142–3, 147, 150, 152,
    154, 194
Cheltenham, 176, 184, 186
Cholmeley, Penelope, and brother, 70
Chute, Thomas, 73
Clarke, Mr. (Prince Regent's librarian)
    22, 51, 165–8, 174, 183
Clarkson (*Abolition of the African Slave
    Trade; Life of William Penn*), 133
Clewes, Miss, 154
Clifton (Bristol), 92
Cobbett, William, 27, 29
Cochrane, Lord, 119
Coffee, Charles (*The Devil to Pay*), 152
Coke of Holkham, 29
Coleridge, Samuel Taylor, 87, 105